T0386665

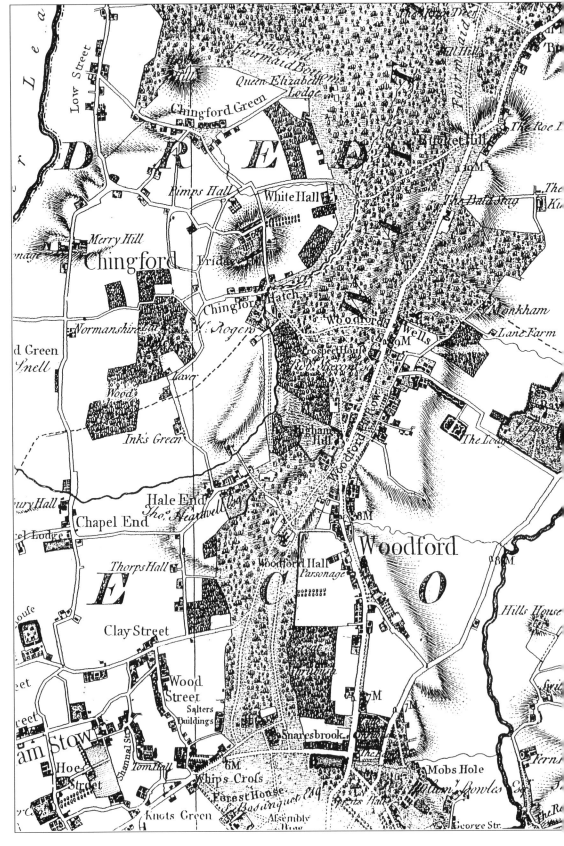

From 'A map of the county of Essex from an actual survey taken in 1772, 1773, 1774, by John Chapman and Peter André'.

In the north-east section of this map of 1932, a plan for the Montalt Estate is shown, proposing that houses would be built on some of the forest land by Highams Park Lane ('the pond') and over the large field to the east. Only Keynsham Avenue, Lichfield Road, Mason Road and Marion Grove were built because the economic slump in the 1930s made these houses difficult to sell. Walthamstow Council bought the undeveloped land to be preserved as a green space for recreation, and is now known as 'The Highams Park'.

A HISTORY OF
HIGHAMS PARK
AND
HALE END

The first boathouse at Highams Park Lake which would have been visible from Highams Manor House.

A HISTORY OF
HIGHAMS PARK
AND
HALE END

M. L. DUNHILL

First published in 2005
This paperback edition first published in 2019

The History Press
The Mill, Brimscombe Port,
Stroud, Gloucestershire, GL5 2QG
www.thehistorypress.co.uk

British Library Cataloguing in Publication Data.
A catalogue record for this book is available from the British Library.

ISBN 978 0 7509 9190 2

Typesetting and origination by The History Press
Printed and bound in Great Britain by TJ International Ltd

Contents

Dedications

This book is dedicated to my husband, Ron, for his help and support throughout the years spent on this project, and to other members of my family: Melanie, who taught her mother how to use a computer; to Ian Dunhill and Dr Deborah Hicks-Clarke, who gave moral support and practical advice, and to Julia Thomson and the late Mrs Betty Grantham, who found rare and useful books.

Special thanks are due to Edith Upton and to Cliff Payling, who made his own research material freely available to me and offered constructive criticism after reading through the draft of the book, and to Fred Revell, the late Barbara Ray and Roger Gillham, who gave me a lot of encouragement to finish. Roger also helped with printouts of the text. The late Dr Douglas Woolf OBE also gave his time to read and make useful comments on the content of some chapters.

Last – but not least – thank you to all the kind people of Highams Park and Woodford Green, whose memories made this book.

Acknowledgements

The Airship Heritage Trust, 69; Mrs Sylvia Ayling (S.D.F. history); Mr A.L.C. Benjamin (technical advice and loan of a computer); Mrs Sylvia Bird, 64; J.A. Bocking, 6; Camilla Branson, indexing; British Aerospace Airbus, Filton, Bristol, 70; John Diamond (journalist, *The Times* newspaper); M.J. Dunhill, 106; R.F. Dunhill, 29; Miss Marjorie Emery (WCHS); Miss C. Ercolani; Mr T. L'Estrange; John Farr (Scouts); Mr and Mrs Fox (deeds of 'Eureka'); Harry Grantham, 98-9; Guardian Newspapers (Newsquest Media Group Ltd), 44; Hale End Library, Highams Park; Paul Hancock, photographer, 35, 51, 72; Ms J. Hawkins (The Regal); D. Insole, 68, 100; Mrs Irene Knight, 46; Peter Lawrence (Tottenham Outrage); J. Leatherland, 40, 42, 45, 47, 82; Mrs Elsie Legg, 73; The Linnean Society of London, 7; The London Borough of Waltham Forest: Building and Legal Depts.; S. Marchant, 101; Mrs W. Marchant, 53; Mrs Mary Martin (finding maps); Mrs Vera Mason, 91; Mrs E. Maynard (bombs at Halex); Mrs. J. McCabe, 79, 86; Dr and Mrs M. Morris, 76; the Rev. Melvin Oakes; Miss H. Oliver, 94, 105; Guy Osborne; C. Payling, 50; Mr Percy Reboul; F. Revell, 77; Mrs Kathleen Rhys (The Rolls); Mr Ring, 62; Mr K. Roberts (Dr M. Ercolani) and Mrs Linda Smith (translations from Latin); S. Skinner, 21; Derek Smith, 43; Mrs E. Stevens, 33; Mrs E. Upton, 23, 28, 32, 48, 97; Vestry House Museum, Walthamstow, 2, 4, 8, 14, 15, 31, 37-8, 41, 48, 52, 88; Mrs Daphne Warner, 83; D. Webb, 18, 78; Dr Douglas Woolf, 84-5.

Contributors

The Rt. Hon. Lord Bottomley of Middlesbrough PC, OBE (1907-95)
Lady Bottomley DBE
Sir George Robert Edwards OM, CBE, FRS, FEng., DL
Sir Fred Pontin
Douglas Insole CBE
Chris Moncrieff CBE
Douglas L. Woolf OBE, FRCP, DPhy Med
Drummond Clapp FRIBA

Mrs Jessie Allen (née Wison)
Mr S. (Stan) Batson
Miss Sylvia Bird
Miss Jennifer A. Bocking
Miss L. Frances Bowler
Mr James (Jim) Davis
Mr John Edwards
Mr Leslie Felgate
Mrs Olive Fewell
Mr Ken Ford
Mr Leon Frank
Mr Melvin Harrison
Mr H. William Hebbard
Mr Arthur Hemmings
Mr Edward (Ted) Jones
Mrs Doris Jones
Mrs Irene Knight
Mr John Leatherland
Mr Sidney Marchant
Mrs Win Marchant (née Bradley)
Mr Alan Marshall
Mrs Edith May Upton (née Lane)
Mrs Vera Mason
Mrs Jane F. Matthews (née Child)
Mrs Jeanne May (née Payling)
Mrs Jean McCabe (née French)

Mrs Jenny Miller (née Cooke)
Mrs Barbara Millett (née Smith-Pryor)
Mrs Maggie Moncrieff
Mr Cyril J. Moody
Mrs Letitia F. Morris (née Luttrell)
Miss Hilda Oliver
Mr R. (Dick) Oliver
Mrs Irene Owen (née Matthews)
Mrs Margaret Page
Mr Clifford Payling
Mr Frank Payling
Mr Douglas Presland
Mr Donald E. Ray
Mr Fred Revell
Mr K. (Ken) Roberts
Mr Charles Rolstone
Miss J. Rolstone
Mr Jan (John) Salamonowicz
Mrs Maria Salamonowicz
Mr Donald Spellman
Mrs Evelyn Stevens (née Walker)
Mr Gerald Verrier
Mr Dennis Webb
Mrs Joyce Webb (née Tayler)
Miss Renee Weller

Preface

Hale End Road, The Hale, Hale End Library, Hale End Sports Ground, Hale End Ward, and the Hale End Horticultural Society were named after a small Anglo-Saxon settlement in the Becontree Hundred and the later Tudor hamlet of Hale End in Walthamstow, Essex. (In 1477, it was also known as 'Wood End'.) The origin of the name 'Hale' may be 'long haul' (i.e. up-hill) or 'a corner of land in the bend of a river' from old Anglo-Saxon words. Hale End and Chapel End used to be in the Manor of Hecham, known later as Higham Bensted(e), but in about 1303 Higham Bensted was divided and they were then in the Manor of Salisbury Hall. At the beginning of the 20th century, Hale End was overwhelmed by the new urban village of Highams Park.

By 1870, the Great Eastern Railway line from Liverpool Street, London, had reached Shernhall Street. The owners of many fine country houses in the area began to leave Walthamstow and artisans, postal workers and clerks moved into the newly-built housing estates. The railway was not extended to Chingford until 1873, and a small wooden station was built in a field, about three quarters of a mile away from Hale End, but cheap workmen's fares were not available there. It was another 24 years before the British Xylonite Company built a factory on Jack's Farm and the urban village began to develop, adopting the name of Highams Park from the renamed railway station.

Until the 1950s, the end of The Avenue, Highams Park, was still a rough track but the farms had been sold off for housing or playing fields. The BX Co. provided employment for local people who worked in a happy environment, created by the spacious grounds of the factory and the caring attitude of the factory's owners, the Merriam family. Steam trains thundered over the level crossing, thrilling the children and allowing people to stop and pass the time of day with their neighbours, and a friendly community developed around the station and thriving shopping centre.

In 1965, Hale End and Highams Park became part of the London Borough of Waltham Forest. Three different postal addresses now encompass the area. Hale End (around Oak Hill) is part of Woodford Green, Essex: the area around Highams Park station is Chingford, London, E.4, and other parts are in London, E.17. (Confusing, isn't it!)

This book is based on oral history. Ten years ago, I asked some older friends if they would record their memories about Highams Park. This opened the flood gates. These very kind people were curious to know more about the old farms and large houses, which they remembered: they found old photographs, books and pamphlets, and contacted other helpful people, and some real local historians emerged. Information came pouring in, but when I tried to confirm stories, it was difficult to locate any history books with titles containing Hale End or Highams Park. However, a great deal has been written about the area, if you know where to find it. I hope that people will forgive me if not everything they told me has been included, but sources of information are given to help future researchers.

1

Rural Hale End

'Highams Park – where's that? Never heard of it!' is the usual response from strangers, suggesting that this must be one of the best-kept secrets of Outer London. Perhaps it is.

The Greenwich Meridian plaque in the pavement by the shops near the station helps to pinpoint Highams Park on a map, and it takes only 20 minutes to get there by train from Liverpool Street station. Since the rebuilding of the North Circular Road (linked with the M11), there is no exit from the east into Hale End Road, so visitors to Highams Park often get lost as they try to double back from the busy Billet Roundabout at Chapel End. From the *Napier Arms* in Woodford (where the old tram and trolley bus routes from Bloomsbury, The Manor House and Wood Green used to terminate), Oak Hill goes down the hill through woodland. A bus route from Woodford High Road to Highams Park goes down Chingford Lane, past forest and common land on the way. From Chingford the buses go by Larks Wood, where bluebells grow in the spring.

About 100 years ago the families of many people who are mentioned in this book came to live in a new urban village, which grew up very quickly around a factory and the railway station near the hamlet of Hale End. The people who lived there would have said that the name adopted for the new development – 'Highams Park' – really referred to the grounds of 'Highams', the last manor house of Higham Bensted(e), which was built in the 18th century.

Hale End hamlet was a sparsely populated farming community and the newcomers saw country lanes, little weather-boarded cottages, a few large, old houses with servants, horses and carriages, and working farms with footpaths and stiles to cross the fields. They were also able to walk for many miles through Epping Forest or hire a rowing boat on Highams Park Lake.

Nowadays most of Highams Park has the postal address of Chingford, London, and old Hale End is said to be a part of Woodford Green, Essex, but in the 19th century they were both within an area described as 'a far-flung part of the Parish of St Mary's Church, Walthamstow' in Essex. The early history of rural Hale End is connected to the Saxon manor of Hecham, later named Higham Bensted(e), which stretched from the great Forest of Waltham in Essex down to the marshes, or Lammas Lands, of the Lea Valley.

Many thousands of years before Highams Park, Hale End or even Walthamstow existed, this part of the world was near the southernmost tip of huge Ice-Age glaciers which ground down mountains and even altered the course of the River Thames. Like the Thames, the River Lea, its tributary, is tidal in its lower reaches and about 25,000 years ago so much water was trapped in the ice that the sea level was extremely low. The land would have been tundra, cold and wet with arctic vegetation, but between the Ice Ages there were periods when the temperatures rose and the glaciers began to melt, bringing down debris and flood waters which scoured out the Thames Valley and the wide valley of the River Lea and deposited sediment over the flood plains. As

1 *A pollarded Hornbeam tree near to Highams Park Lake (1996). 'The good effects of the movement in favour of the preservation of Epping Forest for the Public are already becoming apparent. The trees have this year thrown out a profusion of new wood, which will never be subject to lopping, and a large increase has taken place both amongst the four footed and feathered denizens of the wood.' (1876 Report in the* Walthamstow and Leyton Guardian *newspaper)*

the water levels rose and fell, the River Lea eroded the remains of old flood plains, which can be seen as terraces on the sides of the valley.

In 1868, when the Maynard Reservoirs were built in the Lea Valley, the Walthamstow Marshes began to reveal the remains of animals that had foraged in the swampy lands around the river. As they dug deeper for the foundations of the walls of the reservoirs, workmen found bones of an extinct giant ox, woolly rhinoceros and mammoths.

Archaeological finds from the London clay and gravel of the higher ground in Walthamstow included the flint chippings and tools of Stone-Age hunter-gatherers. In the marshes, Bronze-Age spears and many Iron-Age tools and weapons made with bone and antlers of red deer were found. Roman brooches and pottery were also discovered, indicating that man has occupied the area continuously from very early times. (In the 18th century workmen uncovered extensive Roman remains, including mosaics and masonry, at nearby Wanstead Park but, unfortunately, they were not properly excavated at the time and the area was built over. When a swimming pool was excavated in Oak Hill, Hale End, a shard of the Romano-British period was found, and very recently there was great excitement when a section of a previously unknown Roman road was discovered on the Leyton/Leytonstone boundary, about three miles from the Hale End area.)

As the climate warmed up, England was covered by dense forests. It has been discovered that early Iron-Age settlers in the Walthamstow area chose to live by the river, where they drove wooden piles into the marshy land to support platforms. The remains of beaver, and teeth and bones chewed by wolves, have been found and there is evidence of large herds of wild boar, which rooted about the forest floor for beech nuts and acorns and roamed on to the Lea Marshes at the western end of what eventually became the Saxon manor of Hecham.

Manors were usually described as parishes before the Saxons lost their lands to the Norman invaders in 1066. The people of the parish were able to graze their animals on common land and had strips of land for cultivation which were not enclosed. However, the Saxon inhabitants of Hecham had often to hide themselves away from Viking invaders from Denmark who had discovered the River Lea. Evidence of their landings was discovered when the Lockwood Reservoir was dug out in 1900-1. As well as Anglo-Saxon spearheads and swords and a well-preserved woodsman's axe, remains were found of a clinker-built boat of Viking design. The Danelaw reached as far as the River Lea and it is believed that some Vikings made their homes in the fertile Lea Valley.

The Saxon lords of Hecham lived on the higher ground to the west of their lands, which later came to be known as Higham Hill. (Unfortunately, the name was also used later for the high land at the other end of the manor.) There was a plentiful supply of fresh, clear spring water (later known as Queen Elizabeth's Well) and the air was healthier than on the marshes; there was also a good view across the valley and they were near to the river for fishing.

The Ching Brook is a tributary of the River Lea which now supplies water to the reservoirs in the Lea Valley but it used to join the Lea just to the north of Higham Hill. To find refuge from the Vikings it would have been possible to scramble along the banks of the Ching, or even wade upstream towards the forest round Hale End. Early settlers found a sheltered little valley there, with fresh spring water flowing from the slopes of the forest above the Ching Brook, and later farmers constructed weirs to make fish ponds and provide easier access to water for their animals.

The Manors

In 1086, after the Norman invasion, the Domesday Inquest described the two manors, Hecham and Wilcumstou (Walthamstow, later known as Toni or Toney), in the Hundred of Becontree. The lands of Toni Manor lay to the south, and Hale End was at the eastern end of the smaller manor of Hecham, which was closely associated with the history of Epping Forest.

Until 1066 Hecham had been held by Haldan, a Saxon freeman, and his property was listed as a manor and five hides. There was woodland for 300 swine, more than in the adjoining manor of Wilcumstou, probably because Hecham had more forest, two ploughs of the demesne, four ploughs of the men, eight villagers, two smallholders, four slaves, 18 acres of meadow and three and a half fisheries. Haldan had one ox, one acre sown, one rouncy and two hives of bees. The 'one ox' may actually have meant

2 *Salisbury Hall Manor House was described by Morant in 1768 as 'old and mean', but by 1817 it had been made into a very comfortable farmhouse with a garden, barns and a farmyard. Until 1952, the ruins of the Manor House could still be seen on Chingford Road, behind the* Crooked Billet *public house, opposite Walthamstow Stadium.*

3 *The 18th-century 'Manor House' at Hale End. Records show that, from the year 1500, a house on this site was known as 'Stretmans Farm', where three generations of the de Hale family lived for about one hundred years.*

a team of eight oxen and the rouncy was a horse for riding. After the Norman, Peter de Valognes, had ousted Haldan, two more villagers were listed, but fewer swine and no fisheries. The whole estate was worth £4 and 10 shillings.

At the end of the 13th century, Sir John de Benstede, who was then lord of the manor of Hecham, changed its name to 'Higham Benstede', using the names of two of his estates – Waterhall (known as Higham) and Benstede. Disputes about the boundaries of this manor and ownership of some of the fields caused problems for the next five centuries! It is easy to imagine that the lord of the manor spent all his time hunting with hounds and ambling about his estate on horseback to see the peasants working hard for the harvest, but it is doubtful whether Sir John de Benstede ever found time to be at home. He seems to have been a great favourite of King Edward II, who appointed him Chancellor of the Exchequer and then Keeper of the Wardrobe from 1305-7. He was one of the Justices of Court of Common Bench in 1307, then of Common Pleas in 1309, and he was among the Barons of the Realm who were summoned to Parliament. Afterwards he was sent to Scotland upon the King's Service and the King chose him to be one of the commissioners to negotiate peace between Edward II and Robert Bruce in 1317. (The spelling of Benstede varies, according to different sources, including

4 *A later view of 'The Manor House' (where the flats in Vincent Road are now), showing that it was in a poor state of repair even before bomb damage in the Second World War.*

Benstead and later, Bensted. Hecham also had variations: Heycham, Heyham Comyn and Heyham Balliol. Eventually it became Higham Hill.)

Dennis Webb, an amateur local historian of the 20th century, drew attention to the fact that many streets in Walthamstow today have names connected with the Warner family, who were the last to hold the manorial rights of Higham Bensted, but other local road names, such as Betoyne and Balliol Avenues, are associated with Salisbury Hall Manor. There is also a Saxon name. 'The Lord of the Manor of Hecham in 1066 was a man called Haldan – hence "Haldan Road" in Highams Park. It used to be called Wilton Road, but it was renamed after the Second World War.'

Salisbury Hall Manor House and Moons Farm

In about 1303 the manor of Higham Benstede was divided into two parts. Alexander de Balliol and William le Plomer owned the land and Salisbury Hall became a manor in its own right. Higham Hill to the west and the area to the east where the manor house and also Highams Park lake would be built in the 18th century remained in Higham Benstede. Hale End and Chapel End were both within the manor of Salisbury Hall.

The Salisbury Hall lands followed the Chingford parish boundaries west from the Ching Brook at Chingford Hatch, stopped before Higham Hill and curved south-west to Billet Road, turned east past Chapel End up to Hale End, went along Oak Hill to just past Brookfield Path and around Forest Field to cross the Ching (also known as 'The Bourne') and then followed the brook upstream.

There have been several theories about how Salisbury Hall got its name. One historian claims that in about 1323 Adam de Salesbury used his name for his new manor; another suggests that it was named after Thomas Salisbury in 1346.

Apparently, Sir Thomas de Salesbury's son, Paul, who had succeeded his father and grandfather to Salisbury Hall Manor, 'became involved in lawless adventures at the time of the Peasants' Revolt' and, although he was pardoned for his misdemeanours, he was debarred from the government of the City of London.

An account by William Morris, the 19th-century artist, designer, socialist idealist and poet (who was born in Walthamstow in 1834), was used for one of the historical scenes performed in the 'Walthamstow Pageant', a dramatic production of 1930. It told how Brentwood and Waltham had risen up and the citizens of Walthamstow had been incited to join the angry hordes of protesters led by a man named John Ball, who forfeited his life for his part in the 1381 peasants' uprising.

A later theory (hotly denied by some historians, but too interesting to ignore) about the possible origin of the name of Salisbury Hall was offered by Ebenezer Clarke in his *History of Walthamstow*: it was 'so-called from the unfortunate Margaret Plantagenet, Countess of Salisbury, under whom the manor was held by the Tyrwhit [or Tirwhit] family' from 1450-1541. Lady Margaret married Sir Robert Pole and was described by Henry VIII as 'the most saintly woman in England', but her sons were arrested for treason and executed and Lady Margaret was taken to the Tower of London where, in 1541, she lost her head on the block in a ghastly execution performed by an incompetent executioner.

At this time, the monarch of the day distributed manors and lands as rewards to those who had been of some service to him, and after disposing of poor Lady Margaret, Henry VIII passed 'Sallesburye Hall Manor' to 'Richard Johnson of Waltham Stowe' in 1542. Walthamstow was fast becoming the 'stockbroker belt' of London as its beautiful surroundings attracted many important City bankers and merchants.

The lord of the manor of Salisbury Hall in 1558 was Sir Thomas White (1492-1567), a wealthy merchant described as 'a man of sane judgement and genuine piety'. He had been Sheriff, Alderman and Lord Mayor of London in 1553 and had sat on the trial of Lady Jane Grey. As an important member of the Merchant Taylors' Company, he was instrumental in forming the Merchant Taylors' School and he founded and endowed St John's College, Oxford.

The great Elizabethan scholar, Roger Ascham (1515-68), who was tutor to the last three Tudor monarchs, was never lord of the manor but he spent the last years of his life at Salisbury Hall, which was described as 'a house near "Moones" at Chapel End', given to him by Queen Mary as a reward for his services. (The Roger Ascham School in Billet Road, Walthamstow, which opened in 1929, was named in his honour.)

Thomas Rampston was given a lease from Queen Elizabeth I as 'Fermour' of the manor of Salisbury Hall, but he seems to have aggravated the uncertainties of life under Tudor rule by being involved in all kinds of malicious and bad-tempered disputes with his neighbours before his death in 1599:

> He endeavoured to put a specious colouring upon his encroachments and unjust proceedings by a tyrannical oppression of his juries, whom his steward, one Francis Oxenham, did usually compel by locking them up, starving them, frightening them with threats of imprisonment, the Star Chamber fines and the loss of their copyholds to pass verdicts ready-drawn for the service of his master.

Life in the 16th century was equally precarious in the adjoining manor of Higham Bensted, where Sir John Heron's son, Giles, married Cecilia, the daughter of Sir Thomas Moore, and having been 'attainted of Treason' lost the manor to the Crown. After Cuthbert Hutton's occupation of the land, the manor was restored to Giles' son, Thomas Heron, by Queen Mary in 1556.

Salisbury Hall had many owners in the following years, some living there, whereas others rented out the hall and lands and lived elsewhere. The last lord of the manor to live in the house was Edward Ward Oliver, but after his death in 1917 the ancient timber-framed manor house was neglected. In the early 1920s there was a fire in the kitchen which damaged the wainscot panelling but uncovered an unknown staircase and the remains of a bricked-up secret tunnel entrance. By 1937 the manor house had fallen into such a bad state of repair that a public enquiry was held and it was decided that the house should be protected. Unfortunately, during the war several bombs fell nearby, causing even more damage to the manor house, and after the war the priorities were to rebuild and repair bomb-damaged homes – not to renovate historic houses – so Salisbury Hall was demolished in 1952. (The site of the manor house is now a car park for Walthamstow Stadium, and the quiet little crossroads near Salisbury Hall by the old *Crooked Billet* public house has become a very busy roundabout for local traffic and an underpass for the North Circular Road.

Moones

On the other side of Billet Road (once called Moons Lane) was a moated mansion with 11 acres of land called 'Moones' (or Moons), and later this property was added to the manor of Salisbury Hall by Sir William Rowe, lord of the manor of Higham Bensted, which the Rowe family held for 200 years.

One of the previous owners was a very wealthy and influential man, Sir George Monoux, who was born in about 1465. He used 'Moones' as his country residence and its name may have been a corruption of his. In 1490 Monoux had been Bailiff of Bristol, and then its Mayor in 1501, and when he came back to London he was Master of the Drapers' Company six times during the period 1506-39, then Sheriff of London in 1509 and Lord Mayor in 1514 and 1523. In Walthamstow he is remembered as a great benefactor, who founded the Sir George Monoux Grammar School in a room above his Monoux Alms Houses, which are still there, and in 1513 he was responsible for building the tower of St Mary's Church, using orange-red bricks. The tower was said to have looked beautiful in the light of the setting sun before the Victorians covered the bricks with cement! Sir George Monoux was buried in St Mary's in 1544, and a brass memorial to him and his wife can still be seen there.

After Monoux, the Hale family of Hale End had possession of Moones until 1596. It is very likely that the family needed secret hiding places from time to time (as will be seen later in this chapter), and many years later, in 1861 when a Mr Charlton was living at Moons Farm, it was described by Ebenezer Clarke as having 'some remains of a crypt, and it is thought the relics of an entrance to a subterranean passage or vault'.

Moons continued to be a working farm until 1928. Its ancient tithe barn was said to have been used by the Knights Templar, and when the farm buildings were demolished by Walthamstow Council in the 1930s to make way for a housing estate, the great barn was dismantled with the intention of rebuilding it elsewhere, but unfortunately, during the Second World War, a bomb fell near the carefully stacked timbers and smashed them into pieces.

After the dissolution of the Knights Templar in 1312 their estates were taken over by the Order of the Hospital of St John of Jerusalem, and most, if not all, of the estates in southern Essex were administered by the great priory at Clerkenwell. Two of the clerks there were Alfred of Walthamstow and Peter, also of Walthamstow. The historian Michael Gervers has suggested that 'Randal of Salisbury', a witness to a grant of land elsewhere in Essex (probably Widdington), may also have been from Walthamstow. In these records other names appear which may have connections with the Hale End area, such as 'Brethren; Nicholas of Hales, Walter de Hale and Samson de la Hale'. Other names associated with Salisbury Hall Manor are Balliol and, possibly, William, Richard and Theobald Sorrell, as well as Walter and William Scott.

Hales Brinks and 'The Sale'

At the eastern boundaries of Salisbury Hall Manor, the woodland and 'waste land' from Hale End to Chingford Hatch remained within the manor of Higham Bensted and was known as Highams Bushes and Hales Brinks. 'The Sale' appeared on the map of the Foresters' Walks in the Forest of Waltham, dated about 1641. (The name is still used and refers to the strip of forest land from Oak Hill, Woodford Green, towards Highams Park lake. It borders the grounds of the White House, then continues between the Ching Brook and Forest Glade to The Avenue, Highams Park.)

In 1650, about 16 years before the Great Fire of London, all the timber from 150 acres of woodland in the area known as 'The Sale' was sold off by the lord of the manor, Sir William Rowe. As a result, there are no very old oak trees and the woodland has many hornbeams – some pollarded.

During the 18th century the lords of the manor erected fences to stop deer grazing on their land, and this led to many disagreements between them and the Verderers of Epping Forest, especially when one owner of Highams began to enclose the area around his new lake and The Sale as a private park in 1768. In 1821 the lord of the manor was Jeremiah Harman, who bought the Crown's forest rights to his land and put an end to all the disputes.

Mrs Edith Upton, a local historian, who was born in 1907, had memories of walking along the old forest paths as a child. She commented that one way into the forest was known as 'The Slip', and that by the end of the century all of these paths were very overgrown:

> Between the houses at the back of Sky Peals Road, there is a very narrow path and it's a bit rocky with nettles on both sides – quite a favourite dog-walk. As children, we knew it as 'The Slip', and it goes straight up into the forest – to Mill Plain. There were other paths, but I must admit that they've got very worn out and are overgrown. (Forest Mount Road was a pretty lane and Mr Ruda's house, 'Sky Peals', used to be up there.)

Early maps show that the Walthamstow Mill was on Mill Plain and many paths led up to what was probably a wooden post-mill. Unfortunately, it fell into disrepair and was blown down at the beginning of the 19th century.

The word 'slip' was used to describe several other wide strips of land in Walthamstow. Coe's Map of 1822 showed land along the Ching Brook near Highams Park lake as 'The Slip'. It is now used for allotments. The widest of these old ways, the 'Walthamstow Slip', went from the River Lea, through Leyton and up to the Eagle Pond at Snaresbrook.

In the court rolls of Salisbury Hall (dated 1499-1507) complaints were made in the manorial court about the neglect of ditches, which would lead to local flooding. John Pynder failed to clear out his ditch at Woodende (Hale End), Richard Gosenall's ditch opposite 'Jakes' (Jack's Farm in what is now Larkshall Road) also needed clearing, and the daughter of Symon Pynder, the widow Joan Gylle, had not scoured her ditch opposite Spittescroft. John Hale's ditch at Stonedales was described as 'unscoured to the injury of all the tenants of this manor'; this was probably because he lived near the Ching Brook, which was prone to flooding. All the offenders were told to go away and clear out their ditches or else pay a fine.

Freeholders were obliged to attend the manorial courts and take on posts of responsibility so that law and order and good husbandry ensured the welfare of the people and crops. There was a limited choice of people able to undertake the offices because there were only 60 men and women tenants in the manor. One of the appointments was that of an aleconner who, for a period of two years, was expected to taste all the new batches of beer, brewed and sold by the local women. During the period 1502-7 John Wynde, William Browne, John Jakes and John Skott were appointed as aleconners, sometimes serving in office more than once.

'The Manor House' alias 'Stretmans'

The 'Manor House' in Hale End was a name accepted by the farming community but puzzling for newcomers to the urban village of Highams Park in the 20th century because records show that Hale End did not have a manor house of its own. As the mystery was gradually unravelled, it was revealed that the farmhouse had an interesting history.

Will Hebbard remembered playing in the fields of the farmhouse by the Ching before the First World War:

> The flats at the end of Vincent Road are on the site of the 'Manor House'. It was in a bad state when I first knew it but it was let out to one or two families, King, Sivyer(?) and Williams, who kept pigs in the barns. There was also a market garden, where locals came for home-grown produce and fresh tomatoes and cucumbers cut while you wait.

Dennis Webb knew all about this market garden by the fields of the 'Manor House':

> My uncle-by-marriage was Charlie Everett and he was born in 1865, in one of the Oak Hill Cottages, and was the local florist, down near the *County Arms*, Hale End Road, until about 1927. If you wanted to buy a cucumber from him (and you were not one of the 'hobbledehoys' – you mustn't be one of those!) he would take you down to his greenhouse and cut a cucumber, and wrap it up in a cucumber leaf.

Charles Everett is mentioned in *Across the Years*, a book by Annie Hatley, who knew him as a retired gardener. As a child he went to the school at Hale End, in another of the Oak Hill cottages, run by Mrs Andrews, 'who was a governess and taught young children, giving them a piece of cake if they were good'; when he was older he walked to the National School by St Mary's Church, Walthamstow.

Jim Davis used to visit his grandparents' home in Church Avenue, opposite farmland belonging to the 'Manor House', before Highams Park School was built:

When you looked across the road, you didn't have any kind of school there. All you had was a big hedge going right down Church Avenue, near to where that wire fence is now, by the school. From the top of the road at Handsworth Avenue, down to the bottom, was a gigantic field that went across to Silverdale Road but you had a hedge that went right across the field and split it into two halves. That hedge went right across the hill, right up to the top of Silverdale and Vincent Road, and there was a big ditch around the edge, and a lot of trees along the hedge – big trees – we used to climb right out the top of them. You can still walk through, by the Ching, but you could cut across the big field diagonally, and come out in Handsworth Avenue between the Nursery School and the Hitchman's Milk Yard.

There used to be a lot of goats grazing on there, but I don't know who owned them. They used to come up to you and they were quite tame. There was some kind of a fence on that side of Handsworth Avenue, and a couple of times a year, they used to come down and put a Fair on the field.

I remember the 'Manor House' in the 1920s. As you got to the bottom [of the hill], the farm was right on the corner, on the edge of the field. There was a house and a farm – derelict – and an old wooden place. An old lady lived in there on her own and we were rather frightened of her when we were boys. We used to go down there and look, and she used to shout out from upstairs, but I never really saw her properly.

Mrs Irene Owen lived near the farm in about 1940:

> The Drinkwaters' orchard and farm were where the flats are now in Vincent Road. Their house was rather a tumble-down sort of place. If you went down Brookfield Path, over the bridge, to where the path goes round, there was a farm gate and a big old house and the orchard, where the kids used to go 'scrumping'. You couldn't get through from Vincent Road then: you would have to go round Handsworth, or down Brookfield Path to get to the Drinkwaters' farm. (I know there were a lot of Drinkwater kids – and Jimmy Drinkwater was in our class at school.)
>
> The Council bought the farm. Someone had started to build a block of flats, but they ran out of money, and the flats were left standing for ages. I think the Council took them over and they were occupied in 1956.

The 'Manor House' was previously known as 'Stretmans' and was a copyhold farm with lands of about thirty acres, which were held from the manors of Higham Bensted and Salisbury Hall until 1715, when the property was purchased as an investment by the trustees of Henry Maynard, the lord of the manor of Toni, whose will was dated 1686. It seems likely that from that time, the property was the manor farm and known as the 'Manor House', referring to Toni Manor. Eleven acres of the farm were divided into Home Field, Four Acre Field and the Mead.

In 1752-67 Stretmans was described as 'the Parish Farm, tenanted by Mrs Hester Collard', who was constantly ordered to carry out urgent repairs to the house, which she failed to do. By 1784 a yeoman, Joseph Davis, was living at the farm, followed by Thomas Browne in 1814. The name Edward Forster appeared in 1819, and Thomas Cox had an 18-year lease in 1834.

The next tenant of the 'Manor House' at Hale End was a very distinguished man, John Gurney Fry, who not only had very 'good connections' with many noble English families and was descended on his mother's side from the royal family, but was also the eldest son of the famous Elizabeth Fry, a Quaker who was very well known for her work for prison reform.

In the census of 1851 the residents of 'The Manor House in Walthamstow Forest' were: John Wilson (48), Surveyor of Metropolitan Roads, who had been born in Scotland, his wife, Mary Anne, from Greenwich, and their servants, Eliz. Cracknell from Ongar, Sarah Matthew from Takeley, and the groom, John Mitchell from Little Hadham, Herts. There were many more tenants until in the Second World War a bomb fell, which almost destroyed the house.

Walthamstow Corporation bought the 'Manor House' and a council report of 1932 described the property as a brick-built, two-storey house, 'mostly roofed with slates, partly tiles, partly roofed with corrugated and sheet iron, being the original Manor House now let in 7 tenements'. There was a one-storey stable, made of brick and flint, and 'a range of old farm buildings mostly timber built, roofed with timber, corrugated iron and felt with most parts constructed of brick and flint'. The stable, a garage and the farm buildings were used at that time by a haulage contractor named Williams, who used them as storage, workshops and for keeping pigs. There was an old timber wash house with a brick-built copper and a brick flue, and another building, 'once a coach house, timber built with slate roof, but now falling into ruins'. The comment on the house and outbuildings (excluding a lot of dilapidated buildings which Williams had erected) was, 'These premises are very old, in a very bad state of repair and are not at all a good risk.'

Stretmans and the farm track from the old Woodford High Road appear on the earliest maps, and the road to the 'Manor House' can still be walked, down Brookfield Path and over the Ching.

Hale End and the family de Hale

Quite a lot is known about members of the Hale family, who lived on this farm from the early 16th century. A will, proven in 1433, suggests that there were Hales living in Walthamstow even earlier. In 1500 John Hale (or 'de Hale'), who took his name from Hale End, appears in the court rolls of Salisbury Hall when he rented a half-acre field, named le Brodemede, from Thomas Webbe and rented land from John and Joan Scott in 1507 described as '1 tenement, w. garden and 3 closes and 12 acres of land at Higham Hill ende'. In 1552 John Hale was said to have had 'Hardens' in the west field and houses called 'Skotte and Mowers and Christian Martensfield'.

In 1573 Thomas Halles, Gent. of Walthamstow, was a Catholic and would not (or could not) go to services at St Mary's Church and, after this date, members of the Hale family were hounded to attend services, take communion and pay dues to the parish. At first Thomas excused himself on the grounds of ill-health and the fact that he was a younger son without a living. (The family seems to have been connected to the manor of Giles [Gylls or Gills] in Epping, which is thought to have passed by fine to Anthony Browne, KC, another Catholic, and it has been suggested that this could have been a way of protecting the Hale family money.) In 1582 a writ for the arrest of Thomas was made, but he avoided imprisonment and in 1588 a letter of complaint about Thomas Hale was sent to the Archbishop of Canterbury. Two years later he was denounced as 'a papist' and in 1594 'Thomas Halse of Waltamstoe' and an Edward Hales were listed as Recusants and put into Bridewell Prison.

The Hale family had possession of Moones at Chapel End until 1596, and in about 1594 a long and anguished 'wrytten ballad or Ryme' was discovered in the Hales' house. It began:

> Weepe, weepe, and still I weepe,
> For who can chuse but weepe,
> To thyncke how England styll
> In synne and heresye doth sleepe.

5   *Thomas de Hale took his name from Hale End and lived at 'Stretmans'. He was buried with his wife, Ann (née Porter of Grantham) at St Mary's parish church, Walthamstow in 1588. There is also a Latin inscription on this splendid brass memorial but the picture is unlikely to be a portrait of Thomas. (Brass rubbing taken by permission of the Rev. Canon Paul Butler.)*

Later, in 1607/8, Augustine Hale of Walthamstow, who fled to Ireland, and Richard Hale had to surrender lands, but the family fortune was inherited by Richard's son, Thomas, who lived until 1645. Otherwise, little is known of the Hale family after 1629.

The first reference to 'The Rolls' was in 1537, then 1640, when it was '"Rolles" lying at Hale End held by Thomas Hales': it also appeared in documents relating to St Paul's Manor.

In 1874, the estate was described in the Codicil of a Will made by the widow of Charles, Mrs Frances Whitehurst of Churchfields, Woodford, who was the granddaughter of Gen. George Ainslie; '… the mansion house called the Rolls with the stableyards outhouses gardens and pleasure grounds and the woodland farms lands and tenements and hereditaments thereto belonging containing altogether 67 acres 1 rood and 78 perches or thereabouts situate in the Parishes of Chingford and Walthamstow and the County of Essex … .').

Tracks and By-ways

Dennis Webb lived near the Manor House and within 100 yards of where his grandfather, William Webb, had lived. With the help of an excellent collection of documents about Hale End and family stories, he was able to picture Hale End when it was entirely surrounded by forest and farmland:

> Forest Road was called Hagger Lane in those days, meaning a hill on a slope with trees. If you stand on Hagger Lane Bridge (I always know it as 'Hagger Lane' because that's what my father called it), imagine a little track running across there, to where Wood Street School is, across to Wyatt's Lane, then up Wyatt's Lane (a very old road), across Shernhall Street (Filth Street, as it used to be called) and Prospect Hill, and there you are at St Mary's Church and the Rectory Manor. You can still walk along some of the old tracks.

There seem to be no records of the Rectory Manor, Walthamstow before 1554, when Edmund Withypoll held his first court there, but it was reputed to have been an ancient ecclesiastical manor. It was given to Edmund's father by Henry VIII and its lands stretched from St Mary's Church, Walthamstow down the steep hill to Forest Road. Samuel Pepys made entries in his Diary recording frequent and enjoyable visits to his friend, Sir William Batten, an Admiral of the Fleet, at the Rectory Manor.

Dennis Webb remembered a description of what would have been seen going up the hill towards Hale End Road long before the railway was built. The path went across fields behind Wadham Road (which now runs parallel with the very busy North Circular Road) from Chapel End, where Walthamstow Stadium would be built many years later.

> There's a wonderful letter that was written in 1847 by the Vicar of St John's, Walthamstow, the Rev. John Bull, and he was talking of how he walked from Chapel End, and when he came to Wadham Farm, he saw grouse! It was all wildness at the time, less polluted, and kingfishers were seen there along the Ching.
> If you walk down Hale End Road [from Oak Hill] there are a lot of houses where you have to walk up some steps. Well, that's because there were hills, which have been levelled. There was a lane down there and you can imagine walking along that lane towards Waltham Abbey. In 1865 the Ching bridge along Hale End Road was just a little wooden bridge, just room enough for a cart to go across, and in the summer, when the stream was very low, the kids used to paddle across it.

The main route from Stratford Langthorne Abbey to Waltham Abbey was an old road, now known as Hoe Street in Walthamstow. In 1209 King John travelled along it and is reputed to have stayed overnight in an early house on the site of Salisbury Hall, which was further along the road.

In 1762 the unpopular Window Tax was levied, but only 204 houses of the 301 houses and 94 cottages in the whole of Walthamstow were eligible, and in 1801 the

6 *Beech Hall was built at Hale End in 1782 and was privately owned until after the Second World War. The house was used as a Conservative Association Club but was then sold in the mid-1960s and Swallow Court flats were built on the site. (There is a print showing the back of the house, dated 1800, with the title, 'Hale End House' (see Bosworth), which may have been its name at that time because a later photograph of the back of Beech Hall is very similar.)*

entire population was estimated at 3,006. By 1812 it had increased to 3,777, and at that time, to quote Ebenezer Clarke, '220 families were employed in agriculture and 253 in trade and manufacture and the remainder were variously occupied'.

Beech Hall Farm and Beech Hall

In the 19th century many people moved away from agriculture into towns, but in 1886 some of the Webb family found farm work in Hale End at Beech Hall Farm. At first, they lived in one of the tiny Oak Hill Cottages at Hale End, but William Webb moved into the cottage next door to Beech Hall Farm. Dennis Webb (1924-2004) talked about his family's life on the farm at Hale End:

> My grandfather worked at Beech Hall Farm and my father helped him to drive cattle across the fields to the Caledonian Market! When my grandfather and grandmother were there, they lived in the cottage by the farm, which originally was one bungalow, but they made it into two (at the side of where the fire was). The cottage is still there and so are the cow sheds. That's where, in the time of my father and grandfather, a cow kicked a bucket of milk over, and my father got into trouble because he laughed!
>
> Beech Hall Farm stretched from Studley Avenue and Beech Hall Road right round to where there were level-crossing gates, before Wadham Bridge was built in 1929.
>
> Henry Halfhead was a very wealthy man who lived in Beech Hall House and – rumour had it – one of his ancestors was connected with the Roosevelts in America. At the end, the old house was used as a workmen's club and the condition of the building was allowed to deteriorate, and it was pulled down – not many years ago – and 'Swallow Court' built on that land.

(Unfortunately the 18th-century cow sheds were not protected by a preservation order, and they too were demolished, in December 1999.)

Cliff Payling was one of a large family (all born in Hale End) and he has done a great deal of research about the area:

> I came across the Halfheads first on the 1881 census. There were three brothers, John, Robert and Henry, all in their twenties, and they were described as Farm Managers. They had another farm, Salisbury Hall, and they had a younger sister, who was their housekeeper. By 1891 the census named Robert Halfhead, his wife, four children, and brother Henry, with two servants, as living in Beech Hall, and John, his wife, three children and one servant, living next door in Beech Hall Farm.

Sid Marchant came to live in Hale End in the early 1920s:

> Where the hairdressers and the video shop were, that was the farm shop, which sold the milk, eggs, bread and groceries.
>
> Mr Halfhead owned it all but he rented out the farm. I used to 'live' on that farm as a kid. It had about five cows, which used to graze on that field, where Beech Hall Crescent is now, and horses, and a chap kept some pigs there, and in the yard were over a hundred chickens. I used to go and collect the eggs. I remember putting six ducklings' eggs under one broody hen and she hatched out six little ducklings, and we had to mash the food to feed them. When they were old enough, I took them through the meadow, down to the Ching. The little ducklings went straight into the water, and the old hen went up and down squawking away. She just couldn't understand it. But the sad part about all this is, come Christmas, all those little ducklings were slaughtered, and also the little chicks we reared.
>
> I remember one morning on the farm, Mrs Outhwaite asked me to go in to Beech Hall to see Mr Halfhead to ask him if he'd send his gardener in, because they had a sick cow. I remember going in the lovely gate up the drive – and it was summer. The windows were open, and the family were sitting there having breakfast. The maid was coming in, and at the back the French windows were open looking on to a most beautiful garden. (Mr Halfhead asked me what I wanted, and he was so nice. I told him, and he said, yes, he'd send the gardener in, so I went back to the farm.)
>
> We used to go in a horse and cart to Ponders End to get grain for the animals. I well remember going down Hale End Road, and it was just a country lane, over the old railway crossing and down what is now Larkshall Road, where there were just fields on the right-hand side and the Xylonite (factory, established in 1897) on the left. Past Roper's Farm we came to that part where the trees used to meet overhead in an archway, and then we used to go up to Endlebury Road, which was a little track, just wide enough for one cart to go through. When we came to the Ridgeway there was chickens all over the road and we used to have to make our way through, and the old chickens used to squawk, protesting at what we were doing, and then down Mansfield Hill. That was just like a Devon lane, really beautiful. We used to go on down to Ponders End to load up with grain and then came back again. It was a really lovely afternoon's outing. I was only 11 or 12 and enjoyed helping – but I loved the farm.

Frank Payling knew the Outhwaites, a North Country family, who sold milk: 'Mr Outhwaite told me that at the end of the First World War, in Walthamstow there were three hundred head of cattle and at the start of the Second World War, there were six – and they would be at Chingford Hatch.' Kathleen Hewitt remembered the milk round and the farm in 'Memories of Beech Hall Road about 1922-25', part of a booklet about Highams Park entitled *Bits and Pieces*, which she wrote with Joan Hewitt, Kathleen Howell, Mary Rampton, Ivy Reynolds and Frances Bowler '… at random during afternoon tea'.

> The road was very quiet, though an occasional motor car gave much excitement to the children. Mr Kay, the Milkman (people were known by their proper titles then) delivered milk in a churn on a horse-drawn vehicle. He loved to give children rides [but] the floor of his vehicle sloped alarmingly, although there were fixed seats on either side to cling on to tightly. He kept cows in a nearby field and his cow shed still stands near the top of Malvern Avenue.

Cliff Payling recalls:

> I knew Mr Kay in the 1930s. He sold milk to my mother at the back doorstep. How pure it was I don't know, but it was straight from the cow to the churn! I can remember him now, a tall man, oh, a very elderly man, but my brother and I loved him because he used to bring us conkers and cigarette pictures because he used to smoke like a chimney – they all did!

7 *Edward Forster (the Younger) was a wealthy banker and also a well-known botanist who lived at Beech Hall at the beginning of the 19th century. (Painting in oil on canvas by Eden Upton Eddis.)*

Mrs Edith Upton's husband found going to Beech Hall rather intimidating:

At one time, one of the owners, Mr Halfhead, had shares in Glovers (where my husband was apprenticed when he left school. Well, his father was a buyer there, and he used to have to do business with Mr Halfhead.) He used to say to Leslie, when he was about nine years old, that he wanted him to go up to Mr Halfhead and take some papers to him. So Leslie would scamper up Malvern Avenue, and he'd turn and he'd go to the old house, where there was quite a big gate in the Hale End Road, with a bell that you pulled, and it clanged away in the distance, and you waited some time, and you heard shuffling, and then a little spy hole opened, and an old man would say, 'Well – what?'

Leslie used to earn a penny, but he hated doing it, because it was all so spooky and dark! But there were wonderful lime trees there – gorgeous lime trees! They lined the wooden fence, which was round the property, and in later days it was a favourite courting place because it was so thick and quiet and peaceful, with the lovely scent of the lime blossom. The trees were on the other side of the fence, but they did spread over. Nobody cut them back. You walked beneath them – almost down to the Ching. There was also a beautiful chestnut tree on the Green. It doesn't look a bit like a 'Green' now: it's full of black boxes!

(Hale End village green was a triangle of land, with trees by the *Royal Oak* public house and Oak Hill Cottages.)

In later years various barns, pigsties and other Beech Hall farm buildings were used for small businesses, and Mrs Upton mentioned that two brothers named Smith ran a window-replacement firm there for about ten years around 1976. In the space behind the farm there was a working garage, and a few years ago the local *Guardian* newspaper reported that a collection of obsolete Russian missile carriers was being stored there.

The Forster Family of Beech Hall, Scott's and Mill Cottage

Many people remembered Beech Hall because it survived until 1967, but it might have surprised some of them to discover that it has an important place in the history of Science. Two members of the Forster family, who were notable botanists and scientists, lived in Hale End, Edward Forster at Beech Hall (and later at 'Mill Cottage') and his brother, Benjamin, at 'Scott's'.

Beech Hall was built in 1782, twenty years after the Window Tax, and it was enlarged in 1804, but for hundreds of years before the Georgian house was built other houses had been on the site or nearby (probably at the top of Brookfield Path). Records show that the 12 acres of farmland adjoining the house included Punch Hale in Hale End, Punch Hale Mead, the Moors and a piece of Commons Meadow.

In 1816 Beech Hall was leased to Edward Forster 'the Younger' (1765-1849), and by 1832 he also had possession of Wadham Farm, which he rented from the Master and Wardens of Wadham College. This land had been left to the college in the will of John Goodridge in 1652 and, according to the Tithe Map, the fields were Brook Field, Thorny Croft, Long Downs, Longdown Wood, Lady Crofts and Benstead by Inks Lane.

Edward the Younger was a very wealthy and successful banker, a partner in the London banking house of Forster, Lubbock & Co., the head of three great City corporations and the Deputy Governor of the London Docks, but he had time for charity work and founded a Refuge for the Destitute in Hackney. By 1800 he was also a well-known botanist and had been made a Fellow of the Linnaean Society. He became its Treasurer in 1816 and Vice-President in 1828, and in 1821 he was elected a Fellow of the Royal Society.

Every morning, before travelling to work in the City, Edward Forster got up at 6 o'clock to study his collections of rare British plants. He spent the evenings reading and tending his large herbarium. He and his wife, Mary, were unusually fortunate because they both enjoyed good health and were happily married for 56 years, living at Beech Hall and later at Mill Cottage in 'Woodford, Hale End' until 1836. In their latter years they moved to Ivy House, Woodford, where Edward died of cholera.

Mill Cottage was the only thatched house in the neighbourhood, situated in about an acre of land by Oak Hill Lodge (nearly opposite the *Napier Arms*) and with forest land all around it. Mill Cottage may have developed around the cottages which appear in an old picture of the Walthamstow Windmill, but it was a large house. (In the censuses of 1851 and 1861 Mellor Hetherington, an 'American Merchant' from Stoke Newington, and his wife, Mary, from Winchelsea were living here. James Fenning was another name associated with the last days of Mill Cottage and Thomas Denman lived there from 1890-1907. Much later the houses of Oak Hill Gardens and Gascoigne Gardens were built on this site.)

Edward Forster's father (also named Edward) was a rich City merchant who lived in Wood Street, then at 'Clevelands' in Hoe Street, Walthamstow, and he had two older sons, Thomas Furley Forster and Benjamin Meggott Forster. All loved country life and shared an interest in studying nature, particularly plants. Benjamin M. Forster lived at 'Scotts', Hale End, from 1811-29, and was a celebrated botanist, scientist and inventor, who published scientific books and articles. Like all the Forster family, he was also a philanthropist and became an early member of the Anti-Slavery Committee, and near

8   *Edward and Mary Forster moved from Beech Hall to Mill Cottage, Oak Hill, where they lived until 1836.*

TAM MARTI QVAM MERCVRIO:

9   George Gascoigne, soldier, poet and a courtier of Queen Elizabeth 1, lived at Thorpe Hall in Hale End Road until 1577.

the end of what is described as 'a well-spent life', he framed the Child Stealing Act. Some of the Forster family were buried at St Mary's Church, Walthamstow, and their name has been given to Forster Close, a new housing development on the site of the farm buildings of Beech Hall Farm.

'Scotts' is described in manorial records as a 'handsome cottage at Hale End' which belonged to Salisbury Hall Manor and was named after its first tenant, John, and his wife, Joan Scott(e), in about 1507. The house was somewhere near Hale End Road and the 20 acres of fields belonging to it were called Home Field, Sky Peals, Middle Field and Further Field.

It has not been possible to confirm exactly where 'Scotts' was in Hale End. The house may have been opposite the Oak Hill Cottages and renamed 'Willow Cottage'. Two jewellers, Joshua Horton and his son, also Joshua, lived there in the 1880s. Another possibility for the site could have been on 'Scott's Hoppet' (or Scotchman's Hoppet), just off Oak Hill, to the left of the Bridle Path, near to where the Tile Kiln house used to be.

A tower block named St Patrick's Court and other blocks of flats have now replaced the pleasant large houses by the Bridle Path, which were named 'Ashleigh, Wood Advent', 'The Oaks', 'Villette' and 'Matson's'. These were built by the Warner family on 'Scott's Hoppet' in Cottingham Road, later renamed the Bridle Path.

The Tile Kiln, Fields and the Ching Brook

The borderlands of Walthamstow known as Hales Brinks (or Halebrains – even 'Hell's Brain') and the manorial waste land of Highams Bushes were regarded as being the least productive areas. Deforestation took place from 1713 to 1750: John Hawkins felled 30 acres of Hell Brinks Grove in 1722; 40 acres of the Sale Grove went in 1736, and Long Downs Grove was felled in 1739.

In 1756 Catherine Woolball, daughter of the late William Woolball of Walthamstow, was considering marriage to Sir Hanson Berney, Bart. of Norfolk. Documents show that she had inherited a considerable amount of land in Low Leyton and all over Walthamstow, including Heathcroft Grove, which was eight acres, 'and also all that close, coppice and wood ground called Hell Banks or Hale Brinks containing 38 acres'. This was higher land, and was composed of water-worn gravel and clay that was used for brick and tile-making at the kiln above the Bridle Path. In 1654/5 John Russel had obtained a long lease from William Rowe, lord of the manor of Higham Bensted, for the brick kiln and a cottage, but by 1814 the site was deserted, and the cottage had been pulled down by 1820. (Clay and gravel pits account for some of the hollows and ponds in the forest but others are bomb craters from the Second World War. The remains of banks and ditches excavated by troops in the war have now become overgrown and disappeared.)

Thorpe Hall

Thorpe Hall Farm was another house along Hale End Road, to the south-west of the forest around Mill Plain and opposite Longacre and the Bellevue Estate. It was probably built on the site of another house, where the Elizabethan courtier, soldier and poet, George Gascoigne, had come to live. In 1566 he married a rich widow, Elizabeth Breton, and remained at Thorpe Hall until his death in 1577. The later farmhouse was described as 'a comfortable, roomy building of the early 18th century', and in 1832 it was farmed by William Clark, but from 1826-40 the house was occupied by the Rev. Noel, whose son, the Hon. Baptist Wriothesley Noel, was one of the first pupils of Forest School.

In 1840 an American visitor to Thorpe Hall found the estate 'situated in a most romantic spot; environed with ten thousand rural beauties. On one side is the border of an extended forest, and on the other a smooth and closely-shorn lawn of the most exquisite green; gardens and fields, shrubbery and trees, and all the varied groupings of rural scenery are spread in delightful prospect around this dwelling.' Thorpe Hall School was built on the site of Thorpe Hall, and the railway now passes over where the gardens used to be.

'Belle Vue' alias 'Cooke's Folly'

Mrs Edith Upton remembered a very grand house which stood on the hill near the forest by Beacontree Avenue, Upper Walthamstow:

> Where there are allotments now, it was still forest land and at one time, the North Circular wasn't there. When I was very young, we used to go for walks, and in my mind's eye I can see the house, 'Cook's Folly', and it had posts outside with chains round it, and a flight of steps that went up to a lovely big door. When we came back here, after the war, we had a dog, and my daughter Jane and I went out walking, and we went round all those roads up there, and we couldn't find it! Cook's Folly had gone!

'Cook(e)'s Folly' was another name for 'Belle Vue' (sometimes referred to as 'Bellevue') House, which was built in 1803 on 75 acres of the former Heathcroft Grove Estate and situated on the land which rises from Hale End Road up to the forest and to Hagger Lane on the south side. It was designed by the architect Edward Gyfford for Mr Charles Cooke, a publisher in the City of London, who was delighted with his newly built country house and printed a detailed description of it in one of his own publications, *The Topography of Essex*: 'The house is an elegant brick building, with stone dressings; the

10 *'Belle Vue House' (also known as 'Bellevue' or 'Cook's Folly') survived until 1935.*

11   *Sailing on the artificial lake behind 'Belle Vue House'.*

principal front has a semi-circular portico of Portland stone, supported by columns twenty-two feet high of the Ionic order.' Inside, there were no back stairs but one great mahogany staircase with a square handrail and wrought-iron balustrade, illuminated by a 'rising-sun' window. Most of the windows of the house were almost full-length, and there were window seats – to enjoy the view.

The house was well-named because there were beautiful views from it across bluebell woods and fields of buttercups and daisies, along the Lea Valley and over Epping Forest. Mr Sandys of Pownall Terrace, Lambeth organised the excavation of a three-acre boating-lake on the hillside but, unfortunately, Charles Cooke did not have long to enjoy his splendid home because he died in 1816.

He had two sons and was succeeded by Captain Charles Augustus Cooke, the father of another Charles Cooke. An inscription on the family monument in St Mary's churchyard, Walthamstow was full of praise for the first Charles Cooke but passed no comment about his descendants, who did not manage to maintain the estate well and had a dubious reputation in the neighbourhood. Captain C.A. Cooke died in 1867, 'late of Bellevue on the Forest Walthamstow in the County of Essex', and in the Abstract of his Will, his assets were shown to be under £600. The sole executrix of the Will was Miss Helen Isabel O'Flaherty, the housekeeper, whose name was shown in the census of 1851 as O'Flahertie. The debts grew, and by 1868 the property had passed into the Court of Chancery and a detective known as 'Paddy' Nunan was made caretaker of the house.

Frank Payling said that the local children were scared of 'Bellevue':

> In the area we lived in when we were young, there was our group of five houses in Hale End Road (begun in 1896) and in the rest of the neighbourhood there were large houses – mansions like 'Bellevue'. Now, we were always afraid to go by there because we had heard on good authority that it was haunted. We were told that one of the members of the family said in his will that he wanted to be buried sitting on his favourite charger! I can still remember that it looked very gloomy. Of course, it was derelict then, and had a thicket of wood all round it.

'Highams'

Sid Marchant was always puzzled by some decorative rocks beside Highams Park lake: 'What I could never fathom is, how did they get those stones round the lake? I was told they had come from the old London Bridge.' The stones by the lake and the stone summerhouse which used to stand on the east side of the lake were said to have been built with material taken from the old London Bridge in 1831. Unfortunately, tramps and the general public found uses for the little retreat other than admiring the view and it was demolished at least forty years ago.

Cliff Payling explained the origins of 'Highams':

> The original manor house at Higham Hill in Walthamstow was called Higham Bensted, but the new owner, Anthony Bacon MP, decided he would like a better house and he had one built in 1768. Later, the famous landscape gardener, Humphry Repton, laid out the garden and ornamental lake, with two islands, which was shown on old OS maps as the Fish Pond. It's not a natural lake but was man-made.

12 *'Highams' before 1793. This was the last Manor House of Higham Bensted to be built in Walthamstow, Essex, replacing the old house at the western end of the manor at Higham Hill. The building was extended and it is now used as the Woodford High School for Girls.*

The architect William Newton designed the new house on the hill at the eastern end of the manor, which included the wooded land where Highams Park lake is now and fields bordering Chingford Lane. At first there was some confusion because the house was also named 'Higham Hill', but it was soon renamed 'Highams'.

In 1790 'Highams' was sold to John Harman, a banker, and in 1793 he employed Humphry Repton to alter his imposing house and pleasure gardens. Repton immediately ordered the planting of trees to screen what he described as 'the naked village of Woodford'. His trade card pictures him supervising work on a site, and makes it obvious that every spade and barrowful of earth for his lakes had to be moved by hand! His 'Red Book' of designs for 'Highams' still exists.

Repton was interested in waterways. He was an artist who did a lot of sketching in East Anglia after his family moved to Norwich from Bury St Edmunds, and he went to school for two years in Rotterdam, Holland. He was apprenticed to a textile merchant in Norwich but he did not start his landscape-gardening business in Hare Street, near Romford, Essex, until 1788, when he was 36 years old. His work at 'Highams' was one of his earlier designs.

By the end of his life, in 1818, Repton had completed many successful projects at various houses all over England, including the grounds of Claybury, and even some in Scotland and Anglesey. He left instructions that when he died roses should be planted on his family grave by the door of St Michael's Church, Aylsham, in Norfolk, and the bed of roses is still there.

The Ching Brook used to meander over the land where the artificial lake for 'Highams' was excavated, but to keep the water in the lake fresh Repton altered the course of the Ching and put a small sluice-gate across the north end of the lake, so that, after rain, water could be flushed into it through a channel. Early photographs show there was a rustic bridge over this channel, and until the 1960s another wooden bridge crossed the Ching about halfway along the length of the lake.

The site of the sluice across the Ching Brook was about six feet downstream from where the new footbridge was constructed in 1999 to replace other wooden bridges

13 *'There's the bridge, right at the end of the lake, where the water used to come right across from the Ching and they built a sluice gate. We used to play all round there. I used to come down to see my Grandma – leave my push-bike and go rowing on the lake.' (J. Davis)*

built since the 1950s. Traces of its base can still be seen on the riverbed in dry weather. For many years the only way to get across the Ching at the top end of the lake was to walk along a narrow plank. By then the sluice was never used, and the central panel was raised and the sections on either side dropped to water level.

In 1849 'Highams' was sold by John Harman's son, Jeremiah, to Edward Warner, whose second son, T. Courtenay T. Warner, built the Warner Estate houses. Cliff Payling told the story of a famous Prime Minister's visit to 'Highams' by train in the time of Edward Warner's son: 'Sir Courtenay Warner, who was a Liberal MP, entertained Mr Gladstone at "Highams". He was taken from Highams Park Station and back in a pony and trap.' Miss Margery M. Smith wrote, 'On this occasion great excitement was caused because while being driven down to Hale End Station (as it was then) Mr Gladstone found he had left important papers behind in the house. The papers were hastily sent for and Mr Gladstone caught his train.'

The Warner family, like many other landowners, developed their property: roads were cut, houses built, and in the 1880s the Warner Estates Co. Ltd was established to manage the property.' Cliff Payling wrote,

> Of course, the Warners were speculators and they started to build on their land. They built a line of very large six-bedroom houses in Montalt Road (which have been converted into council flats); they built flats in Chingford Lane, near Mill Lane, which bordered their property, and they built all the 'Warner' Roads and Warner flats in Walthamstow. They would have built all over the entire area, but for the 'Epping Forest Act'! That stopped them building any more, and left us the lake and our forest land.

The Warners had planned to build on forest land and Hales Brinks, from the old Woodford High Road down to Hale End Road, but fortunately these plans were not carried out.

Sir Courtenay married into an aristocratic family, and all the roads in Walthamstow which the Warners developed still bear the surnames of that family, the names of villages and places where they had their estates, and the Christian names of his own family. They left in 1902 and 'Highams' was rented out. One of the tenants was the Bishop of St Albans. Apparently we were in the Diocese of St Albans in those days, before there was a Diocese of Chelmsford.

When the Warner family moved away, to Brettenham Park in Suffolk, 'Highams' was leased at first to Lady Somerset, who soon went to live in the White House, Woodford Green, which was built in the Arts and Crafts style on 11 acres of the estate and sold in 1906, and then to Dr Jacobs, Bishop of St Albans. One of the bishops of St Albans lived for several years in Castle Avenue, Highams Park. (The Rev. Melvin Oakes, Vicar of All Saints Church, Highams Park from 1982-96, confirmed that in 1905 the first move was made to establish the Diocese of Chelmsford in a Private Member's Bill in Parliament. The first Bishop of Chelmsford, the Rev. John Ditchfield, was enthroned on 23 February 1914.)

During the First World War 'Highams' was used as a hospital for wounded soldiers, and in 1919 the house was rented (and eventually bought) by Essex County Council to reopen as a school within Walthamstow. It was named 'Woodford County High School for Girls', with Miss Janet M. Gordon as its first headmistress. Margery M. Smith wrote two publications about 'Highams' for the Walthamstow Antiquarian Society: the first describes the many alterations to the manor house, and the second gives the history of Woodford County High School from 1919-69. Miss M.M.Smith also wrote papers for the Woodford Historical Society and was a teacher of History at the school from 1927-62.

The Chestnuts

Will Hebbard remembered seeing an old house in about 1910:

> 'The Chestnuts' in Oak Hill, Hale End stood where the houses at the end of Hollywood Way and Holly Crescent, Woodford Green are now. On fine days an open landau came from the large house, driven by a coachman with cockade and breeches, and Mrs Glanfield would go out for her drive, looking for all the world like Queen Victoria in bonnet and pelisse. In the grounds of the house was a large pond which intrigued me.

Sid Marchant also had clear memories of Mrs Glanfield, the widow of George Glanfield, a wholesale clothier who had owned and lived at 'The Chestnuts' from at least 1882.

> During the holidays we used to walk along Hale End Road and then through to Oak Hill and then on a glade there, which is still in existence, next to where the Kingfisher Pool was, we used to play cricket and football. An old lady owned the big house in Oak Hill, 'The Chestnuts', and she used to drive up in her carriage with her parasol, and she had a coachman, all dressed up in uniform and a top hat. She used to drive up to the top of the hill there, stop him, and watch us play for about an hour, then drive back.
>
> After she died her nephew took over her house and it was a school for a while [Oak Hill School], and we rented the field from him and played football. Then it was all sold for building – just beyond Holly Crescent – all along there. She owned all that land. That all went when the builders came.

Annie Hatley recorded earlier memories of 'The Chestnuts' by asking Charles Everitt (Everett) to 'take her on a walk' around Oak Hill in 1880:

> We started our journey up Oak Hill from his cottage, first passing 'The Chestnuts', owned by Miss Hillyard and later by Mr Glanfield. We then came to the path leading to the so-called 'Manor House', owned by Mr Berthon, a Swiss, whose family were very good people.

14   *'The Chestnuts' was in Oak Hill, where Holly Crescent is now.*

'The Chestnuts' in Hale End appeared on the 1822 'Map of the Country 12 miles round London', but a 1746 entry for Hale End in the parish of St Mary's Poor Rate Book shows that a rent of £20 was paid by a Mr Laybanks for a property in Hale End. The next year the rent was paid by William Loxham Esq., the new owner of this 'copyhold House and land at Hale End, Essex, held of the manor of Salisbury Hall', and Mr Loxham is known to have lived at The Chestnuts. William Loxham (the second son of Edward Loxham of Kirkham, Lancashire) was a very wealthy 'Hatter and Sword Cutler, under the Royal Exchange', who retired to Hale End some time between 1744-7. He had married Lydia Hargraves (or Hargrove) but unfortunately all of their three children died in infancy, so, after William died in 1780, aged 85 years old, the son of his brother (the Rev. Robert), Edward Loxham, who was also a Sword Cutler, inherited The Chestnuts. In 1782 the house was leased for 15 years to Francis Hanrott. Lydia was left two cottages in Hale End, where Henry Mills and Adam Furnace had possession for life, and two freehold houses in Shoe Lane, London, which were in possession of a widow, Eleanor Gyles.

The Chestnuts had been offered for sale in 1781 and was described as a brick house, having four rooms on each floor, with a cart yard, rick yards, two pleasure gardens, a kitchen garden and an orchard, a canal and two fish ponds, with adjoining meadow land (West Field, Middle Field and East Field), of 15 acres 20 perches. Edward Loxham and his wife Jane lived in Woodford until his death in 1798. Their son, Robert, married his cousin, Elizabeth Loxham, and they lived at The Chestnuts until he died in 1845. One of their two daughters, Elizabeth, was unmarried and died in 1861, but Jane married George Hildyard.

Forest Hall in Oak Hill

On the opposite side of the road to The Chestnuts was Forest Hall, built in the 18th century with about 13 acres of land and described by Frank Payling as 'a very large

15 *Until 1844, St Mary's Church in Walthamstow was also the parish church of Hale End, over two miles away. This early view shows the tower, Alms Houses, and a chapel, which were built in the late 15th to early 16th centuries. Today, trees line the paths through the churchyard, making the centre of Walthamstow village very attractive.*

red-brick Georgian place, that became an orphanage, and was where the council housing is now'. Seen from the road, there was a high wall and a long stable block on the right-hand side (shown on maps from 1822), and in about 1830 it was owned by Mr Arthur Ryder.

Probably the most interesting resident of Forest Hall was the poet, Mrs Harriet Hamilton-King (1840-1920), who was the daughter of Lady Harriet and Admiral William Alexander Baillee Hamilton. She had lived at the Manor House, Chigwell after marrying the banker, Henry Samuel King, and had the means to employ servants and nannies to care for their seven children. She moved to Forest Hall with four daughters after Henry died in 1878.

From 1869 she had become passionately interested in the 'cause' of Italian Unification, which inspired her work *Aspromonte and other Poems*, and her correspondence with the Italian patriot, Guiseppe Mazzini, was used later in his *Letters and Recollections* of 1912. Her poetry was published between 1862 and 1902 and was very well received by Victorian readers, her most popular work being 'The Disciples'. She became a Roman Catholic later in life and wrote *The Prophecy of Westminster and Other Poems* in honour of Cardinal Manning.

Forest Hall was used as a children's home (noted in the Selwyn Avenue School log book as 'Mrs Steer's') until the Second World War, when it was destroyed in a devastating fly-bomb explosion. By 1930 12 acres of the estate had been sold for 130 building plots and Oak Hill Court now stands on the site.

Mapperley House and Forest Lodge in Oak Hill

Will Hebbard remembered other people who lived on Oak Hill:

> Councillor Watkins had a groom to take him in his governess cart to and from the station when he went to the city every day from his Bridle Path home.

The Thomas family at Mapperley House were furniture wholesalers who, knowing father in Custan Road, got him to do their furniture repairs, and I was sent with the bill, which was never sent when the repair was done and often involved a golden half-sovereign or a sovereign in payment. In their grounds on the bend of Oak Hill were about twelve lime trees with an excellent perfume when in bloom.

Mapperley House was built in 1860 and demolished in 1936.

Higher up on the other side of the road was a large house owned by the Manders family, whose only son I knew, and he was killed by a kick from a horse about 1913.

This was Forest Lodge, which in 1846 had been the home of John Hetherington with Mellor and Mary. The house was later sold and became the Kingfisher Pool, and later *Waltham Forest Hotel*. Afterwards it was named the *Woodford Moat House*, then the *County Hotel, Epping Forest*. In 2005 plans are afoot to demolish the hotel for housing.

'Sky Peals Farm'

'Sky Peals' is a fascinating name, originally given to a field and then to a mid-19th-century house by the forest, and it continues today in Sky Peals Road. A reference (with two spellings) in the court rolls of Salisbury Hall to lands acquired by George Monoux in 1518 shows 'a close called Sykales (*c.*8 acres) from Margaret Skerne and William Dryclow, her son and heir; 3 acres in Bromland on the north of Milfield; a tenement called Normans land and 13 acres in Bradfield abutting on Sylkales'. This may refer to Sky Peals, although 'Milfield' seems to be at the western end of the manor.

Dennis Webb wrote,

In 1844 a new house was built on the field called Sky Peals, to the south of the forest. This became later 'Sky Peals Farm' and the first occupant was George Augustus Clark, who lived there for 20 years. Sky Peals was built on land belonging to Scotts and took over as the farm.

The Census of 1881 showed that Sky Peals was being farmed by John Gregory, a 75-year-old retired butcher from Poplar, and he and his wife Harriett and their married daughter were living in the house. The farm's Bailiff, Abraham Bull, and Charles Bull, an agricultural labourer born in Colne, lived next door to each other in two of the little Oak Hill Cottages near the Webb family and Beech Hall. Another large family which lived for several generations from at least 1841 in the Oak Hill Cottages was that of William Sheridan, the chimney sweep.

Frank Payling remembered fields behind a 19th-century house:

On the opposite side of Hale End Road [from Beech Hall farm] is the three-storey house which is still known as 'Montserrat'. It was bounded on one side by the driveway up to Sky Peals house, which is now known as Forest Mount Road, and the other side extended as far as Mapperley House. Hooper's field was most attractive, sloped right up to the forest and on one side of it had a beautiful row of aspen trees. You used to get a lovely shade. The owner of the house and field was Mr Hooper, a wealthy man, who made umbrellas.

Churches and Chapels

Mrs Edith Upton wrote,

There were beautiful bluebells in Larks Wood – and anemones – which are coming back. Through the Ching passage, from Beech Hall into Winchester Road, it was golden with celandines. I remember it when it was a slippery bank, with a little path.

Winchester Road was not 'tar-macadamised', and my relatives, who lived in Walthamstow, used to walk over to see granddad. When they got down to where the Ching Bridge is, they took a diagonal line, right across fields to Walthamstow, and there were not any houses there. All those fields belonged to Hitchman, who gave the ground that the Methodist Church in Winchester Road is on.

This church was built after John Hitchman (1834-1911) approached William Mallinson of 'The Limes' in Shernhall, Walthamstow, with an offer of land so that provision could be made for church services for the growing population of Hale End. In 1902 a trust was set up and a small iron hall was erected, but it soon proved to be inadequate for a congregation of 150 and Sunday school of 100, so a better building was built and opened in 1904, with the Rev. H.J. Watts as the minister in charge, 'with Shernhall Church having the oversight'.

William Mallinson (1854-1936) founded a very successful hardwood firm, which produced the first plywood. He was known as a great benefactor to London churches, and in 1935 he was elevated to a barony. His son, Sir Stuart Mallinson, lived at the White House, Woodford Green, where he invited many famous visitors to plant trees in his arboretum. After Sir Stuart's death the White House was used as a Respite Care Centre. Unfortunately a serious fire damaged the building, but the house was restored and is now known as Haven House Children's Hospice.

Larks Wood is just over the old parish boundaries in Chingford, and is part of the manor of Chingford Earls, which was owned by the Boothby-Heathcote family of Friday Hill House. Ropers Farm backed on to the wood, and before the Roper family came the farm was known as Inks Green.

Chingford and Hale End were near neighbours but they had separate manors and churches and developed in very different ways. Records show that there was a chapel in 1442, which gave its name to neighbouring Chapel End, but the building was a ruin by 1650. Dennis Webb was very interested in the complicated history of the local churches and their parishes, beginning with St Mary's parish church, Walthamstow, which was in the manor of Toni and dates from at least 1108, although it is thought that an earlier place of worship may have been founded in the seventh century after Cedd had converted the people of East Anglia to Christianity:

> When you had a manor you generally had a church, but you did not have a church here at all, so loyalty was to St Mary's, Walthamstow. Hale End had no church, but you looked to Walthamstow rather than to Chingford. The land between Hale End and

16   *Roper's Farm, Inks Green by Larks Wood (c.1909). 'Larks Wood was known as "Hungry Hill" from the Saxon word "hunway" meaning a forest on a slope.' (D. Webb)*

17   *The entrance to Roper's Field, where Roper's Avenue is now. The path on the right still leads into Larks Wood.*

All Saints-on-the-Hill on Chingford Mount (which was the old manor church of the Chingford Hall Manor) was partly owned by the Canons of St Paul's Cathedral and partly by the Chingford Manor. Chingford parish church wasn't built until much later on, when Heathcote took it over. He was the rector, and the lord of the manor.

All Saints, Highams Park is a very unusual church, because Hale End was split between two parishes, St John's, on the Winchester Road side, and St Peter's-in-the-Forest this side; this was a 'Conventional District' and it was the vicar of St Peter's-in-the-Forest who used to hold the services. All the weddings went to St Peter's-in-the-Forest. I have a map of 1897 showing that in the Parish of St John's there wasn't anything at all on that side of the railway line, right over to Edmonton, just ordinary farmland!

In 1840 St Peter's-in-the Forest was built as a chapel of rest for St Mary's Church, Walthamstow, but in 1844 St Peter's became the parish church of Hale End. More people moved into the area with the coming of the BX Co. Factory, and in 1898 All Saints Church was built in Castle Avenue and it was dedicated as a chapel of rest for St Peter's-in-the-Forest.

By 1912 there were four well-established nonconformist churches in Highams Park, as well as All Saints in Castle Avenue, and the huge All Saints parish church began to rise in Selwyn Avenue. But only one part, because fewer houses were built than expected and the congregation was always quite small. A very large parish church was not needed.

All Saints Church was originally named St Matthew's, but the name had to be changed because the money bequeathed in the wills of Canon Ainslie, and his sister, Miss Elizabeth Ainslie of 'The Rolls', and intended for the church in Castle Avenue could only be used for 'All Saints Church'. In 1978 the All Saints Church in Selwyn Avenue was pulled down and All Saints, Castle Avenue became the church of the parish.

Dennis Webb used to go to All Saints Church in Selwyn Avenue:

I always thought the font was beautiful there. The seating was hand-made and it was given at the time of the Consecration of the Parish Church by the wife of the Bishop of St Albans. (Last time I saw it, it was resting in St Catherine's Church, Leyton.) When the Rev. Jeffries came in 1953 there were 500 chairs – and woodworm! The old church hall was purchased from the Chingford Airfield, which is now under a reservoir.

The original War Memorial has been copied and is now in All Saints on the Hill – they are all Highams Park people. There was a little stained-glass window, and I was very, very upset about that, because it was given in memory of a little girl who died. I think she was killed by a horse and cart in Forest Road. I

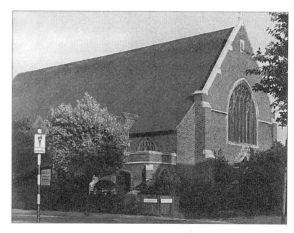

18 *The parish church of All Saints, Selwyn Avenue, was named St Andrew's at first, but when it became apparent that Miss Ainslie's donation could only be used for 'All Saints Church', the name was hastily changed!*

wanted John Crump to bring the window up to All Saints on the Hill but the builders wouldn't get it out.

The Rev. John Crump, AKC, RD (1927-98) was the Vicar of All Saints, Highams Park from 1965-78 and the Rural Dean for Waltham Forest for 13 years. He was loved by the congregation of All Saints for his gentle manner, jovial remarks and great kindness, especially to the older folk. When he and his wife, Brenda, moved on to another church at Abridge, then to Walton-on-the-Naze, it needed a coach to accommodate the many parishioners from Highams Park who wanted to visit them and wish them well.

Romany Gypsies

Renee Weller came with her parents to live near Oak Hill in Woodford Green in 1932, when gypsies still camped in the Forest. Her interest in local history led her to give talks to school children:

19 *All Saints Church on the hill, built in 1897. 'That picture is pre 1911 – There's no flagpole,' said Dennis Webb. In 1903, the church had no vestry or organ: that was built in 1911. The church hall followed in 1908, and the vicarage in 1920-1.'*

20 *Gypsy Rodney Smith, OBE. In the forest by the old Woodford High Road on Mill Plain, a stone commemorates the birth in the forest of Rodney Smith, who became the world famous preacher known as Gypsy Smith. He died while he was travelling on the liner, the* Queen Mary.

When we first moved here it was not unusual to see the gypsies – real Romany gypsies – coming around, and they were building the trellis-work and the woodwork for the gardens. Dad had both sides of the garden trellised and an arch at the top of the garden for a swing for us children, and they were made by the gypsies. I also have memories of us going out, when Dad finally got a car, and we used to go round the country lanes. It was nothing unusual to see a genuine Romany caravan. Of course, it's recorded that Gypsy Smith was born in the forest by Mill Plain in 1860, right up at the top by the High Road.

In his book, *The History of Woodford Green United Free Church*, R.L. Galey mentioned that some time between 1906 and 1916 Gypsy Rodney Smith had 'visited the church, which was filled to capacity to hear him', and that in 1869 'a Gypsy Tea Party on Mill Plain was organised by Mr Longmore for 300 gypsies'. The famous preacher from the Forest, Gypsy Rodney Smith, OBE, travelled far and wide, and when he died in 1947 he was on board the ocean liner the *Queen Mary*.

Woodford Row and Woodford Side

Barbara Millett lived in Chingford Lane, Woodford Green during the 1940s and '50s, '... next door but one to Chapman's Farm and their pigsty! We used fly papers constantly!' This was in Woodford Row, part of the small settlement at Woodford Side, which grew up around the Woodford Windmill on the old mail coach route. The boundary between Walthamstow and Woodford ran along what is now called Savill Row. Opposite Mrs Millett's home was a piece of derelict land with fruit trees and the foundations

21 *Samuel Skinner, aged six, taking the reins of the goat cart with 'Nanny', the family's goat, in Spencer Road (off Macdonald Road) in the 1920s.*

22 *The Walthamstow Mill. This stood on Mill Plain at the top of Oak Hill by the old Woodford High Road (now a forest track). John Hawkes, a millwright from Whitechapel, built this post mill in 1676 but it is thought to have blown down in about 1800. Another mill, the Woodford Mill, was at the top of Mill Lane, Woodford Row, probably just the other side of the Walthamstow boundary line.*

of a house which local people called 'the farm'. A map of 1865-76 names it as 'Park Farm' on the Highams Estate, and in 1882 the occupant was C. Hodges. (OS maps of 1930 showed several buildings on the site but now there is a large block of flats there, erected by Waltham Forest Council.)

At the back of Mrs Millett's house was Ashman's allotment, and she remembers that the lawn tennis courts behind the church and old houses of High Elms were also used as allotments during the Second World War:

> There were lots of little cottages dotted around, including Faery's Row Cottages with no roadway, and people did their washing out at the back of the fenced cottages along Savill Row. I knew the man who had stables by the *Golden Cross* public house on the corner of Mill Lane and Savill Row. His name was Horace and he used to graze his goats on the green by the school. The blacksmith's shop was at the end of an alleyway and I sometimes watched him working at his forge but the entrance to the alleyway now has a building on it.
>
> The shop on the corner of Elm Grove and Chingford Lane has gone back to being a private house. When I was little it was a greengrocer's shop run by the Knights, and they kept a horse to pull their cart in the stable just up from the shop. Before the Knights took it over it was a butcher's shop, and Knights sold their greengrocery from the little hut on derelict land on the corner of Mill Lane and Chingford Lane.
>
> The people who owned 'the farm' were the Chapmans. Old Mr Chapman lived in the side of the farm house next to the abattoir and his married daughter lived in the other side of the house. The son, David, and three of his sons ran the butcher's shop in the High Road which is still there.

Higham Lodge and Highams Cottages were built by the Woodford High Road near to 'Highams', just past the entrance of the lane to the present rugby club, and over the years additions were made to the small cottages until they became one sizeable dwelling named 'St Margarets'.

2

'Haile' to the Newcomers

'Eureka' was the name given in 1926 to a small school in Falmouth Avenue which was built on land belonging to the Collard family within the manor of Salisbury Hall. The building of the bungalow began in 1924 but its present owners have kept the deeds of their house, which give a fascinating history of the site and indicate how the building of a railway to Hale End led to the development of the first suburban estate and the last days of the manor. The plot of land for 'Eureka' was on 'The Haile Park Estate' plans of 1880, which showed that some of the fields were about to be covered by the first new roads: Handsworth Avenue, Falmouth Avenue, part of The Avenue (from the station to Falmouth Avenue) and Castle Avenue.

Events in the lives of the Collard family of Walthamstow are recorded from 1541, but the story outlined in the 'Eureka' house deeds begins in 1855, when the last of the family line, George Collard, died and his wife, Jane Sabina, inherited 59 acres of land within Salisbury Hall Manor, including fields of arable land called Gaffings Birch, Barne, Harp and Scurl's, and Castle Field, which measured 7 acres 2 rods 9 poles. Castle Field was also known as 'Castle Cold William'. It began to the east of Jack's Green Lane (now Larkshall Road) and went up and over the hill where Castle Avenue was to be built and down to The Sale near the Ching Brook. At that time it was part of a farm let on lease to a Mr Wicks.

Jane Sabina inherited a very attractive acreage of land, and after the death of her husband she married again, twice. Mrs Jane Sabina Collard – ultimately Burton – lived in a house named 'Brookfield', in Shernhall Street, Walthamstow, and seems to have had an on-going battle of wills with the local Catholic priest. She had given money towards a place of worship, but after bitter disagreements withdrew her support. In her Will she left money for charity and eventually the Collard Alms Houses were built in Maynard Road, Walthamstow. The Will of 1865 also showed that Salisbury Hall Farm had been leased to Francis Wragg, yeoman, of Walthamstow for £120 per annum.

Francis Wragg was one of the famous coaching and carrier family which farmed in Clay Street and had livery stables in Wood Street, running coaches to London seven times a day until 1870. This was near the end of the romantic but uncomfortable era of the stage coach, a time when coaching inns and their stables flourished. Anyone intending to travel into London from Essex had to cross the River Lea via 'Stratford-ate-Bow' or the Lea Bridge Turnpike Road. In 1839 Robert Wragg's coaches, in their distinctive yellow and brown livery, provided frequent services from Leyton to the Royal Exchange and from Walthamstow to Bishopsgate, which enabled businessmen, huddled in greatcoats under their travelling rugs, to make daily trips into London. However, competition from other coaching firms was so fierce that eventually Wragg's coaches went only to Stratford.

Stage coaches stopped at Woodford, and until about 1845 this was also the boarding point for one of the busy short-stage coaching routes to the Royal Exchange. The coach service ran along Woodford High Road, but in the 18th century passengers from Epping and beyond would have faced the possibility of attack by Dick Turpin. Many highwaymen lurked in the Epping Forest area, but as more and more coaches and carriers filled the roads travelling became safer.

But the age of steam was coming, and when Walter Hancock tried out his 'Automaton' steam coach along the unmade High Road to Epping in 1836, it was probably not only passing horses that were startled! In 1840 the first railway near Walthamstow opened, operated by the Northern & Eastern Company. The Lea Valley Line was planned to leave London and run along the valley to Broxbourne and Cambridge. There was no railway to Hale End but people from the Walthamstow area were able to board the trains at Lea Bridge Station, which was built at the old turnpike. The trains had an immediate affect on Wragg's coach services, although horse buses providing transport home to Walthamstow from the station operated for many years after the coming of the railway.

The future of Epping Forest was already threatened because people were encouraged to enclose acres of forest land for building projects, but the railways posed an even greater threat to the Forest and also to large houses with estates. In 1864 Parliament gave its approval to the Great Eastern Railway Company's plans to build a railway through Epping Forest to High Beach, and this would open up the whole Forest for building. It was proposed that two lines would be built, one from Stratford and Leyton via the Hall Farm and Coppermill Junction to Chingford and High Beach, the second beginning at Bishopsgate and going to Bethnal Green and Hackney Downs. It would then cross

23 *Hale End railway station was surrounded by fields for 20 years after it was erected. G.E.R. renamed this station, 'Highams Park (Hale End)' in 1894.*

the marshes and join the first line at Shern Hall Street in Walthamstow. The railway line was to cut across farmland near Hale End, with stations at Inks Green Farm by Larks Wood and at Chingford Hatch. Fortunately, due to 'cash-flow' problems at crucial moments in other GER railway building projects, these plans had to be modified.

Eventually a railway line was built from London to Shernhall Station in Walthamstow, and it opened in 1870. It started from Bishopsgate, but almost immediately trains were moved to the new terminus at Liverpool Street (which was more conveniently placed for the City). Shernhall closed in 1873 when the line was extended to Chingford, and trains stopped at Wood Street and the wooden station named Hale End, which was over half a mile away from the hamlet.

Unlike many districts within easy reach of London, the coming of the railway made surprisingly little impact on the local farming community for the next few years, apart from as a way of transporting coal and churns of milk, but in 1875 Salisbury Hall Farm was broken up by the sale of land to the Great Eastern Railway Company, and in 1877 Castle Field in Hale End was sold for building to J. Haile and Richard Crossley for £8,600. 'The Haile Park Freehold Building Estate' of 1880 was on the other side of the valley to the cottages and houses of old Hale End, which was not really affected by redevelopment for another 50 years.

The deeds of 'Eureka' in Falmouth Avenue mention that Mr Augustus W.O. Burton either lived or had offices at 106 Falmouth Road, Great Dover Street, Southwark in 1879, and this may be how Falmouth Avenue got its name. 'Haile Avenue' appears in Shillinglaw's *Directory* of 1882, but it is not clear if it refers to Handsworth Avenue or 'The

24   *The marshalling yard and the old signal box at Highams Park and Hale End station.*

Avenue'. Nowadays the only written reminder of the 'Haile Estate' is 'Haile House', a semi-detached house next to 'Rye House', on the brow of the hill in Handsworth Avenue.

Cheap workmen's tickets were not available from Hale End Station and so there was little demand for the proposed terraces of small houses on the Haile Estate plan aimed at people with modest incomes. Instead the history of Hale End repeated itself, as wealthy businessmen were attracted by the area's beautiful surroundings and the short journey, now by train, into the City of London. These buyers chose several adjoining plots in Castle Avenue to build large houses with long gardens and stables: on the south side of the road some plots of land included gardens going all the way to Handsworth Avenue. A row of big houses with attics for the servants were built over the hill in Handsworth Avenue, with pleasant views over the fields of the 'Manor House' to Hale End and the Forest. Down the hill towards the station in Castle Avenue there was another big house (now replaced by flats), and two three-storey semi-detached houses were built which also had a fine view across the fields to 'Rolls' and Larks Wood.

Margaret Page said that one of the houses, 'Zeta Villa', was built in 1880 for a sea captain, who named it after his ship. She also heard about some later owners of the house from her neighbour, Bob Izod, who was 96 years old when he died in 1994.

> Bob Izod said that they were theatrical people (Watson Music), who used to do
> pantomimes. They were in pantomime with Lupino Lane. Bob saw all the little
> costumes on a line in the garden, and great big vans arrived for the props, including
> a throne. Up the hill by the Vicarage, where the flats are now, was a double-fronted
> house and Mr Evans Peachey lived there. In the first house [after Church Avenue]
> in Castle Avenue lived Mrs Anne Frazer, the Scottish fashion journalist, who worked
> in Fleet Street. Her husband was Wing Commander (Bill) Frazer, who flew notable
> people like Sir Winston Churchill.

Some houses had a stable and, on the 1880 plan of the Haile Estate, stables and a small garden with a pond are shown on the corner of The Avenue and Hale End Road, near the station and level crossing at the bottom of a hill where, many years later, a branch of Barclay's Bank was built. It is not surprising to learn that there were problems with water under the bank building. Dick Oliver was the manager of Barclay's Bank for several years and he had lived in the Highams Park area all his life:

> I remember a garden with a brick wall in front of it in the space between the shops and the bank on this corner. The bank was extended into The Avenue and when they excavated the garden, digging a hole about twenty feet deep, there was no water. But no sooner did they put a strong room down there and it rained than it filled up with water! We had to have pumps in the strong rooms of the bank, which started up each time it rained and the water began to rise. There have always been springs round here.

The present occupants of the building, which is no longer a bank, say that the pumping equipment still has to be used occasionally.

Epping Forest and Builders

Larks Wood and High Beach had been saved from railways and building developments, almost by accident, but towards the end of the 19th century an alert group of people woke up to the fact that the entire Forest could disappear if the many proposed building developments were allowed. They formed the 'Epping Forest Fund Committee' and fought a furious battle through Parliament to preserve the Forest. They claimed that commoners had the right to allow their cattle to roam over all the forest lands – not just within their manors' boundaries – and they won the case. This led to the Epping Forest Act of 1878. Land which had been enclosed recently was returned to the Forest, and in 1882 Queen Victoria declared that Epping Forest should be 'free and open for ever'.

After this there was no longer a 'free-for-all' situation in Epping Forest. A few speculative builders from London began to show interest in the 'Haile Park Estate', but building was erratic. In 1885 plot no. 66 in The Avenue was bought by a refreshment stall-holder of the Balls Pond Road area of London, Daniel Appleing, and Oscar Watling a builder. Seven years after buying the ground, Watling built one side of a pair of 'semis', and this stood as a detached house for about ten years before half the garden was sold and the other semi-detached house was added.

Records of buildings and alterations to houses in Waltham Forest Planning Department Archives show that several large houses in Castle Avenue, such as 'Crest

25 *The old* Royal Oak *public house, pre-1906, at the junction of Hale End Road and Oak Hill.*

View House', owned by Robert Flint, were built in 1881, probably without mains drainage as cesspools were being installed for Nos. 16 and 18 Castle Avenue, but by 1891 drainage was installed by J.C. Warner at Nos. 8 and 10.

The first house to be built in The Avenue was 'Redthorne', a large house on a big plot of land where, in 1891, a looking-glass manufacturer from Shoreditch, Fred Vincent, lived with his wife, his son, Leonard, and Rosa Vincent (who was 80 years old and had an income of her own). The house still stands but most of its land has been sold for development.

That year was a very significant one in the history of Hale End because the City of London Conservators of Epping Forest, with the help of contributions from the local boards of Walthamstow and Woodford, bought the lake belonging to 'Highams' and the land around it from Sir Thomas Courtenay Warner, Bart. The Conservators also purchased the land by Chingford Lane, 'The Lops', now the golf links and common, and the narrow strip of land from the lake to Oak Hill, part of The Sale. In 1894 Hale End railway station was re-named 'Highams Park (Hale End)' to encourage day-trippers to come and enjoy the lake in the newly opened Highams Park.

Miss F. Bowler knew most of the people who had lived in Falmouth Avenue. The booklet *Bits and Pieces*, which she helped to compile, said that the oldest house in Falmouth Avenue (No. 73), known as 'The Farmhouse', was built in 1892 and had two natural wells in the garden.

> There was an open space, a bit of rough ground that wasn't built on, and Stone, the builder (a very nice man), built those two houses which are joined together. The Stones lived in one, and the Ratners, who I knew very well, lived next door. Then of course, it was the Smee estate with the yew trees – and that *was* a big garden!
>
> The gardens of 'Normanhurst', where 'Sheldon House' now stands, went through to St Leonards and across the back of the gardens of Nos 30, 32, 34 and 36. 'Normanhurst' became a nursing home, and then during the war the Home Guard had it. Graham Smee returned for a while after 1945, then it was demolished. 'Biddington', a detached house, was also part of Smee's estate and was occupied by their chauffeur!
>
> Mr Exley was a schoolmaster and his wife was a schoolmistress. They had a son and a daughter and their home was on the right-hand side down Falmouth Avenue, but their house is now down: it's a block of flats.
>
> Where Amanda Court now stands there was a house called 'St Moritz'. This was part of the other Smee's estate – Walter Smee's. They lived there with their daughter, Hilda. Later, when the Hodgsons had it, they had tennis courts.

Donald Ray recalled 'St Moritz' because when he was very young he sometimes visited the house with his grandfather, who was the gardener. Before the First World War his grandfather had been Head Stockman at Copped Hall, the beautiful country house near Epping, which is gradually being restored by the Copped Hall Trust:

> Before the war, in Falmouth Avenue there were a lot of older houses, which I think of as being Victorian, though the one the Hodgsons lived in was probably late Edwardian. It was one of the houses on the left-hand side going down the hill towards the lake. The garden was not only behind the big, detached house but on both sides of it as well, and it stretched down behind several other houses to the pathway which runs along by the Ching. I went there as a small boy with my grandfather, Walter Walker.
>
> My memories are of cycling over to Highams Park with my grandfather at about eight o'clock in the morning, and having lunch with him in the summer-house or in the shed in which they kept potatoes and things, and thinking this is absolutely *marvellous*, and having quite foul cold tea in a milk bottle! (He 'didn't hold' with modern things like thermos flasks.) I spent long days 'helping' with cutting the lawns, which for years grandfather did with a hand mower! It seemed to me there were acres and *acres* of it as well as lots of garden.

26   *The* Royal Oak *was rebuilt in 1906 and is still there.*

The names of the people my grandfather worked for were Hodgson and Clark, the firm of Clark, the Estate Agents, in Hoe Street, Walthamstow.

Today Donald Ray, BA, FRCO, who still lives in Chingford, is better known as a musician than a gardener. He has performed in countless concerts and string ensembles and has travelled all over the world as an Examiner in Music. His late wife, Barbara Ray, published several local history books about Chingford, a village about three miles from Hale End. Their three daughters all went to the Highams Park School and one of them, Jane Ray, is now a very successful artist and book illustrator.

A more ambitious Haile Estate plan appeared in 1897 after the arrival of the British Xylonite Company's factory workers. It proposed more roads, builders being expected to buy small plots for little houses, and one of the new roads was planned to run along the banks of the Ching. St Leonards Avenue was a road where the vendors hoped to sell 46 plots but, once again, things did not go as expected and St Leonards Avenue stayed a dirt track until after the Second World War, when only 26 houses were built.

As more farm land was sold, building began in earnest in the new urban village. In 1899 the name of the station was changed again, to 'Highams Park & Hale End'. This lasted until 1969, when the '& Hale End' was removed, by which time the whole area was known as Highams Park and the whereabouts of old Hale End was almost forgotten.

Oscar Watling and his brothers set up a builders merchants' business in The Avenue and by 1903, until about 1917, he was the owner of 'Cove Hithe' in Castle Avenue. In 1908 Oscar Watling is mentioned as the builder of No. 38, and in 1910 he built a 'motor house' for No. 40, but he was also the builder of the Beech Hall Estate on the fields of Beech Hall Farm.

Newcomers to Hale End

At the end of the 19th century there were still shoemakers, coachmen, chimney sweeps, a thatcher, a carriage-painter and grooms providing services to the large houses in old Hale End, and the earlier entries in the parish registers of St Peter's in the Forest show that the majority of people in the Hale End area worked as gardeners or 'Ag Labs' (agricultural labourers). In 1851 Mrs Hills was publican of the *Royal Oak*, but local directories of 1882-7 listed the beerhouse keeper at the *Royal Oak* public house

27 *Thorpe Hall Cottages, Hale End Road. The Bradley family moved into the first cottage on the left in the late 1890s, and Mrs Win Marchant was born there in 1903.*

in Hale End Road as James Charlton, whose birthplace is shown as Edmonton in the census of 1881.

Cliff Payling's father came to live in Hale End Road in 1897, and at that time his house was surrounded by fields:

> By 1881 there were more people in the Walthamstow census for this area than there had been in 1871, but even then there were only about 30 houses listed in Hale End! It doesn't mention any addresses at all, unless it was a big house like 'Sky Peals' or the farms, so pin-pointing exactly where the buildings were from the census can only be done by looking at the order in which they were listed.
>
> I found that there was a complete mixture of people – something like half of them were quite wealthy, living in not particularly big houses but they had live-in servants, and the other half were agricultural labourers. You name it and they were there. The interesting thing was, hardly any of them were born in this area.

Mrs Win Marchant, like the Payling family, *was* born in the Hale End area, where she lived for 99 years until she died in the extremely hot summer of 2003. In 1996 Mrs Marchant enjoyed telling the story about her father, William Eli Bradley, a master glass-cutter of decorative glass, who had travelled to London for work but found that the polluted air affected the health of his children:

> My father came from Kidderminster, the country part of the Midlands, where he was apprenticed. He came to live in Dalston, London, after finishing his apprenticeship. He married my mother and started his little family, and they had two children there.
>
> One day, in the late 1890s, father got on the train from Liverpool Street, intending to go to Chingford, just to look around, because his doctor recommended that he should come to a country place to get the fresh air for the sake of the children. Of course, that suited him! He wanted to do it as well – he was a countryman.
>
> He got off the train before he reached Chingford, at Highams Park, and he crossed the fields and found four little cottages in Hale End Road. One was to let, and that cottage, which he decided to rent, is still there. [It is at the end of Thorpe Hall Terrace.]

Next door to our house was a yard, then two wooden cottages: typical Essex Board, tarred black, where the Young family and the Sorrels lived. There was a row of about eight cottages a little farther along, named Berry Grove. Mr and Mrs Sinfield ran the Laundry at the back of the field behind Berry Grove, and they had a nice house near the railway bridge – all pulled down now. Hitchman's Cottages, in Hale End Road, near where Wadham Bridge was built later, were built to house the workers from Hitchman's Farm and Dairy at Wadham Lodge. (Later, Collinson's Precision Screw Company, which removed to Fulbourne Road, was built on the corner of Hale End Road and MacDonald Road.)

Our family grew, and after two more children I arrived, the middle one. Eventually there were eight children (sadly, my parents lost

28 *Miss Muddiman photographed children running up Wadham Road to see the trains (c.1923). This is now part of the North Circular Road! 'There was a level-crossing at the top of Winchester Road and, in the lane that led to it, were some cottages. They had a lovely shrub in the gardens that my mother called a Tea plant. It had a very thin leaf and it grew as a hedge in these little cottages. You'll find a reference to those cottages in Annie Hatley's book.' (Mrs E. Upton)*

another child), and we moved to a bigger house a few doors along Hale End Road, on the corner of Thorpe Hall Road [Ursula House]. The old coach-house halfway down our garden, where we used to play, is still standing.

Cliff Payling recalled:

> At the Hagger Lane end of Hale End Road was Berry Grove. Before her marriage in 1906 my mother used to live in one of the tiny terraced houses in Berry Grove (which became 33 Hale End Road). It wasn't weather-boarded like the house where the Sorrels used to live. One of my cousins, who went to school in the old 'Tin Hut', lived next door until about 1908 (our mothers were sisters), but the houses of Berry Grove were demolished many years ago.
>
> Hitchman's Cottages were opposite Woodland View, the name originally given to the houses that stretched from Cobham Road to Wadham Bridge, some of which were pulled down when the new [North Circular] road was built recently.

The farmer of King's Farm at Chapel End was Mr Stevens, but Wadham Road and Wadham Bridge took their names from Wadham Lodge, which was farmed by John Hitchman. In the 1881 census the farm was said to cover 280 acres (some of which remain as playing fields today), and there was enough work for 16 men and two boys. The census included two stockmen, Charles Poulter, born in Walthamstow, and Mr Garmerd, born in Guildford, and the farmer, John Hitchman, who was then 46 years old and had been born in Longford, Glamorgan. John Hitchman bought Wadham Lodge Farm from the College in 1898 and became a great benefactor to the Hale End area. He also gave money towards the building of Moreia Welsh Presbyterian Church in Walthamstow.

Several houses in Castle Avenue had Welsh names, and census returns show that at Bellevue House in 1851 the cook and housemaid, Ann and Kate Jones, had both been born in Wales. Quite a large number of Welsh people came to settle in Walthamstow. Oswald Rees Owen, BA, BD explained the 19th-century Welsh settlement in his history of Moreia Welsh Presbyterian Church, Walthamstow, *Hanes yr Achos* 1903-1953 (translated from Welsh in 1992 and 1995 by members of the congregation).

At the end of the last century and the beginning of this one there was a large exodus from Wales to London, especially from Cardiganshire. There was a crisis in agriculture in the old country and it was difficult to make ends meet. People heard of great possibilities in the milk and other businesses in London and many Cardiganshire people left to try their luck. I heard of some, who met many years afterwards and found that they had left Tregaron for London on the same train.

At this time there was a big change in Walthamstow. The Great Eastern Railway started running cheap trains to Walthamstow, and thousands of people left Central London for the suburbs.

Thousands of new houses were built in Walthamstow (e.g. the Warner Estate) and many came from Wales to start businesses in the town. There were several clothiers and milk rounds in Hoe Street and High Street, and with them came Mr and Mrs Vaughan, who became active members of the church later on.

The Welsh-speaking church first met in 1901, above a restaurant in St Mary's Road, Walthamstow, but in 1932 Moreia Church was established in the converted stable block of 'Church House' in Church Hill. In the early 1950s 'Moreia' moved to Leytonstone High Road and the new buildings were built on the site of the house where the famous surgeon, Sir Joseph Lister, had lived.

Stan Batson's family moved to Winchester Road, Highams Park in 1929, but he had lived as a child in Fulbourne Road, which he described as 'a quiet little road':

When we were very young there was very little traffic, so the streets were our playground and we would roller-skate, play football – all sorts of things – with no traffic about. We would go round into Garner Road, next to Franklins, the Bakers, and old Mrs Jones' haberdashery, on the other corner there, and we were never any trouble to anybody in the cul-de-sac there. It just led into fields before they built any houses.

At the back of Fulbourne Road (where Bridge End and Queenswood Avenue are now), there were allotments and a tiny cul de sac – another little playground for us. On the left, going towards Highams Park and Wadham Road, were allotments and on the right-hand side (where the newer houses are now) it was just open fields and all of Wadham Road was nothing more than a country lane. Wadham Road ran up to a level-crossing where the railway cut through it. Of course there was no Wadham Bridge at all. We used the 'top field', as we called it, as our playground and also the open fields on the other side of Wadham Road.

There was some kind of farmhouse and buildings [Wadham Lodge] going down towards the *Crooked Billet* pub in those days. Chingford Road and Chingford Mount Road were partly built-up, but once you got to the end of Fulbourne Road, you were more or less in the country.

Cliff Payling talked about an inrush of lively families who quickly established a flourishing community, living and trading near the railway station in the new urban village of Highams Park. The little backwater known for centuries as Hale End quietly faded away.

Up to a few years ago half the people in Highams Park came from Hackney. My wife's family and our next-door neighbours on both sides originated from Hackney. It's amazing – people came from all over the country, some from other parts of Essex, obviously coming in towards London, but others came from the north of England, the West Country and Scotland. There were a few who named their birthplace as Walthamstow, but not many. Our family came from the Homerton area.

Jane Matthews (1894-1997) lived for 57 years in Vincent Road, Highams Park, and when she was in her 101st year she talked about her father's long journey to London in the 1880s, when he found work in Hackney.

When my father was fifteen he came down from Sunderland with a pony and trap. Yes, they walked it, although the road was so long, and they travelled all night. He was a cabinet-maker – furniture, you know – wardrobes and that sort of thing. He started for himself, then he worked for somebody else, then he started for himself again, and that's how he went on. He lived in Hackney – I think all cabinet-makers had lived in Hackney. It was the wood-section of the country: for woodwork and polishing and that sort of thing Hackney was the place. Dad was a good worker, a nice worker, and he used to go to Auction Rooms, called Tooth & Tooth, in Tottenham Court Road, and that's where he used to send most of his furniture for sale.

Miss L. Frances Bowler, born in 1906, lived in Highams Park for nearly 94 years:

My father came from Hackney, which was rather smart in those days. He used to go by horse-bus into the City. My mother (née Nash) lived down at Hatfield Peverel, near Chelmsford – farming folk – and I think that her mother had a small public house, called *The Swan*, which went very well. My father went down there with his cycling friends, and he called into *The Swan* and that's how it all started – all very romantic. But when she came from the country to live in Beech Hall Road my mother said, 'Oh – all those trains!' but she soon got used to them.

Father used to go up to the city every day – first class. Mother used to ask him why he went first class? (He thoroughly enjoyed it – that's why!) My father really did know the timber trade, about all the stuff coming from Russia, and he enjoyed working for London Timber Brokers. He was very good at it: he knew about every bit of wood – what it was – and in the First World War they called him to the War Office because they found that the best mahogany was being used to make cases to send out guns! He helped them to put a stop to that. They used ordinary wood afterwards (I don't think plywood had been invented) but *not* the very best mahogany.

Will Hebbard (1904-90) and his wife Dorrie (1903-98) were business people who lived for over 60 years in Manor Way, near the old level crossing at Chingford Hatch (now closed), but Will spent his childhood in Highams Park and went to school at the Sir George Monoux Grammar School. When he was about 12 years old, Will lost an eye in a terrible accident with an axe, but that did not stop him driving the many cars he owned during his lifetime. Will's father, Harry Hebbard, was in the furniture trade, and in about 1925 he moved to a larger house in The Avenue, appropriately named 'Chippendale', which is still there.

Will and Dorrie's two sons, Geoffrey (1934-99) and Bruce Hebbard, also went to the Monoux School, and in 1972 Bruce persuaded his father to write down some of his early memories of Highams Park:

I was born in Highams Park in 1904 in the last house in Silverdale Road (No.25) and I do not lay claim to remember much before say four to five years of age, but there were paraffin lamps on the station and over the rural parts like Larkshall Road, then a continuation of Hale End Road. The latter existed well into the 1930s. The Oak Hill area was lighted in this way for many years.

Most of my childhood playground was the 16-acre field now occupied by Sydney Burnell School, it being very easy to jump the fence from the garden to the field. The local kids all met there and made dens in the hedges and climbed all the trees, searched for birds' eggs and played in the hay. As soon as the hay-cutter appeared, the children went mad and stayed out until dark.

This was one of the 'Manor House' fields before Sidney Burnell School – now the Highams Park School in Handsworth Avenue – was built.

Miss Bowler remembered that horses were part of everyday life:

I used to feed the horse when the baker took the bread round. On the corner of Handsworth Avenue and Hale End Road there was another horse – at Barratt's. He must have had a stable somewhere because he had a pony and trap, and mother hired that and she took us out occasionally. That was great fun. She'd always had a pony and trap down in the country and we went to Epping Forest once or twice, and it was lovely. Once she got as far as Epping, rested the pony, fed him and watered him, and then we trotted back. It was so quiet – gorgeous! We would have a picnic, and sometimes you would see French's men with their horses going back up to Loughton and Buckhurst Hill – and

nothing on the road – so quiet! But the roads were not made up, and I remember saying
– wasn't everywhere dusty!

Frank Payling recalled:

Where Pamphilon's shop used to be (in The Avenue), there was a shop run by a man
named Watling, and at the rear of the shop he had a forge, and he repaired horse
shoes: the boys would bring their iron hoops to be re-welded, and you got there by
going through the alleyway from Handsworth Avenue. He shoed the horses and the
oven was right at the back of Pamphilon's shop.

Mrs Jessie Allen (1892-1996) was interviewed in her 105th year. She and her husband
had worked at the BX Co. Factory in Larkshall Road, Highams Park, but for the last
four years of her life Jessie was a resident at the St Francis Rest Home in Falmouth
Avenue, Highams Park, where she talked about her childhood in London and her
family's move to Walthamstow in 1901:

My father was a tailor and he worked at home and we used to have to take his work
to the City, through Bunhill Row. I remember once, when I got to the corner of
Bunhill Row, there was a crowd and it was a battalion of soldiers – CIVs (City Imperial
Volunteers) leaving their barracks to go to the Boer War.
    My mum used to do her washing at the baths in Pitfield Street, Hoxton. I was
the eldest of seven children, and I used to have to take my little baby brother in the
bassinet down to her for her to feed him.
    I really don't know why my father decided to move, but I didn't like where we
lived in some buildings in Great Eastern Street, London, and we came to live in
Walthamstow in 1901. A new estate had been built and we lived at number 71 in
Chingford Road. (You know the *Bell* public house? Well, it was near there, down on the
left-hand side.)
    It was all country – oh, it was beautiful! We used to walk from our home right up
to North Chingford – go over the Mount. It was a long walk, but we loved it, and just
as you turned the corner in Chingford Road (just past where the rubbish tip was),
you came to a little brook, the Ching, and we used to tie a rope on there and have a
swing. Where the rubbish tip was (and we used to go on it and rake it over to see what
we could find), I remember the Bus Garage being built, and Clover House.
    I remember Salisbury Hall very well. The people's name was Ferguson and I used to
go to school with one of the daughters, Jeannie Ferguson. I was one of the first pupils
when Chapel End School opened in 1903 and I can remember a lot of the girls there.
It was an Elementary School and I left when I was 14.

(The School Board had come to an agreement with the dairy farmer, John Hitchman,
to purchase land at Chapel End in 1898.)
    Miss Hilda Oliver remembered another aspect of life in the early days of Highams
Park – housework without electricity:

Nobody had electricity. In our house we had gas – in some places it was on the wall
– with these mantles and, of course, you lit them with a match. Every time you put a
match through the mantle-net, it tore because it was only like a fine mesh. Yes, they
were very delicate. You had to light them every evening and all the streets were lit with
gas lamps. Someone had to come round and light them.
    We had our electricity just after the war in 1945 (we were a bit late, I think, because
our neighbours probably had it earlier) but we cooked on gas. Originally Mummy used
to cook quite a bit on the oven here in the kitchen – a sort of grate with a coal fire
and an oven beside it. That was all black-leaded and emery-papered on the steel. It was
a lot of work! Things are so much easier in that way now.

James Davis (Jim) lived for over 40 years in the same house in Church Avenue, Highams
Park that had been owned by his grandparents. As a child in the 1920s, he used to come
from Walthamstow to visit them. He recalled that The Avenue was not only without the
present bus route but was unsuitable for any vehicles near Chingford Lane:

The end of The Avenue wasn't made up when I was a boy – it ended near the bridge (over the Ching), and then you had a little dusty road that took you into Chingford Lane. We used to climb along the sides of the banks and hop over the Ching at the bottom of Falmouth Avenue. I remember that bridge being built and Charter Road being made up: it used to be a rough road, the Charter Road.

The road commemorates the Borough Charter for Walthamstow in 1929. It had been an unmade track for carriages and carts to reach the lake from 'Highams'.

Well into the 20th century people continued to find work in Hackney and then move out to Highams Park or Woodford Green in Essex. The late John Diamond, the winner of the 'Journalist of the Year' award in 1998, used to live with his family in Lichfield Road, Woodford Green, near Highams Park lake. He said that for years he spent many hours waiting for the 275 bus at the Chingford Lane end of The Avenue:

We moved there from Hackney when I was 16 – some 28 years ago – and although my youngest brother went to a local school, I went to the City of London on a Hackney Scholarship.

He left school early and, before becoming a journalist, tried other ways of making a living – some more successful than others:

I went out to work locally when I was 16, serving as the only Jewish bacon slicer at Edwards the grocers in South Woodford. And much later, when I was trying to teach, I spent six weeks teaching at a South Woodford school (the name of which I just can't remember).

Two Notable Residents, Lord and Lady Bottomley

In 1936 two remarkable people married and came to live in Sunnydene Road, Highams Park. Arthur Bottomley was a dignified but friendly man, who could often be seen (even after he had been honoured with a Life Peerage) waiting at the bus stop in The Avenue on his way to the House of Lords. He was happy to be known locally as Arthur Bottomley. His wife had also been honoured by the Queen and was Dame Bessie Bottomley, who chose to be known as Lady Bottomley. Lord Bottomley was interviewed in his old age and asked how his career had begun and whether he had lived all his life in the Walthamstow area:

I was born in Tottenham, in Sutton Grove, near St Anne's Station. I came to Walthamstow when I was twelve months old (to Longfellow Road). First I went to Gamuel Road School and then we moved and I went to Pretoria Avenue School, and I owe a lot to Pretoria Avenue School because there was a teacher there who was a remarkable personality, quiet and unassuming, and he made such an impact on me that I think he encouraged me to go into public life although he wasn't in public life himself – a teacher named Thorpe. He was very good. I got a job in the City, in an office, and then I left the City to get a job on the railway and I worked on the LMS in the workshops for many years.

Arthur Bottomley left school when he was 14 years old. He was asked why he had become so interested in politics:

I suppose the simple way of explaining it is that my father was a very hard-working person and couldn't get a job, and I thought, what kind of society is this when it doesn't enable a man to look after his family, and I got associated with a railwayman and he said that if I wanted to *do* something about it I should join the Labour Party, which I did, and from then I got on to the Walthamstow Council when I was 21, very young.

He remained on the council for 21 years until he was chosen to be mayor.

Afterwards I got a job as a trade union official and went into politics in a big way, becoming a parliamentary candidate but not getting elected. In due course I was elected as a Member of Parliament for Rochester and Chatham, lost the seat in 1959, but succeeded in winning a by-election in 1962: that was for Middlesbrough and I remained there for 21 years.

I first met Clement Attlee when he was a social worker in Stepney. He became the Mayor of Stepney before he became a Member of Parliament, and I worked a little with him during the war. I was a trade union officer and he used to seek my help in solving particular difficulties in Stepney, but then of course, in 1945, I got into Parliament and he invited me to join the government.

I lived here in Highams Park as it was easy enough to travel to Rochester and Chatham, but it was a bit more difficult to Middlesbrough. We spent a good time in Highams Park, particularly with friends.

Lady Bottomley, who served as a councillor and county councillor, talked about some of the older houses in Walthamstow:

My great-grandfather was an Estall (my mother's family). He lived in Westminster and he went to church at St Margaret's, Westminster, where there is a plaque on the wall to the family, and then, when Walthamstow was expanding, he moved over here and built those lovely Victorian houses in East and West Avenue.

My grandfather went to the Sir George Monoux School when it was in the churchyard [in a room over the Alms Houses by St Mary's Church]. My cousin, Ted, went to the second Monoux School, which was built in High Street, Walthamstow. I was a governor of the school when it was rebuilt again.

Cattle and Commoners' Rights

For centuries Epping Forest has been grazed by cattle owned by certain individuals who have Commoners' Rights. In the forest by Oak Hill there are traces of the metal fence which replaced the wooden pound for cattle. Ebenezer Clark's *History of Walthamstow* of 1861 stated, 'In order to keep the cattle under due discipline pounds have been constructed for all animals that are found straying without the forest mark. The cattle are impounded until owned and the expenses and damage paid.'

Unfenced roads through the Forest allow cattle (and deer) to roam freely, but several years ago bullocks became uneconomical because they took too long to achieve the correct weight for market. As the cattle were withdrawn, shrubs and trees quickly re-established themselves in the grassland areas of Epping Forest. A small herd of longhorn cattle was recently reintroduced to graze and save the habitat. An elderly cow that had been reprieved from the knackers yard to graze in Epping Forest immediately disappeared. To the delight of the forest workers, she reappeared a few days later much slimmer and with a healthy little calf!

Jeanne May, who was born in Hale End and was a head teacher in Walthamstow, talked about Commoners' cattle:

We haven't seen the cattle so much lately. They are still around, but now there are cattle grids around the Waterworks [at the Woodford end of Forest Road]. They would come down the roads and eat things out of people's front gardens and leave their 'calling cards' all over the place, but I haven't seen them for some time. They nearly got a Bill through Parliament a few years ago, but at the last moment somebody saved the Commoners' Rights.

Maggie Moncrieff talked about her first experience of the Forest's wandering cattle in 1962, soon after she and her husband, Chris, who was then a Fleet Street journalist, had come to live in Woodford Green. Many journalists and printers have come to live near Highams Park Station because the trains ran all through the night.

In the very early morning I heard this sort of rustling noise, and there was a herd of cattle walking down Hale End Road, now and then taking a good mouthful of aubretia out of the front gardens. They looked so peaceful! One or two of them wandered off

29   *Commoners' cattle, c.1965. (Waiting for Hale End Library to open? If so, it would not have been the first time that a cow had wandered in.)*

on their own and one had to be chased out of somebody's front garden. But they've not come for ages. I think maybe the traffic keeps them more confined now.

Mrs Moncrieff came from Scotland as a child when she won a scholarship to dance at the famous Sadlers Wells Ballet School, when Dame Ninette de Valois was 'Madame'. She joined the prestigious Perth Repertory Company as an actor and first met her husband as she travelled to find work in the London theatres.

Chris Moncrieff is a very well-known journalist who for many years made regular TV appearances as Chief Political Correspondent to the Press Association. He has travelled all over the world to report on the important stories of the day, sometimes with barely time to pack a bag. When he retired from Westminster in 1994 he received a Book of Tributes written and signed by past and present Prime Ministers and many other distinguished parliamentarians, showing appreciation and respect for his commentaries. He continues to work for the Press Association and can often be heard on radio.

He remembered that some years ago there was a tragic accident caused by local Forest cattle. The dispute about Commoners' Rights that followed made him think about ways of preventing similar accidents, but his solution to the problem led to a bizarre story which made the headlines world-wide:

> One day, about twenty years ago, a motorcyclist was killed by these cows, by running into them up Oak Hill, and apparently there was no redress against the owners because of these ancient rights (which you all know about). Anyway, I approached a Member of Parliament, namely Marcus Lipton, who was MP for Vauxhall, and said, why don't we get a Question tabled in the House of Commons, so that these cows must have luminous paint on their horns and their tail and haunches, so that motorcyclists can see them in the dark? Marcus Lipton thought this was a splendid idea. A House of Commons Question was duly tabled, and the Minister said no! But it made a very good story. The *Evening Standard* headline was, 'By the Light of the Silvery Moo', and a minister told me later that he was on a trip to Africa, and he bought an English-language paper, and the only story from the entire United Kingdom on that day was the story of the cows at Highams Park!

3

Builders and Bandits

Woodford Row and St Andrew's Church, Woodford Green

Olive Fewell was interviewed in 1995, when she talked about one of the early building projects at Woodford Green, in the area shown on old maps as part of Woodford Row near to where the Woodford Windmill used to stand:

> I go to St Andrew's Church in Chingford Lane, which was originally called St Andrew's Mission Church, and its centenary was in 1988. It is in the 'lost area' of Chingford Lane – sometimes in Walthamstow, sometimes Woodford Green. It used to be the daughter church of All Saints but now it comes into the boundaries of Woodford Wells and we are with All Saints, Woodford Wells. We are together now, and about to have a team curacy. Actually, it was first built so that servants of the houses in Woodford would go to St Andrew's, and the 'others' – their employers – would go to All Saints, Woodford Wells.

St Andrew's was built in 1888 and it has a curious history. The second vicar of All Saints, Woodford Wells, the Rev. N.R. Fitzpatrick, had three missions built in Woodford Green. St Andrew's remained his property until he died in 1917, when it was bought by Mr F. Gardner and leased to the vicar of the time. It is a wooden-framed building, which was covered with corrugated iron (like the 'Tin Hall' in Hale End); it had a wooden bell tower, and was built near the pavement of Elm Grove, with the front door facing Chingford Lane. Like Woodford Green Primary School, it is within the boundaries of Walthamstow, and was also in the parish of St Peter's in the Forest but an arrangement was made to transfer its allegiance to All Saints Church, Woodford Wells.

Up to 1923 there was no real church hall, and the church was in such a bad state of repair that it would have been demolished if Mr John Collyer Mead had not come to the rescue, undertaking to repair the property and move it to a new position to make room for a church hall. After stripping off the cladding, iron rollers were placed under the wooden framework and the whole structure was rolled on to its new foundations! It was then covered with what is described as expanded metal and rendered with cement and pebble-dash outside. Although the bell-tower was not rebuilt, the interior of the church was completely lined with hardboard. A church hall was added and a flourishing church was re-born. During the last 75 years the church and its hall have had several 'face-lifts', and the many additional features, donated by members of the congregation, give it the appearance of a very well established church.

The official centenary history of St Andrew's describes what might have been, but for the Second World War:

> In 1939 a letter from the Bishop of Barking was received by All Saints Church Council, saying that for some time the Bishop of Chelmsford had under consideration the forming of an Ecclesiastical District to be known as St Andrew's, out of the eastern end of the parish of St Peter's, Walthamstow, and a small part of All Saints' adjoining.

30 *These houses in Montalt Road, Woodford Green, were some of the first to be built on the Warner family's estate and, at first, they had an uninterrupted view over the park land of 'Highams' to the lake.*

Sir Edward Warner had offered two sites – on the corner of Henry's Avenue, where Park Farm had been, and by The Charter Road – for a Church and Parsonage. A sum of £1,300 would be available towards the cost, with a stipend allowance of £200 per annum. All Saints' PCC were in favour of the scheme, and St Andrew's were very pleased to think that a larger Church and parish of its own might be possible. However, the war came along and the scheme was shelved. After the war, the LCC built a large housing estate at Chingford Hatch, and St Anne's Church was built, so that the scheme was dropped.

In 1975 the vicar was the Rev. John Taylor, who is now the Bishop of St Albans. He requested (and was granted) a Pastoral Order to re-draw the parish boundaries to include St Andrew's, part of St Peter's, and part of St Anne's Church, Chingford Hatch, within the parish of All Saints, Woodford Wells.

Farms and Houses near Chingford Lane

Maps of 1897 show Higham Farm, 'Brook House' (where Betoyne Avenue is now) and two other houses, 'Sunnydene' and 'Nightingale Hall', at the other end of Chingford Lane, between Hatch Lane and where The Avenue is now. The fields of Higham Farm were referred to as Housefield, Stackyard field, House buildings, Chase, enclosures with ponds, and two fields named Cardmakers Branches (where the roads Sunnydene, Clivedon and Nightingale were built). In 1881 a Mr C. Hodges lived at Higham Farm House, and until about 1949 the ruined house could still be seen from The Avenue). The farm and its buildings stood below the brow of the hill on the right of where The Avenue is now, and was reached by a short farm track from Chingford Lane, because at that time The Avenue had not been extended from the end of Falmouth Avenue.

The census of 1861 recorded that William George Fish, a pawnbroker who had been born in Finsbury, was living at 'Nightingale Hall' with his children (Mary Ann, Kate, Henry, Algernon, William, Herbert and baby Frank – all born in Hackney), and in about 1903 it appears that George Whitley sold Higham Farm to Henry Fish, who

31   *A view over The Avenue, Highams Park, showing building plots for sale – looking across the railway and part of Castle Cold William field towards Rolls Cottage and Larks Wood, as seen from Castle Avenue.*

lived near the farm in the house called 'Sunnydene'. (The Fish family established the well-known jewellers' shops in Walthamstow.) In the mid-1920s a George Whitley sold land to Frank Abbott and others (hence Abbotts Crescent).

Farmland and Builders

In the late 19th century some of Wadham Farm and Thorpe Hall (which had been bought by John Hitchman), Jack's Farm and then the farmland around Beech Hall were used for building, but it is only very recently that some of the Salisbury Hall Manor playing fields have been lost to supermarkets because, for many years, the local branch of the National Playing Fields Association fought hard to keep these fields for sporting activities.

Edith Upton was born in the newly built village of Highams Park in Winchester Road, the house being built by her grandfather:

> Mr William Thomas Lane was a London man, from Bethnal Green. He was building houses in Highams Park in the early 1900s, and he built in Handsworth Avenue, Winchester Road and in Castle Avenue (the two houses next to Hale End Library, up the hill).
>
> On the left hand side of Handsworth Avenue there is still one called 'Handsworth Villa', and I think it was a Mr Bradbrook, or some such name, who lived there. He had two daughters, and in our family we had a picture of the father, with the daughters in their long black frocks and big white aprons.
>
> In Winchester Road grandfather built three groups of houses: they were numbers 65, 67, 69, 71 and 73, and there were two more lower down, namely 89 and 91. After crossing the River Ching there was a large area of vacant land, which remained so for many years, and I can remember marguerites, buttercups and red clover – a profusion of wild flowers growing there. Grandfather's next group adjoined this land and were numbered 141 to 151, and finished opposite the Methodist Church. He and Grandmother then left London and came to Highams Park and lived in one of his own houses, No. 149, Winchester Road.

Grandfather used the same design for all of his houses, whether big or small; all had back additions, and where there was a flank wall they were always windowless. His belief was that windows weakened a wall, and he always used chestnut-coloured bricks around the front porches: these 'bull-nosed' bricks were smooth and glazed and have withstood the ravages of time.

In 1903 Mr and Mrs Samuel Johnson Upton bought one of these houses and raised their family of five boys, and in 1904 Mr and Mrs Thomas Henry Lane also bought a house from his father, W.T.Lane. I was born in 1907, and then my brothers, Ernest Thomas in 1911 and William Joseph in 1913. Being near-neighbours, we children played together and went to Selwyn Avenue School together until I was 13 years old, when I went to the 'Brown School', the Commercial Secondary School, Walthamstow.

32 *Mr William Thomas Lane was one of the builders who went to the Wadham Estate sale of 1898. He bought two parcels of land and then, just before the turn of the century, he built houses in Winchester Road.*

John Edwards recalls:

We bought 25 Handsworth Avenue in 1937 from a man called Kohl, who left a lot of letters and postcards which suggested he was of German origins. I would imagine that he took the house over in 1919, some time after the First World War anyway, and before that it was owned or occupied by Dr Rogers, who was a well-known medical practitioner in Highams Park. As for the age of the house, I was given to believe by my father that it was built round about the turn of the century. Most of the houses were of that design and, so far as I know, there are only about three of them left. But Handsworth Avenue was by no means a road with the same type of architecture. Some of the houses that were pulled down for the new Medical Centre were of an entirely different design. They were much lower, probably only two storeys, whereas our house was three storeys high.

33 *Some large houses, part of the Haile Estate, were in Castle Avenue. 'Dr Rogers lived in Castle Avenue, afterwards Dr Cuddon-Large's house and later, the "Richmond Fellowship" had that house.' (D. Webb)*

34 *'This photograph was taken by my father in about 1905 from the back bedroom of 65, Winchester Road, built by my grandfather, W.T. Lane – where we lived. (Beech Hall and the farm were up the hill on the other side of the railway line.) My mother (Edith Eliza Davis) is on the left with her youngest sister, May, who was crippled. The others are Mr and Mrs Arnold and Jim and the daughter of his first marriage. I think they were Christian Scientists – that sort of religion and they used to have meetings and the harmonium in the front room – so, on Sunday evenings, we used to close our windows if we didn't want to join in!' (Mrs E. Upton)*

I do know something about building in Highams Park because on the other side of the level crossing, in Selwyn Avenue, there are two houses: one's called 'Daisy Villa', and the other one is 'Catherine Villa', and they are named after my grandmother, who died in 1901, and Daisy, my aunt, who died only four years ago, round about 1990, at the age of 100. They were built by my grandfather, Alexander Edwards, who was a builder.

The Level Crossings

Will Hebbard has described level crossings early in the 20th century:

From Hale End Road to the level crossing at Wadham Road were two cottages. The Fosters lived in one of them and Mr Foster was a keen gardener and kept a very fine garden. All three of the level crossing gates (Wadham, Highams Park and Chingford Hatch) were of the older crossover type and all originally had 'kissing gates' for foot passengers. The kissing gates at Highams Park were removed when the subway was built about 1908, those at Wadham Road when the bridge was built (1927), while those at Chingford Hatch were altered about 1935, and all were removed in 1971-2.

Until the electrification of the line began in 1960, and the mechanical barriers were installed at Highams Park level crossing, the crossing man had to close the gates by hand. People used to walk across the railway line by using the wicket side gates until just before the train came into view, when the gates were locked from the signal box.

Hale End and Highams Park Garden Village

Will Hebbard added:

We always talk of the district as Highams Park but in fact it should be Hale End. The former description only covers a small area round the Park itself. Nearly all the roads were in existence by 1907-8 but the buildings have been filled in since then.

35 *The construction of the subway must have been the most ambitious and probably the most expensive building project in Highams Park. In 1907, an agreement to start work was made between the Great Eastern Railway and Walthamstow Council and the total cost was estimated to be £2,150, of which the Council had to contribute £1,434. The signal box was removed from its position by the station and was rebuilt by the level-crossing. The subway was in use by 1909.*

The Avenue ended at Trumans Sports Ground [now the Jubilee Sports Ground], while only Rolls Cottage and Ropers Farm and the large house, Woodlands, now used by Waltham Forest Borough Council, were beyond Halex.

Beech Hall Road was started in 1906, but I can remember some houses were still being built near the River Ching, together with all the houses beyond the river, and the council estate which was not built until after the first war.

There was a large mortar mixer on the corner of Studley Avenue when Robinson built Preston Avenue, which was afterwards taken to Empress Avenue for that estate.

Sid Marchant mentioned his wife's father, one of the craftsmen who helped to build the new houses in Beech Hall Road, Highams Park: 'Win's father, William E. Bradley, was a master glass-cutter of decorative glass, and the "brilliant-cut" glass panels in the front doors of Beech Hall Road were all worked by him.'

The next wave of building came in about 1906 and the land agents, Messrs Rayner and Brilmayer of Walbrook, London, E.C., produced a brochure showing detached houses designed by E.C.P. Monson, FRIBA, FSI, for the 'Highams Park Garden Village'. These houses, with a starting price of £275, were to be sold as 'artistic detached houses in charming situation and unique neighbourhood instead of terrace houses in monotonous streets'.

Their close proximity to the lake and the 'superior houses in the vicinity' were not the only attraction. The brochure stated, 'Highams Park Garden Village is only about 8 miles from the City, is close to the Railway Station, which has [an] excellent train service and cheap fares. It is in a charming and healthy situation adjoining the beautiful forest and has abundant recreations.'

Highams Park Garden Village houses are still popular and it is rather surprising that only a small estate was built in Clivedon Road and in Sheredan Road, which included a very attractive little crescent of six houses. A few houses in the Garden Village style

The HIGHAMS PARK GARDEN VILLAGE.

Situate within 5 minutes' walk of Highams Park Station (G.E.R.), with excellent train service to Liverpool Street

36 *Highams Park Garden Village, from the brochure that advertised houses to be built in Sheredan Road and Clivedon Road. Tennis courts were planned for the space at the back of the houses but garages were built.*

were also built in Gordon Avenue. Tennis courts in the open area behind Clivedon Road were planned, but eventually garages were built there. Several bombs and a number of 'friendly fire' shells fell on the little Garden Village Estate in Highams Park during the Second World War, but repairs to most of the houses were made without altering their character.

'The Tottenham Outrage'

As more houses were being built in Beech Hall Road in the winter of 1909, some extraordinary events took place under the railway bridge by the Ching Brook and then in one of the old Oak Hill Cottages at Hale End. This was the final episode of the infamous gun-battle, remembered as the 'Tottenham Outrage' (or 'The Walthamstow Tram Chase'), in which four people died, including the two villains, and 25 people were injured. (Some of the following information refers to the marvellously lively account in *The Houndsditch Murders and the Siege of Sidney Street* by W.H.Allen, which is based on contemporary police records. Information about the first part of the chase was found in one of two articles entitled 'Don't go too near, they've got shooters', from the *Guardian & Gazette* newspaper of January 1989, which were written by Peter Lawrence of the Woodford Historical Society.)

In January 1909 Jacob Lepidus and another revolutionary from Latvia, Paul Hefeld, who had been employed at Schnurmann's rubber factory in Tottenham, used guns to threaten and rob the factory's wages clerk of £80 – a daring crime because Schnurmann's was opposite a police station! The robbers ran down Chestnut Road, shooting wildly at their pursuers (including armed police on bicycles) as they headed for the marshes. On the way they killed one of the policemen and a ten-year-old boy, and other people were badly wounded.

Hefeld and Lepidus crossed the marshes and the River Lea and reached Salisbury Hall Manor House, where they hid behind a haystack, shooting at anyone who approached them. They broke cover into Chingford Road and hijacked a tram. The terrified driver hid upstairs and a woman and child managed to get off, but the conductor was forced to try to drive. Hefeld killed the pony of a cart commandeered by an armed policeman which had nearly caught up with the tram, and at this point an elderly passenger became very agitated and appeared to try to take the gun from Hefeld, who shot him in the throat. The conductor told the anarchists they were about to come to a police station, and at this they jumped off the tram.

The next victim was a milkman, who was also shot and wounded. Hefeld and Lepidus soon overturned his milk cart by taking a corner too quickly so used their guns to threaten the young driver in charge of a greengrocer's horse and van. With Hefeld shooting both pistols from the back of the van at men chasing them in another cart, Lepidus drove the stolen vehicle along Forest Road. They turned into Fulbourne Road towards Highams Park but had not released the brake on the van and, as they turned into Winchester Road, the horse began to tire and the gunmen to run out of ammunition. They leapt from the van and ran along the path by the Ching and under the railway bridge, but this is where their luck ran out.

The builders in Beech Hall Road had erected a high fence around the building site, barring the way, and Hefeld was too heavy and too tired to climb over. He shouted to Jacob Lepidus to go on. It is said that Hefeld used one of his two remaining bullets in an attempt to shoot himself in the head, and that the police arrived and took him to hospital in Tottenham where he died later of an infection, but Lepidus ran on, taking refuge in the Oak Hill Cottage, where Mrs Rolstone and her children were at home. Miss Joan M. Rolstone, now living in Rustington, Sussex, has very kindly allowed her father's account of the event to be printed here. He was the elder of the two little boys in the cottage when the gunman burst in, and, although his story

37   *Mr and Mrs Rolstone with their two sons some years after the drama of the Tottenham Massacre, which ended violently in their Oak Hill cottage.*

(probably told and retold during his lifetime) may contain some inaccuracies, it gives a vivid impression of the terror felt by his mother and the children and the excitement of the people of Highams Park:

There have been many articles printed from time to time regarding 'The Tottenham Outrage' of 1909, but below are the true facts of the events, which took place in the cottage on Oak Hill. Relating to the chase from Tottenham to the River Ching, I know very little, but from the River Ching to the time the murderer committed suicide, I can give you the true story.

On 23 January 1909 the two bandits were chased from Tottenham to Oak Hill after a daring robbery. When they got to the railway embankment by the River Ching in Winchester Road, the young man, named Markovitch [*sic*], believed to be 25 years of age, was shot in the back by the police as he climbed the embankment. He was certified as dead by Dr Rogers of Highams Park. Police Constable Bridges of Chingford Police Station remarked to Dr Rogers, 'Shall I send for an ambulance?' and Dr Rogers replied, 'No, he is a murderer. Place him on that plank, stop the first vehicle coming along and take him to the mortuary.'

Meanwhile, the other fugitive – Jacob Labatus – also a Russian Jew [*sic*] believed to be aged 30, made his way across Kay's Farm [Beech Hall Farm, where Beech Hall Crescent is now]. After the long chase from Tottenham, he was obviously feeling the strain and made his way towards the four cottages on Oak Hill near the *Royal Oak* public house. He climbed over the fence of the first cottage he came to, where my mother, myself and my younger brother, William, were in the kitchen.

(It has been said in the press from time to time that there was an 'old lady' in the garden hanging out washing. The 'old lady' was my mother aged 32 and she was scrubbing the kitchen floor at the time.)

On hearing all the commotion, she went out to the front of the cottage and, while she was out there, the bandit came in the rear of the cottage and bolted all the doors. My mother, being outside with the police, soon became hysterical, knowing that her two sons were inside with the killer. Then the trouble started inside. My brother and I, aged three and six respectively, were soon terrified. We

38   *The Rolstone's cottage in Oak Hill, where Jacob Lepidus was shot in 1909.*

were at the table playing with the few toys I had received three days earlier on my
sixth birthday.

I can to this day remember that man's face as he came into the room. His shirt
was open at the neck and he wore no cap and his face was dirty and covered with
perspiration and blood. A ghastly sight. In his left hand he carried a revolver with a
barrel, which was easily eight inches long. He looked at us and then made one grab at
an enamel jug of water which was on the table. After drinking, he then made his way
into the front room.

He must have been seen through the window by the police, for as a result two
or three shots were fired through the window. He fired back and wounded a police
officer in the shoulder. Labatus then came back into the kitchen and our dog was

barking furiously although, unfortunately, chained near the door. Jacob Labatus returned to the front room and my brother and I followed him. When I got to the door I saw him trying to get up the chimney. When he came down, not having got very far, another shot was fired outside and he fired back. He then pushed my brother to one side and said, 'Get out of the way, or I'll shoot you.' We most certainly got out of his way and at the same time, started crying for our Mum! My brother, wearing a white blouse, was covered in soot from the man's jacket. Then the police fired again and the bullet hit the photograph of Queen Victoria which was hanging over the fireplace.

After a while he made his way upstairs and, after a short lull, firing took place through the window. I believe Jacob Labatus only fired twice whilst inside the cottage because by that time we were rescued by an unknown man [reported to be a baker from Tottenham] and taken with my mother to a neighbour's house.

While all this was going on, my father (who was a coalman in the employ of Warrens, the local coal merchants) was found and brought home. When he arrived all was quiet, so the police and my father made their way into the cottage by way of the wash-house. Inside there was silence, and fearing that Labatus may be waiting to ambush them on sight, the police would not venture upstairs. My father suggested sending our collie dog up. This was immediately accepted by the police and so she was sent upstairs. She was so excited by all the fuss she was ready to fight. She went into the front bedroom and sniffed all around, came out and went into our bedroom. They heard the dog jump on to our bed, give one bark, jump off and then she came down. The police were then satisfied that Jacob Labatus was either unconscious or dead, because otherwise the dog would have shown fight. They made their way upstairs, and found him lying on our bed, shot through the head with his last bullet. He was rolled down the stairs and taken away.

Mr Lawrence has researched, lectured and written about the event in great detail and has compiled a more colourful version of Charles Rolstone's story, using police records of the incident. Police Constable Eagles stated that he climbed a ladder and looked into the bedroom, to see the gunman pointing a gun at him. He saw the dog go into the bedroom and then, after clambering down the ladder, borrowed a revolver from Det. Con. Dixon before bravely entering the cottage, where he went up to the bedroom.

I fired two shots at the door panel. The door opened and a man pointed a gun with his left hand. I fired at the man when he threw his arms in the air, staggered and fell on to the bed. I rushed in and took his gun.

Dixon emphasised PC Eagles' bravery:

Without the slightest hesitation, he hurled himself against the door and it burst open. Jacob was leaping about and laughing wildly, shouting, 'Come on now.' Two shots were fired. We rushed into the room. Eagles snatched the gun and I seized him by the throat and dragged him on to the floor. There was blood oozing from his forehead.

Mr Lawrence goes on, 'Jacob had shot himself, obeying the anarchist creed of not being taken alive.'

As any amateur sleuth can detect, there are certain anomalies in the accounts given by Charles Rolstone and by the two policemen and, if Lepidus did kill himself, it seems likely that a certain amount of extra drama was added to this very dangerous event in the lives of the residents of Highams Park and Hale End.

Charles Rolstone's daughter maintains that her father's home was situated in the first house of the next block to the right of the cottage usually identified as the one involved in the shootings.

At the time there was speculation that Lepidus might have hidden the stolen money up the chimney, but the £80 was never recovered and what really happened remains a mystery.

Houses and the Australian Gold Rush

Stan Batson recalls:

> I remember the old level crossing going and the houses at the top there in Wadham
> Road being built. And Wadham Bridge itself being built before the war, so I think it
> must have been the late 1920s. It was our entertainment in those days. When we were
> kids we would go and pretend to 'help' the bricklayers move the bricks. I remember
> on one occasion they came up late one night, unloading bricks on the site (all done
> by hand in those days, of course), and then asked if 'us kids' wanted a ride back on
> their lorry. They took us down Wadham Road to the *Crooked Billet*, about two or three
> hundred yards up towards Edmonton, then turfed us off. And we had to walk back!
> That was quite a bit of fun for us in those days.
>   They resurfaced all the road in Fulbourne Road, round about 1926, and soon after
> that the allotment land was sold. I think it was Gale Bros. who started to build houses
> on the left there, then on the top field, and then Wadham Road started to be built.
>   Highams Park was being built up in those days, so we got in on the act quite
> early. The Warboys family were building extensively, and Gales. Later on, Martins
> were building up in Hollywood Way but, of course, old Mr Warboys, he was building
> Coolgardie Avenue and Warboys Crescent. I was told Warboys got the name
> 'Coolgardie' from Australia.

(Mr Warboys went out to Coolgardie and made some money in the gold fields.) The
Warboys family lived in Selwyn Avenue at one time, then moved to a large house
built by Mr Warboys. He used the name 'Coolgardie' again in another of his roads,
in Chigwell.
    Stan Batson spoke about the Warboys family of Highams Park:

> I knew young Jack Warboys, old Mr Warboys' son, quite well, and his wife, Avril.
> Presumably 'Avril Way' was named after Avril when they knocked down the big
> Warboys' house at the back of Warboys Crescent and new houses were built. Jack
> Warboys' son was a keen tennis player and they had quite a good tennis court in their
> garden in the estate, which lay between Warboys Crescent and Larkshall Road. On
> the edge of the estate, facing into Larkshall Road, there was – and still is – quite a
> substantial chalet-bungalow, where old Mrs Warboys lived for quite a time after old Mr
> Warboys died.
>   I've always been interested in property and I've always had property. Mr Stevens,
> who was a local electrical contractor, and I went into business together twenty-five or
> thirty years ago. We started off by building a little house in Guildford Road. When I
> say 'build', I don't mean we physically built it, but we planned it and got the various
> contractors to do the building and, of course, Mr Stevens did all the electrical work in
> it. That was just a one-off on a plot of land that we acquired. Over the years, we have
> bought and sold many properties in and around Highams Park, a few of which we still
> own. In The Avenue there's a block of ten houses, which included Miss Muddiman's,
> and we've bought nine out of the ten and converted eight of them to flats. The dates
> are on the little stone fascia under the front bays. They were built in pairs between
> 1903 and about 1907. After the war the two bungalows were built on the vacant land
> between numbers 99 and 103. We still own the freehold of the first eight of those
> houses and the ninth one is exactly the same as when it was built. It has all the old
> cornices and the plaster rose in the middle.

Highams Park in the 1920s

Arthur Hemmings lived for many years in Forest Glade, and his wife, Grace, taught
music at Warwick School for Girls in Walthamstow:

> The first time I ever came across to Highams Park was in the 1920s, I suppose, before
> a lot of the property around here was built. I remember Handsworth Avenue, a part
> of it being built on one side but one end not built at all. A place which is called St
> Leonard's Avenue – now that wasn't built. It was just wild you know – trees – just gone

39   *Rowing, in a hired boat on Highams Park Lake, used to be popular, c.1930.*

wild, like one end of The Avenue. Highams Park Station end was built, but towards the other end of The Avenue, towards Chingford Lane, it wasn't built at all in those days. At the top end of Forest Glade, by The Avenue, they had built some bungalows on the right-hand side, but on the opposite side, there was nothing at all, just wild land all those years ago.

I married Grace in 1937 and we rented a place at Queens Road, Leytonstone, and we stayed there for ten years. The war came along, and when it was over we decided we wanted to move and liked the Highams Park district. It was a more rural area, more countrified too, and what took my attention (you wouldn't believe this) was the old railway crossing – typical rural England, I thought! And we also liked the property – looked round and saw the property there and the close proximity to the Forest, and that really appealed to us – I was a great walker! They had an old Boat House where they hired out boats, and I used to take Grace on the lake, and we used to get tea and coffee there and ice creams. We used to go out there at lunch time.

Road Surfaces and Spackman House

Edith Upton recalls:

> I think Winchester Road was made up round about 1914, just at the beginning of the First World War. I can remember the dust when they were doing it, and the smell of the tar!

Jim Davis talked about Church Avenue:

> Everybody walked across the field, to cut off the corner, because this was a terrible road! It was all mud, and people wouldn't come down here, even the tradesmen, because they used to get stuck in the mud! We used to put out ashes to try to keep the road passable, but many times they've been stuck and they've had to bring vehicles to pull them out. I'm talking about the 1930s, when the cars were a bit ancient to get out of that situation, without towing trucks with the power they have now.
>
> This part of Church Avenue was a lane, right up to when I married, but when we

came to live here, 40 years ago, we had to pay for the road to be made up – so much each, but we all decided to have it done. 'Percy Bilton' built this road, and everybody had to leave their cars around the corner because you couldn't use the road. I didn't have a car then.

Church Avenue was about the only road that had stayed unmade. Friday Hill was done before the war, when it was more of a lane. I remember that being done, up to the top of the hill, then they made it up into one big road.

Gordon Avenue was made up, but down in the corner by the Ching it wasn't and it went straight through into Brookfield Path and [on the left] there was an orthopaedic hospital for children, 'Brookfield'. That was there for many, many years. You used to see all the children as you walked through. Later it was an Old People's Home, 'Spackman House'. It's not there now, but it was.

Spackman House was built in 1916 as 'Brookfield Red Cross Hospital', in memory of Thomas S. Armstrong's son who was killed in the First World War. Mr Armstrong donated the land and money towards the cost of the buildings and the Red Cross equipped and maintained the hospital. Mrs Henry Young of Larkshall Farm in Chingford offered £100 for linen, and further funds for its upkeep were provided by Mr C.P. Merriam of the Xylonite Co. Ltd. Lady Warwick came to open the hospital.

In 1923 it became Brookfield, Hale End, Hospital and School for Crippled Children, later Brookfield Orthopaedic Hospital, and then in 1956 it changed use and was known as Brookfield Hospital for the Aged. The old buildings have now been demolished (although the porch was saved and graces the clubhouse of Wadham Bowling Club) and a small housing estate built on the site.

In the lean years of the 1930s the first of the new houses on Law Land's 'Montalt Estate' (part of the Highams Estate) did not sell well so building stopped. In 1934, Walthamstow Borough Council was offered the chance to buy the 20-acre field by Highams Park lake to preserve it as a green space for ever. This transaction was completed in 1937 and the field is now officially known as 'The Highams Park'.

During the Second World War the field was used as allotments, and at the end of the war 'prefabs' were built there on condition that the land would later be restored as park land. Local residents were successful when they insisted that none of the large trees in the field should be felled.

Post-War Developments

Most of the building in Highams Park and Woodford Green was completed by 1935, but more council houses and some well-designed flats were added over the years. Much to the surprise of local people, the high-rise block of flats by the Forest off Oak Hill, named St Patrick's Court, has recently been renovated instead of being demolished. Other high-rise flats in Waltham Forest have been replaced by smaller blocks or houses.

Miss Renee Weller felt outraged when a post-war council turned down a planning application to build a multi-storeyed hotel on the site of the Kingfishers' Pool and then gave themselves permission to build a tower block to replace the large 19th-century houses by the Bridle Path:

> I mentioned this to a relative of mine, who said to me that you've got to house people, and I said, yes, but it was not necessary to build a tower block! They finally completed the building, and now, if you're at the top of Larkshall Road, or at the top of Hale End Road, or in Forest Road, sticking out, like a sore thumb, across the canopy of the forest is St Patrick's Court.

4

The Factory in a Garden

Will Hebbard remarked:

> The making of Highams Park, as I knew it, was caused by the removal of British Xylonite Company from Homerton to Hale End in 1897, bringing work to hundreds of people in the area. Everyone set their clocks and watches by the 7.55 and 8.00 a.m. hooters and anyone late was shut out and fined before starting the day's work.

Stan Batson's father opened a shop in Winchester Road in 1929.

> Going round the corner into Larkshall Road, we had the well-documented British Xylonite Company, later Halex then BXL. It was the Merriam family business and I knew one of them, Tony Merriam, who often used to come in the shop. BX brought a tremendous amount of trade to Highams Park. The factory workers in those days used to have a lunch hour. All the girls used to come out from work – pour out – dozens and dozens of them, and they'd all come round. There'd be three or four 35 buses, waiting to take them back into Fulbourne Road, MacDonald Road and Victoria Road, where many of them lived. If they could walk home they did, but hundreds of them climbed on to these buses, and they'd go home, have dinner, and then catch a bus back! I don't know how long they had, but the bus service must have been good for them to have got back, because that's what they used to do! They used to bring a lot of trade into Highams Park. We've lost all that.

The British Xylonite Company Ltd, which was the backbone of Highams Park's economic success, began in Homerton, London. It was incorporated 13 June 1877, when it took over the business of Messrs Daniel Spill, H.J. Leigh Bennett and A.D. Mackay at 24 High Street, Homerton. In the same year the Homerton Manufacturing Co. Ltd was established at 122 High Street, Homerton by Mr L.P. Merriam (Managing Director) and his son, Mr C.P. Merriam (Secretary). The object of this firm was to manufacture various articles from the sheet Xylonite made by the BX Co. Ltd, and in 1879 the two companies merged into one. (At this time there were 29 employees, and the hours worked ranged between 55 and 70 per week.)

In 1885 the Holloway Collar Factory was started and rapidly grew in size, and the premises at Homerton were found to be too small for the increasing business. There was also some anxiety about producing inflammable materials in such a built-up area, and the directors began to look about for a site in the country on which to build a factory for the manufacture of sheet Xylonite. They chose Brooklands Farm at Brantham, Suffolk (on the north bank of the River Stour, opposite Manningtree), where a factory was built in 1887.

At Hale End, Thomas Rainbow (or Ranbow) was farming Jacks Farm, which consisted of some 50 acres, from 1873-96, but that year it was bought for redevelopment by the BX Co. The following year work began on the new factory, which had been planned by C.P. Merriam and Mr G.E. Wells. In 1898 the large office block was built and the clerical

40 *Factory workers outside the British Xylonite Co. Ltd near the level-crossing, Highams Park. Mrs E. Upton remembered the crowds passing her house. 'At one time, a thousand people were employed there. There was a stream of people just before 8 o'clock, all walking or cycling up Winchester Road. Before 1914, you could hardly cross for people! It was a good sight.'*

staff moved over from Homerton, followed over the next two or three years by the works department, and Hale End became the London headquarters of the organisation.

The factory was known locally as 'The Xylonite', because Xylonite was the trade name of celluloid, until 1938, when the BX company, now much larger, was restructured and the name 'Halex' was introduced, derived from Hale End plus the X of Xylonite. Part of Hale End Road passed the factory gates (at one time Jacks Lane, and now known as Larkshall Road). The factory at Brantham made the material and Halex made products from the material.

'BEX' and 'Halex' became world-famous names for plastic materials, and a multitude of useful plastic goods were designed and produced by the company at Hale End. The history of its development is described with first-hand knowledge by Mr John Leatherland, and other Highams Park people:

> I started work with Halex in 1947, when I was engaged as the Personnel Manager (having been in that work previously in the Midlands), and after a couple of years the personnel function at the Larkswood factory was added to my duties: in 1961 I became the Xylonite Group Personnel Manager. By that time employees were spread over twelve sites, ranging from the Isle of Wight to Plenmellor, Northumberland.
>
> Natural plastics have always existed in the form of rubber, horn and shellac etc., but the initial synthetic plastic material was 'Parksine', made by a man named Parkes, who was trying to imitate natural horn and shell. He put his material on the market in about 1864, but it wasn't a commercial success. Several other people experimented but were also unsuccessful.
>
> In the early days of celluloid, which was the first man-made plastic, and using a mixture of wood (*xylon* – the Greek word) and nitric acid, Halex made toilet and fancy-ware goods: brooches, hair-slides and toothbrushes, hairbrushes and combs, household brushes, also necklaces and bangles. Imitation coral necklaces were made of celluloid and were very saleable. As a boy, I wore celluloid collars – the ordinary choir-boy type. They were money-spinners, and so were celluloid cuffs for nurses and food shop assistants, who wore them for hygiene and so that their sleeves wouldn't wear out when

they were writing! Men also wore celluloid cuffs, denoting that they were non-manual workers, and also dickeys – imitation stiff shirt-fronts. Later, the only industrial product made with celluloid was cutting-bars for guillotines, because it was strong, resistant and soft.

Then, of course, there were table-tennis balls. Halex was the only factory in the country that made table-tennis balls. You may have seen them under other firms' names, but they were made at Halex from the early years of this [20th] century, when 'Ping-Pong' became the game from which table-tennis developed. Originally the table-tennis lawn was just a board, but later on, as table-tennis became a national and international game with competitions, each ball had to be exact in every detail – size, weight, bias – everything. Nobody ever made a table-tennis ball from any other substance than Celluloid, but for other purposes all sorts of the newer plastics were used.

A quarterly house magazine was published by BX Co. from about 1912, which was known as the *Xylonite Magazine* until about 1963, but later became the *BXL Review*. These magazines were filled with articles about the company, its products and personalities, and social events at the Hale End site and all the other factories owned by the company.

I was in touch with the work-force and the management, and consequently I was asked to write a column for *The Link* (about 1972), a BXL publication for Halex pensioners. One of the two joint-editors was Percy Reboul, who was previously the editor of *Cross Link*, the company newsletter, and had been the Publicity Manager for Bakelite. He did personnel work for Halex and he had also worked for Cadbury Bros. The other editor was John Akers, a scientific writer for British Xylonite.

Several articles refer to the inventor of the table-tennis ball process, Sydney William Snell (1891-1969), who was very important to the international success of the company. John Leatherland described him as 'a very likeable chap, being of medium height, with a slim build – a very quiet and pleasant man'. In 1892 Sydney Snell's father, William,

41 *Jack's Farm, Hale End Road (now Larkshall Road), where the BX Co. factory was built in 1897.*

42 '*At Hale End, there was a department known as the "London Delivery", which comprised a number of horses and carts and later motor vans, which delivered in a wide area of London but otherwise, goods went by train and were delivered by the local Goods Station with their railway goods vehicles – the normal method in those days.' (J. Leatherland)*

joined the British Xylonite Co. Ltd at its original works in Homerton, and Sydney became an apprenticed engineer to his father at Hale End in 1906 at the age of 15. Apart from five years away in the First World War, Sydney worked there until 1952 and, even then, Halex were so reluctant to lose his knowledge and experience that they retained him as a consultant. In 1920 he was appointed Technical Manager with the responsibility of mechanising all the expensive hand-operated processes currently in use on the site. With his mechanical engineering training and special talents as an inventor, he was well equipped to undertake this work and made a resounding success of it. Very soon, 'Ping-Pong' balls were being produced in their millions by the secret 'Snell Process' on Snell-built equipment.

Snell never made elaborate drawings in the earlier stages of development: his men worked from sketches he made on pieces of paper in the place where he found the greatest privacy and inspiration! He travelled in Europe, exchanged information with Du Pont in Canada and bought the first injection moulding machine from Germany. A host of fully-shaped plastic items were soon pouring from Hale End machines.

Sydney Snell saw the great potential of the new polymeric materials and in the 1940s designed lines based on polystyrene and polyethylene. He developed polyethylene household ware, and was the first man to produce a washing up bowl using plastic in place of metal, the Halex round plastic bowl being the first on the market. He also invented the rondating process for smoothing the tips of toothbrush bristles (for which everyone should be grateful!)

Mrs Irene Knight recalled:

> I worked down in Highams Station Avenue for BX Plastics. It was basically the
> British Xylonite Company, but BX Plastics made the raw materials, and Halex made

43   *A 'Halex' van. The trade name 'Halex' was from BX plus Hale End Road.*

the articles from the raw materials. We had celluloid, which was, of course, nitro-cellulose, and there was another one, which was called Bexoid, which was a cellulose acetate. Though they made everything with celluloid, it was very inflammable – *very* inflammable. It didn't seem to worry anybody, and I never remember hearing of an accident related to it! But cellulose acetate was, of course, non-flammable.

John Leatherland explained:

It was in the early years of the century that cellulose acetate was produced, a kind of 'non-flam celluloid'. It had some success but celluloid remained the dominant material used at Halex until after the Second World War, when there was a great expansion of many different plastics, based on oil.

No-one was allowed to take matches or lighters of any kind into the factory – nor pipes, and I am afraid I have had to discharge quite a number of people for doing so. There was no question about it: it was in the Laws. If you did, you were out. After the war the company owned numerous factories and each factory had its own voluntary fire brigade. The men worked at ordinary jobs, but if the fire alarm went they dropped everything and ran! At Hale End there were at least a dozen people involved, and by the time I got there they had learned all about celluloid and how inflammable it was,

44 *Mrs Jessie Allen, on reaching her 104th birthday in 1996. Mrs Allen and her husband had both worked for BX. Co. Ltd.*

so the precautions had been taken and there were only small fire alarms – nothing really serious.

We had Inter-Works Fire Brigade Competitions. Each factory in turn took it upon themselves to be the host and brigades came from other factories, and the main street of the factory, or some other convenient place, was cleared. Portable pumps were set up (the sort we used in the War), and ordinary drills done.

When Mrs Jessie Allen was into her 105th year, in August 1996, she was still an alert, friendly woman with a good memory and was able to talk about her early life and her long association with BXL. She met her husband John Allen, a survivor of the Battle of the Somme, while they were both working at Xylonite, and after beginning married life in Wood Street they moved to Frankland Road, South Chingford in 1937. This was about half a mile from her husband's work at BXL, and she lived there until John died in 1987.

Mrs Allen had been interviewed (as 'our oldest pensioner') by Percy Reboul in 1991 for *The Link* magazine, and also by the *Guardian & Gazette* newspaper on her 104th birthday in July 1996. The following account includes some of her comments from the other articles:

I went to British Xylonite at Hale End in 1916. A number of members of my family already worked there, and the shop was headed by Jack Timms, whose cousin was the charge hand. (The Timms brothers lived in Selwyn Avenue.) They were lovely people.

One day in 1921 I was working in the Battery Shop, making batteries for cars, when someone came out to me and said that I was wanted down at the office, so I went, and Mr Laurence Merriam came out and he asked if I was Jessie Wilton and looked me up and down. I can see him now – a very, very nice man – and there were a lot of fellows there being interviewed as well. I was in there for half an hour or more, then he asked me if I would like to work in the new factory. When he explained that my foreman would be Mr Harry Timms and there would be more money, I agreed, and started on the extrusion machines. So I was the first one to work in the new Lactoid building and I was very happy in my work. I really enjoyed it.

The place was just being built and was in a mess. There were only two fitters, myself and Mr Simmonds, the Chief Chemist, who worked in a tin-pot lean-to 'laboratory' in the corner. I remember the tank room, where the smell of the formaldehyde made your eyes water and even caused visitors to cry! An old sailor, Tug Wilson, worked in that room and he was used to the smell. He was a great character.

We used to walk over the hill that was between the old and the new factories, which was lovely, and there was a very nice old gentleman, Mr Mackay (one of the bosses), who used to see to all the flowers, and if you were going past as he was seeing to the roses he would cut one off and give it to you. I remember Mr Frank Merriam at the factory as well. Oh, they were good people.

Alexander Dunlop Mackay lived from 1854 to 1939, and was known to his friends as Guy because his birthday fell on 5 November! He was a director of the company for nearly 62 years and attended daily at his office until five weeks before he died. At Hale End factory he was a much-loved and respected character. Mr C.F. Merriam remarked in Mr Mackay's obituary of 1939:

I think that the happiest memory I shall retain will be of seeing him pottering round the grounds on a hot summer's afternoon, wearing an ancient and somewhat battered straw hat, cutting roses to distribute to the girls.

Jessie Allen continued:

At first my wage was about £1 a week and it went up to £2, but I had to stop working at BXL when I married in 1924. I liked my job and the company so much that I asked Mr Laurence if I could stay on. He said no, and stressed that the company rule was to not employ married women. It was a pity, but my contacts were maintained because my husband, Jack, worked at the Hale End and Larkswood factories for 49 years, retiring in 1960 as Chief Foreman. I bought him a bicycle for his wedding present and he went to work by bicycle to Highams Park from Wood Street Station. At first we had two rooms with my mother-in-law, which wasn't very nice. They were the coal merchants, Allen Brothers – well-known, and they had this stable with horses in Brandon Road near Wood Street Station.

At the factory an Athletics Club and the Bowls Club were started. My husband was a County Bowler and he played for Essex many times.

We used to go to Brantham with the Bowls Club and the Cricket Club when, once a year, they used to play the people at the Brantham factory, and then they would come up here the next year and be entertained at this end.

Mr and Mrs Allen took part in many sports and dancing activities, and Jessie founded the Ainslie Wood Ladies Bowling Club and a tennis club at the Halex factory.

John Leatherland said:

The company was governed by members of the Merriam family, who had very much the paternalistic outlook of the Quakers, and shortly after the end of the First World War, they bought the Rolls Estate adjacent to the factory, on which were constructed football and cricket pitches, bowling greens and tennis courts, and the clubs used the pavilion for their meetings. I wanted to encourage the social side beyond occasional dances, and started an annual horticultural and handicraft show, a fun sports day and clubs for darts and badminton and old-time dancing, that sort of thing.

He wrote in *The Link* magazine:

By mid-1948 the shortage of items like combs etc. had been met and demand began to drop off, and of about 2,000 people employed at Hale End, we had to make 800 people redundant over 12 months. Traditionally, most of the work had been done by women, with men doing the night shifts, so it was mainly men who lost their jobs on the basis of last in, first out.

45 *Sports were encouraged by the BX Co. 'Those were all the bosses. They took an interest in the teams. Mr Wells was the engineer and his son, Percy, worked with him.' (Mrs J. Allen)*

46   *The Knight family lived in Preston Avenue. Like many families in Highams Park, they had moved from Homerton to work at the BX Co. In 1912, five of the children were christened on the same day at All Saints parish church. The family picture shows Mr Thomas James Knight, who was a clerk, and his wife and three of their sons, Geoff, Tom and Eric and their sister, Edie with their relatives, Bill Harrison and his two aunts, who lived in the same road.*

Irene Knight worked at Halex and married Fred, one of the Knight brothers, who also worked at the factory:

> His father was Thomas James Knight. He came from Clerkenwell, and was married there. When the firm, the British Xylonite, moved from Homerton to Highams Park, a lot of their staff, employees and people, all moved down here with them. That was almost the beginning of 'Highams Park'.
>
> I think that Mrs Knight and her sisters worked for them. In those days whole families worked for British Xylonite, but Mr Knight never worked for them at all. No, he was in the electro-plating business, but the family moved down and *en masse* they all worked there at Xylonite. It was convenient, it was handy.
>
> Families stayed in Highams Park. It was only the war (and the price of houses) that really broke everything up. At the British Xylonite they had practically whole families there; husbands and wives, mothers and fathers and sons and daughters, and they'd be doing various jobs as there were a lot of different workshops.

Vera Mason recalled:

> I met my husband, Len, when we were both working at Halex. We met at the BX Plastics factory, which was at Higham Station Avenue (but of course, Halex was the firm). That's been built on now. There were allotments there too, along Tudor Road, between Selwyn and the factory buildings. Of course, you could go off to the left then, right across the fields where Ropers Avenue is now, almost to Ropers Farm!

After Poland was invaded during the Second World War, many Polish men and women came to Great Britain, and some found employment at Halex in Highams Park. Jan Wladyslaw Salamonowicz, born in 1925, escaped to freedom in England by walking across Russia! Jan (also known as John) found work at the Halex factory, where he met Maria, another worker from Poland, who became his wife. He described his work and how he came to stay and bring up a family in Highams Park:

> I had lived in London, but I worked in Edmonton. Then travel was easier – the 144 bus was running straight to Walthamstow on a direct route from Edmonton – but it was the attraction of the job at Halex which brought me to Highams Park. You see, when I moved to Walthamstow from Stoke Newington I was still working on night shift all the time, so the idea was to find better work and to do away with night shift. We saw newspaper adverts and went to Halex and there was a vacancy, so I started there.
>
> It was a family firm and they were very nice gentlemen, the Merriams. (I knew the elder Mr Merriam.) The younger Mr Merriam served in Burma. He was a Captain in the Tank regiment, so he had a very good reputation among the workers because a few of the men had served under him in the regiment. So there was the family involvement in the firm. Halex was a model firm, recognised for the social arrangements.
>
> The Engineering Union was in a strong position. There were different types of union, but everybody was in a union, and any questions – everything – went through the Workers' Committee. There was a Works Convenor and some Shop Stewards and there was a Workers' Committee. As far as I remember, they paid you for the time you attended Committee, and your wages were not deducted if you were a representative from the workshop.
>
> I did eleven-hour shifts and there was round-the-clock work. That was just after the war. We had a quarter of an hour before dinner and a quarter of an hour after dinner for a tea-break. The time was paid for: it wasn't deducted.

Maria Salamonowicz commented:

> It used to be called 'The Factory in the Garden'. It was lovely – everything was nice. We used to have a 'Dinner Hour', you know – not work through it! At dinnertime we used to go round to the shops in Highams Park. I remember Mr Leatherland, and Mr Lewis was my Foreman. His son became the Conservative Leader of the Waltham Forest Council, and there was a doctor who came to the factory, Dr Marien, the one who died young – a lovely doctor as well.

This reminded her husband about other services:

> Once a week they had a Dental Surgery and they had a doctor twice or three days a week but we had a medical nurse all the time, to see to the smaller things. Everything had to be put down – every scratch – every accident. Yes, you had to be meticulous about that.

John Leatherland praised the social services offered to the workers.

> Dr Sanders was a long-standing doctor in Hale End and he spent a couple of mornings at the factory. He was a character. One day he phoned me and said, 'Leatherland, can you come up to the surgery? I've got a young man here, who thinks that he has got a better barrier cream than ours.' (The workers used cream on their hands to protect the skin when they were using certain substances.) When I got to the surgery Dr Sanders told the man to use his cream, and then the doctor used a brush to cover his hands with paint, but the barrier cream hadn't had time to dry so the unfortunate young man spent the next half hour in the corner of the room vainly trying to wash off the paint!
>
> Pensions went back to the early years of the century. One of my odd jobs was being Secretary of the Xylonite Company's Sick and Provident Society, which had three and a half thousand members and was a registered Friendly Society. Welfare schemes, Dentist, Doctor, Optician and Chiropodist: you name it – they'd got it!
>
> Many workers had their employment safeguarded because the company had a scheme so that people employed for a certain period were there permanently. They had a Works' Committee from 1919, and I recall reading in the old Works' Committee Books that around the period of the General Strike in the 1920s there was an announcement by the Chairman that all salaries and wages would be cut by 5 per cent. I think it was.

The factories at Hale End and Brantham had canteens from the earliest days, these superseding the old mess rooms required under the Factories Act. People could heat up their own food or purchase a full meal at a reasonable price. A two-course meal in the canteen cost 1s. 3d.: menus included the traditional roast, shepherd's pie and stews, with baked jam roly-poly a favourite pudding. Nothing fancy. There was a Canteen Committee to deal with complaints and, because of the widespread nature of the factory buildings, many were about cold tea and coffee served from trolleys. Nothing very serious, though curry was often contentious, whether too hot or not hot enough.

Maria had to learn how to speak English:

> I found people here very friendly. Kind friends in the Halex workshops were very patient, and they used to teach me to speak English. We had lots of 'Sing-songs' in the workshops, you know – working and singing in Halex. It used to be lovely, and through songs I learned a lot. I used to ask them, 'What *means* that?'

Jan did not have so much of a problem:

> I spoke some English as I learned a little bit before I came here. They had 'Music While You Work' from the radio and there was a local radio station in Halex. They used to play their own records, and beamed music to all the workshops in the morning and in the afternoon, so we had about two hours of Halex on transmission.

Peter Simcox was appointed as BXL's first Company Secretary in 1962, a former Managing Director of Halex who had joined British Xylonite in 1955 as Assistant Company Secretary. It was then still a public company, part owned by Distillers, who went on to acquire the whole company in 1961 and, a year later, to combine it with other companies owned by Union Carbide in the U.K. to form Bakelite Xylonite Ltd (BXL).

John Leatherland recalled:

> I ceased to be the Halex Personnel Manager in 1961-2, on becoming the Group Personnel Manager.

47 *The 'Factory in a Garden' – pleasure born of necessity. Workers enjoyed the gardens that separated the buildings to avoid the risk of fire.*

The Merriam family were efficient and active administrators and they were very nice people to deal with. The last of the family to be responsible for the running of the company retired in 1962. Lawrence was the Managing Director of the plastics materials-making division. Charles Coubrough, who became Chairman of the company, was a grandson of the original founder through his mother, who was a Merriam; and his younger brother, Adair Coubrough, who lived in Essex, was the BX Co. Works Director. Frank Merriam (the eldest) lived at East Bergholt, and Laurence Merriam near there.

In 1963 a dramatic change occurred. Union Carbide Corporation of America became the co-owners with Distillers Co., and a merger of BX (Bakelite) and Xylonite took place. What, up to then, had been essentially a family business was pitchforked into a different industrial world. The management style was what might be called 'American chemical' – that is, a large volume of product made by relatively few people – capital intensive in modern terms, whereas most of Xylonite and much of Bakelite was labour intensive.

Halex closed down in 1969-70. By that time BXL had come into operation and my office was in London, near Marylebone Station. Of course, Union Carbide took over the company completely and, in my opinion, they were not so interested in its products as in its value.

The intention to finally close the Hale End site was a well-kept secret and when it did come it was a nasty shock to the people there. Traditionally, a job with 'The Xylonite' meant a job for life, and long service employees felt the company had let them down. At the end there was a shocking amount of redundancy to deal with. About 1,200 people lost their jobs.

After the BXL (Halex) factory closed, a small but densely populated council estate (Aldriche Way) was built on a corner of the factory land at the back of the houses in Selwyn Avenue and Tudor Road, but the rest of the large site was designated Highams Park Light Industrial Estate. This included a small plastics factory which distributed Motherware goods for some years, and Waltham Forest Council arranged that a commemorative plaque for BXL should be placed on this building.

5

A Little Learning

In the rush hour children head for the local primary and secondary schools, buses coming from other boroughs to the Joseph Clarke School for partially sighted children and Brooke House School for physically handicapped children. At the other end of Hale End Road, more buses bring children from far and wide to Whitefield School, another special school with its entrance in MacDonald Road. The many schools make life very different today from what it used to be in old Hale End, especially for children.

The present Whitefield School was built on the site of what had been quite a large Victorian double-fronted house with a carriage drive and gardens around it. This became home to the William Morris School for the Deaf, Hale End Road, which had first opened in Queens Road, Walthamstow in 1900 and then moved to William Morris School in Gainsborough Road two years later, before combining with Hale End Open Air School in 1949 and moving to Hale End Road in 1952. During the mid-1950s it was still being used by Walthamstow Council as a schools' clinic, but it closed in 1969 when Hawkswood School in Chingford was opened.

Education from the Sixteenth to the Nineteenth Centuries

Until 1835 there was no school at all in Hale End. Some children probably learned to read at dame schools, but if they could be spared from working on the farms they had a walk of over two miles across the fields to school. There was a schoolroom over the Almshouses by St Mary's parish church in Walthamstow village. The Sir George Monoux Grammar School was founded in 1527 as a Free School for young children and from about 1782 it accepted girls as pupils. The school moved to new buildings in High Street, Walthamstow and became a very good Grammar School for Boys after the First World War. In 1927 another move took the school to its present site in Chapel End behind the Town Hall. Although the school still exists in name, it is now a Sixth Form College.

However, in the early years of the 19th century all children were given a chance to learn when the National Schools were established, and in 1819 a school was built opposite the Walthamstow Workhouse. The building is now a spiritualist church and the old workhouse was used to house Walthamstow's Vestry House Museum. Hale End's first school was held in one of the little Oak Hill Cottages but did not open until 1835. 'Hale End National Infants' School' appears in records of 1840, but by 1865 this school had closed. St Peter's National School, Woodford New Road was built in 1846-7 by Hale End's new parish church, and by 1889 it had been enlarged to take 190 children. The school closed in 1903.

Woodford Green Primary School

Before either Hale End or St Peter's National Schools opened the children of Hale End area may have been able to go to Woodford Green National School, which was

48 *Woodford Green Board School, c.1891.*

just inside the boundaries of Walthamstow (in Sunset Avenue, near the High Road in Woodford Green), and this school has survived for over 180 years. It was built in 1820 and has the distinction of being one of the earliest schools of its kind in the country because it replaced the National School for Boys of 1814, which had already absorbed the 'Boys' School of Industry' held in the workhouse. But there was a crisis in 1818, when the number of children fell from 90 to 69, and the school had very low funds because some subscribers had withdrawn their financial support on the grounds that it 'encouraged delinquency and impeded juvenile employment'! The new school was built on land belonging to 'Jeremiah Harman of Higham Hills in the parish of Walthamstow in the County of Essex', to teach boys and also girls from the Girls' School of Industry.

Although it is an old building, many improvements have been made to the old National School since my sister, Julia, was a pupil in the 1950s. At that time our mother, Mrs Lettie Grantham, was working there as a part-time teacher in what was known as 'the School on the Green'. I remember her saying that the school building was in desperate need of repair and had been condemned for years. Mr Donald B. Spelman was the Head Teacher from 1950-68 and he wrote a graphic description of the conditions he found at the school:

> When I was appointed in 1950 the older part of the building had remained unaltered and because it was due to be demolished nothing was done to repair the deteriorating fabric nor to introduce modern amenities. Remarkably for an urban school in the mid-20th century, electricity was not laid on and the classrooms were lit by inefficient

49 *Woodford Green Junior School, c.1953.*

gas burners which shed such a poor light that no written work could be attempted in the late afternoons in winter. The heating was even more primitive, consisting of 11 separate units, open fires in the infant rooms and slow combustion cast-iron stoves in the others. The outside toilets were cold and dark and froze up at the slightest hint of frost. The slate roof leaked and the drains were blocked by roots from surrounding trees so that classrooms were flooded after heavy rains.

An even greater problem than the inadequacy of the building was caused by the building of the Highams pre-fab estate and the consequent sudden expansion of the number of children in attendance, from under 300 to over 600.

A total of 176 families were re-housed until 1960 on what had been re-named by Waltham Forest Council as 'The Highams Park'. In 1948 the brick shed near Tamworth Avenue, which had served as a First Aid Post in the war, was converted into Highams Park Community Club, with a kitchen, piano and stage. When it opened it was hoped there would be lectures, whist drives and other social activities.

Mr Spelman went on to say that he was pleased to see that great improvements to the school had been made in the 1970s. Cliff Payling was a young teacher at the school:

I started work as a teacher at the school in 1951 and taught there for seven years. At that time we had those old, high teachers' desks with very tall chairs in the classrooms. I believe the original building of 1820 was enlarged in 1889. It was in a terrible state when I went there. In fact, just prior to that they had had a plague of rats under the floorboards – rats used to come up sometimes!

The post-war 'Bulge' had raised the number of children in the Infants', and it gradually passed through the school. Across the grass of the common land near the golf links, the school rented two classrooms in the building behind the United Free Church, plus the hall, which was used for Assembly and for school dinners.

50 *Woodford Green Junior School, the class of 1953 with their class teacher, Cliff Payling. They posed for the photograph on the Common by the school.*

51 *The hamlet of Hale End, pre-1906. In the 19th century, there was a 'Dame School' in one of the tiny cottages.*

We used to play games behind the school on the scrubby, uneven grass, but we had a ground at Salisbury Hall Playing Fields for the football team to play. We were part of Walthamstow. It was a Walthamstow school! Since then, I believe, it has alternated between Walthamstow and Redbridge (and now it's back in Walthamstow again). The girls played netball in the playground and they visited other schools to play matches, but there wasn't the organisation for the girls' sport that there was for the boys'.

Mrs Kennard, the Deputy Head, always took the 4th year 'A' class, and Ted Harsant had a special post for teaching backward children. Other members of staff at that time were Sheila Hemnal, who taught at Woodford Green for about five years, then spent the rest of her life in Jersey, and Miss Gladys Cobbledick, who became Head of the Infants' School at Thorpe Hall in Hale End Road; there was Mrs Norgate, over in the Infants', who also became a head teacher in Walthamstow, and Miss Margaret Woolstencroft, who became a headmistress at Foulness Island.

We had our ups and downs, but it was a very happy school. Mr Spelman was a very friendly Head, and you didn't leave the school unless you were looking for promotion or were transferred to another school.

Other Early Schools

'Hale School' is mentioned in the Registers of St Peter's-in-the-Forest, in a baptismal entry of 1846 for two pupils (11-year-old George Lucas and his younger brother, James, the sons of an Edmonton carpenter), but it is not certain which school had this name. Another baptismal entry in the Registers of 1848 named a child's father as 'Mr Berthon, a School Attendance man, living in Walthamstow Forest' (a part of Walthamstow at that time). The name 'Berthon' was also closely associated with the early days of Forest School, which was known as 'The Forest Proprietary Grammar School' when it opened in 1834 on land known as Forest Place (near Forest Rise and just within the boundaries of Walthamstow). The new school used the house of a previous one, Exeter College, which had closed soon after it began in 1830. The first headmaster appointed to Forest School was the Rev. Thomas Dry, and the well-known school continues to the present day, taking some pupils as boarders. A Forest School for Girls was established much later in September 1978.

Another Walthamstow school for the sons of gentlemen was within walking distance of Hale End. It was opened in 1841 and run very successfully for nearly twenty years by Dr J. Glennie Grieg, LLD at Walthamstow House in Shernhall Street. The large mansion was rented to Dr Grieg after the death of Lady Wigram, the second wife of Sir Robert Wigram, who fathered 23 children.

The census of 1851 shows that, at Bellevue House, Charles Cooke's young son, George, had his own governess.

Hale End Schools

The communities of Woodford and Hale End were within easy walking distance of each other but they developed differently. A mail-coach route had run through Woodford Row and Woodford Green from 1692, and the railway came to Woodford in 1856, much earlier than to Hale End.

The congregation of Woodford Union Church used to enjoy occasional Sunday School outings down to the lake in the grounds of 'Highams', but when the railway was extended to Hale End in 1873, and the area began to be described as 'ripe for development', two leading members of the Union Church, Henry J. Cook and Edward Tozer, decided that it was time Hale End had its own church. In 1875 they led the formation of a mission at Hale End in a four-roomed cottage next to the *Royal Oak*. What began as a Sunday evening service for adults and a Sunday School rapidly developed into a small day school, and 'concerts were arranged by the people once a month, the entrance fee being one penny'. For five years all went well, but the committee started a Men's Club and this was too much for the landlord of the *Royal Oak*, who gave the superintendent notice to quit the premises.

Mrs Mary Andrews was listed in the 1881 census as the governess of the school, living with Mr Andrews and her seven-year-old granddaughter, Amelia, in the Oak Hill Cottage three doors away from the *Royal Oak*, where she had lived since at least 1877. In 1891, she was described as an Infants' Mistress, and lived in the same cottage.

In 1881 new land was rented to build a small tin building for the school known as the Mission Hall, near the old stone-flagged Beech Hall Farm entrance (which still exists between the houses in Malvern Avenue). The poultry and game salesman who was living at Beech Hall at that time was unimpressed by the new school and continued to employ Miss Edith Harrington, a 24-year-old governess, to teach his eight children. In 1893 Mr Cooke transferred the lease of the Mission Hall to the School Board. Later, Malvern Avenue Congregational Church was built on land behind the Mission building, and when the drains of the 'Tin Hall' were sealed a shepherd's crook was found.

Jeanne May, whose family has lived in or near Hale End Road for three generations, remembers the Mission Hall:

> The building in Hale End Road, which we always called 'The Tin Chapel' or 'The Tin Hall', was where the Old People's Home is now, at the top of Malvern Avenue. It came right on to the pavement – you stepped straight in. It was where we went to vote, and it was also used as the Primary Sunday School and could be divided into two by a partition, and it had at right angles another smaller room, so I think when it was a school it could have had three classes.

Sid Marchant recalls:

> Mr Alfred and Mrs Annie Hatley were both teachers, and they took us for Bible Classes at Highams Park Congregational Church, Malvern Avenue, where there had been a school, and my Sunday School Teacher was Jack Dalton.

Mrs Hatley, who came from Clapton to live in Lyndhurst Road, Highams Park, was also the chairman of the Walthamstow Antiquarian Society after the Second World War. In her book, *Across the Years*, she gives a delightful picture of Hale End as it used

52   *Wood Street School (Junior Boys') celebrating Queen Victoria's Diamond Jubilee in 1897.*

to be, with its 'row of cottages, picturesque but insanitary' and little triangular village green planted with three chestnut trees opposite to Beech Hall Farm. She describes the schoolchildren arriving at their new school, some taken there by a maid.

> The school was set in the loveliest surroundings – buttercup fields, a tall elm opposite and a 'slip' going up the forest, lined on one side with red may bushes.

The green has now been paved over and is cluttered with street furniture; the great elm trees were affected by Dutch Elm disease and have all gone from Highams Park, but there are still some red hawthorn trees along Hale End Road near to Malvern Avenue.

'The Wood Street British School', Shernhall Street was taken over by the School Board in 1880, and in 1899 Wood Street School opened, which was very convenient for the children who lived in Hale End Road near Hagger Lane (Forest Road). Mrs Win Marchant, a pupil there, said, 'All the Bradley brothers and sisters passed through the hands of Miss Shearing, the Headmistress of Wood Street Infants' School'.

Selwyn Avenue Schools

By 1902 the new houses in Highams Park and the resulting increase in the population threatened to overwhelm Hale End's 'Tin Hut' school, which was already full. This state of affairs prompted the School Board to buy a plot of freehold land from John Hitchman (of Wadham Lodge Farm), and Selwyn Avenue Senior Mixed School was built. A year later some of C.J. Geary's land at Thorpe Hall in Hale End Road was also sold to the School Board, but Thorpe Hall School was not built on the site until 1935.

53   *The staff of Wood Street School, c.1908. Standing from left: Mr Walter Hewett (later Deputy Head). Centre: Dr John McCartney, who lived in 'Hale End House', Hale End Road. He went on to take Holy Orders and taught at the Technical College. Seated: Mr Broadhurst is second from left, centre is Mr Butcher, Headmaster. On the left, Mr Sims is sitting cross-legged by the aspidistra.*

54   *Wood Street Boys' School, where all the children in the Bradley family from Hale End Road went to school. Arthur Bradley is sitting behind the cup in Mr Hewett's class, Standard 4, c.1908.*

55 *Selwyn Avenue Senior Boys' School c.1909, seen across Cavendish Road from the banks of the Ching Brook before the houses were built.*

Selwyn Avenue Senior Boys' School opened on 11 April 1904, with T.F. Humphries as its Head Teacher, and the Girls' and Infants' Schools followed soon after.

During the summer holidays the school was closed for four weeks but, by the time it re-opened on 29 August, 21 of the children had measles. Outbreaks of infectious diseases like diphtheria, rheumatic fever and scarlet fever were fairly common, and measles could be fatal; there were even occasional cases of smallpox in Walthamstow, and tuberculosis was dreaded.

Geoffrey Grantham, and his sister, Joan (who died in 2005, aged 99) were both teachers at Selwyn Avenue School during the period 1925-37. They knew how dangerous infectious diseases could be because during their own childhood, when they lived at Higham Hill, their two-year-old sister, Joy, caught a cold and died of pneumonia three days later. Their friend and neighbour, Florrie Sharpe, and all her young brothers and sisters died of tuberculosis.

In 1904 a number of children were excluded from Selwyn Avenue School because younger members of their families were suffering from whooping cough, and one entry in the Log Book noted illness in the local Home for Orphans at Forest Hall in Oak Hill – 'an infectious case at Miss Steer's Home, excluding 29 girls'. At that time quarantine was the only way to stop infectious diseases from spreading and so children missed a lot of schoolwork through family illness.

There were 325 children at the school in June 1908, at which time the roads in Highams Park and the surrounding area were still unmade. On 15 December, the Headmaster wrote, 'Heavy rain – all Home girls absent'.

Activities for Children

The Log Book mentions that during term-time 'scholars' from Selwyn Avenue School had swimming lessons at the Walthamstow Baths and were sent to various woodwork or laundry and cookery centres in Walthamstow. There were also violin classes. My own family knew Reg Adler from the early 1930s until he died in 1982. He started in local schools as a peripatetic violin teacher. My daughter was one of the many lucky children who had violin lessons with Reg in his later years, and we all became very fond of him because he was such a kind, affable man, as well as being a fine musician. He moved from Walthamstow to live in Chingford and at local concerts or other musical events Reg Adler was usually there as leading violinist or musical director of his orchestra. One of his two daughters, Janet Loze, said that, before he began teaching violin classes

56 *'The Log Books of Selwyn Avenue show that children from the school were sent to Violin Classes. This picture shows one of these classes in Leyton, taught by Reg Adler, a violinist, who had played with several well-known orchestras before teaching and moving to Chingford. Later, he founded the Essex Chamber Orchestra. The Head Teacher, sitting by Reg was my grandfather, Walter A. Cooke, who was also an organist.'* (M.L. Dunhill)

in Walthamstow, Reg had studied at Trinity College of Music and played in several well-known orchestras. After the war he trained as a full-time teacher and taught at the McEntee School in Walthamstow, but he continued as a freelance musician and he was involved with Adult Education at the 'Walthamstow Settlement' in Greenleaf Road. This led to the formation of his Essex Chamber Orchestra and his wife, Amy, joined the orchestra as a cellist.

Mrs Loze's daughter, Suzanne, was a pupil at Highams Park School and she and Mr and Mrs Adler's other daughter, Mrs Christine Dalton, both became professional violinists.

Highams Park used to be a very popular place for day-trippers, who came by bus or train from London to 'the most beautiful lake within a day's reach of London', and from 1905 the teachers at Selwyn Avenue began to take classes of children into the Forest and fields for nature study. Ernest Spragg became the Secretary of Walthamstow Natural History Society and joined the staff of Selwyn Avenue School in 1907; entries in the school Log Book from then on show that organised nature study was encouraged. In 1914 the HMI's Report on Selwyn Avenue School mentioned the small school garden and said that 'the long list of wild flowers found by the boys in the locality is proof of the interest aroused'. Frank Payling's experience of nature study was rather painful:

> You went up into the 'big-boys' when you were eight. Mr Spragg was our form-master and he took us for nature study. On one particular hot, sunny day we were taken to a field, roughly where Forest Glade and Nightingale Avenue are now. It was nearly all fields then. Our task was to collect the flowers of different kinds of grass. To collect my flower-heads I had a Bird's Custard tin, to which I had tied a string round my waist. Well, to me in those days grass was just – green! In the afternoon Mr Spragg called us to count how many specimens we had collected, and another boy and I had collected two less than he thought we should have done. We were 'read the Riot Act' and told if we didn't collect a certain number by the next morning we were for 'the stick'!

Whether it was because it was such a hot day that my grasses withered going home, or whether they just jumped out, I don't know, but there were even less than I had had at half-time! Anyway, next day I went to school and I received 'the stick'.

Cliff Payling noted that Ernest R. Spragg was born in the schoolhouse of Woodford Green School, where the census of 1891 shows his father was the Head Teacher.

Schoolchildren still have lessons in the Forest around the Ching and Highams Park lake and little children from the Nursery School in Handsworth Avenue used to 'go down to the woods' for walks and Teddybears' Picnics. In the winter some older children go cross-country running round the lake.

Social and Health Education

Mr Walmsley taught for 20 years at Selwyn Avenue School and his arrival in 1908 coincided with an outbreak of scarlet fever in the junior part of the school. The Medical Officer sent a terse memo to the Headmaster, saying that, in his opinion, there was no risk to the 56 children who had been kept away from school by their parents.

The hard winter of 1909, with bad roads and a heavy fall of snow in early March, kept many children at home. Mr Humphries recorded the funeral of a schoolchild in Standard VI, and he wrote that 35 children were absent from school with mumps. He mentioned that subscriptions to the 'Boot Fund' continued. A notice from the Walthamstow School Board in 1903 reads:

> The Board has allowed the use of school buildings for concerts and entertainment in aid of funds supported by voluntary subscriptions for providing children with boots in deserving cases, and for giving free breakfasts to those children whose parents are in poor circumstances and out of work through no fault of their own. Some hundreds of boots have been supplied and several thousands have received free breakfasts.
> The Board has also arranged for dinners, at the cost of about 1d. or 2d. each, to be provided at the several cookery centres for a limited number of boys and girls from any of the surrounding schools on two days each week.

Arthur Hemmings, who lived in Forest Glade for many years, knew why 'Boot Funds' were necessary:

> I spent a lot of my youth – happy years too – in Stepney. I was a Rover Scout and we used to meet in the Settlement House, Stepney Green. Of course, in those days, things were very hard down there in Stepney. Our boys never got a holiday unless we took them. We used to run Jumble Sales, and things like that, to raise money, and got them away for a fortnight. Some of them used to come without any boots or stockings in those days. Things were bad, and we used to buy shoes or boots for them, and come the next week, the same boots were for sale – Mum had taken them in to the Pawn Shop!

At Selwyn Avenue School in 1910 the last lesson each afternoon for Standards V to VII was 'devoted to special lessons in Citizenship', and Mr G. Avery of the 'Band of Hope Union' lectured the older children on 'Temperance and Hygiene'. It may not have been a coincidence that he gave the talk shortly after the opening of the *County Arms* public house in Hale End Road. The *Great Eastern Hotel*, run by A.M. Jelmoni, nearly opposite Highams Park Station in The Avenue, and the *Wilfred Lawson Hotel*, at the top of Chingford Lane, were both temperance hotels.

There were 391 children at Selwyn Senior Boys School in 1911, but a circular from the Education Office gave instructions to admit some children from Chingford for the first time. Until then the school had only accepted children from Walthamstow, even though the Chingford boundaries were so near. James Knight, born in 1892, of 'The Rolls', which straddled the Chingford/ Walthamstow boundary, seems to have been an exception.

57 *Miss Muddiman's small school in The Avenue, c.1953. Dr Douglas Woolf's daughter, Valerie, is shown, second from left and Dr Marien's daughter, Angela is fourth from left.*

Accidents were recorded in the Log Book. Eleven-year-old Thomas Holyoak, who lived in Winchester Road, was injured in the high winds of February 1911, and in December of the same year there was a 'serious accident during organised games – playing 'Buck Thrust', when a boy fell and broke his leg. A doctor was called and the injured boy was taken home in a cab, which in those days meant bumping over unmade roads in a horse-drawn cab!

One 'school circular' warned about the danger to health from houseflies – and this was still a problem in the 1930s. Miss Renee Weller recalls:

> Of course, they talk about pollution of the streets nowadays, but then the great dread was flies, which used to invade the house in the summertime, and you had fly papers and fly sprays, because of the horses' dung in the road. But then, when these houses were first built, the lady of the house would be at the ready – with a pail and bucket – to fly out into the street to grab the manure, saying, 'That's *mine* – not yours' to fertilise the gardens!

The Misses Hickman and other Schools

In 1886 Thomas Sutcliff Armstrong, JP (1855-1937) came to live at 'Hinkwood', a house in the part of Hale End Road now called Larkshall Road, and became a great benefactor to Hale End and Highams Park. He was the first churchwarden of All Saints Church, Highams Park, and purchased land for a Church Hall at All Saints-on-the-hill which became known as the Church Room. In about 1904 Miss Fanny Hickman rented this hall for use as a private school.

Miss Frances Bowler was a pupil at this school and she remembered being taught French, Scripture, Needlework and Recitation:

> Two maiden ladies, the Misses Hickman, Fanny and Annie, had a school, and their first school room is now used as the Church Hall of All Saints Church, and I went to the school and had lessons there! The youngsters started when they were five or six-ish, and when they got a bit older the boys went on to somewhere else, but we, the older girls, went to where Miss Fanny lived at 31 Handsworth Avenue for lessons, which were given upstairs in her house. [In 1906 the address was 7 Handsworth Avenue.] I went there until I was old enough to go to the High School in 1920. (This was one year after the opening of Woodford County High School for Girls.)
>
> Aglaia Macropoulos whose collection of dolls and family photograph albums are kept at the Vestry House Museum was at Miss Hickman's School. She was just a bit older than I was, and she went on to Walthamstow High School and did very well, matriculated, and I heard that the whole school at Miss Hickman's had a holiday because she had got Matric!

Win Marchant, who lived in the Highams Park area for 99 years, knew another of the Misses Hickman's pupils:

> Miss Olive Muddiman attended the private school in Handsworth Avenue run by two spinster sisters, the Misses Fanny (born in 1855) and Annie Hickman, and when she became old enough to teach other children she did so for Miss Fanny in the school she had opened in All Saints Church Hall in Church Avenue. When Miss Fanny died Olive started her own very successful little school for 25 to 30 children in her home at 121

58 *'Eureka School' (translated, 'I've got it!') in the late 1920s, in Falmouth Avenue. Back row from left: 2nd, Sybil Hooper, 5th, 6th, and 7th are Miss Barham, Miss Dawes and a Miss Koller (Kollar or Collard?), whose parents lived in Ainslie Wood Gardens, where they had a small farm. Second row down from left: 1st and 2nd, Kathleen Lloyd, who became a District Nurse in Highams Park and Peggy Spragg. Maynard twins are in front of Miss Koller. Third row, last right: Douglas Woolf. Front row, last right, Basil Jenkins.*

> The Avenue. She used to describe the two sisters with affection: Miss Fanny Hickman was tall and thin – a real schoolmarm – but Miss Annie was little and demure – very sweet. Their brother, on marriage, went to live in one of the original larger houses in Castle Avenue. I cannot remember meeting him, but people spoke highly of him.

Dennis Webb commented that they all paid fees to attend the school and laughed as he imitated the way in which Miss Fanny used to dismiss the possibility of accepting many of the local children to her school by declaring in polished tones, 'Aie take noe children of the Trade!' (which illustrates the social divisions of that time rather well).

Mrs Diana Oliver (née Ralph), was the sports teacher at Miss Muddiman's school, a charming woman who had trained to be a dancer but, when she was only 17 years old, had left a promising stage career to marry Dick Oliver. He was very well known to local people because he was the manager of Barclays Bank in Highams Park for several years. The Oliver and Ralph families have lived in Highams Park since its earliest days and have supported many local activities, especially at All Saints Church. Mr Oliver was Treasurer of the Woodford Branch of Arthritis Care and Dr Douglas Woolf was its Chairman.

Dr Woolf mentioned another local school:

> In The Avenue, on the corner by the little alleyway next to the solicitor's, there used to be a school called Warner College, where Miss Davis and Miss Parsons were the teachers.

Mrs Joyce Webb (née Tayler) went to Warner College for the last two years before it closed at the beginning of the Second World War:

> We used to go up the alley and use the gate into the garden at the back of the house to get to the classroom. Miss Parsons gave piano lessons and there was a through room to the front, where we used to have 'orchestra' practice with her. (I played the triangle.) She looked very old to me, but I used to be rather scared of Miss Davis, who was short and rather fat with her hair pulled up in a bun, and she wore long black skirts. She dressed as she always had done, I suppose. When the war began, there wasn't an air raid shelter, and the children were sent to the new Infants' and Junior School at Handsworth Avenue.

6

The First World War

In 1914 war was declared on Germany but, at first, life in Highams Park continued peacefully. There were several Sunday School outings and a day-trip to Clacton-on-Sea for the children of Selwyn Avenue School. But in January 1916, conscription was introduced for unmarried men, and in May married men were also obliged to leave their families to fight in the war. (Only miners, factory workers involved in essential war work and men in poor health avoided being sent to the trenches.) School circulars mentioned Belgian refugees and gave suggestions for action in case of air raids. In the spring of 1915 the male staff of Selwyn Avenue School were absent for a day or two, attending medical examinations for military service, after which most of the men went to war and more women teachers had to be employed.

Alan Marshall's father was a Lance Corporal in the First World War, and his grandfather was also in the army:

> My grandmother, Mrs Sloss, used to live in Highams Park, and she was a mid-wife, and my grandfather had been a Medical Dispenser in the Army, on a China station. I always remember going into 133 Winchester Road, and going upstairs to the bathroom, and there, along the side of the bath, were all these Chinese snakes that my grandfather had collected.

Les Felgate lived in Cranston Gardens, built on Ropers' farmland:

> My grandfather went to Canada in 1913, the year after the *Titanic* went down, and his ship stopped where it went down and they had a service there. (If he had gone the year before, it is almost certain that *he* would have been on the *Titanic*.) He was a master craftsman in woodwork, and he was looking for work in Canada with a view to moving his family there, and then the 1914 War started and, being patriotic, he thought he'd better come back and sign up – although I'm not sure if he did.

In 1915 the *Walthamstow, Leyton and Chingford Guardian* newspaper reported on how people in Highams Park were adapting to wartime. A Mr H.V. Wilman of 122 Selwyn Avenue started a Rambling Club, which he hoped would encourage a community spirit in the new urban village. On the military front, the Hale End Volunteers (5th Essex Volunteer Regiment), under their commandant, A.J. Pearce, planned a regimental parade with the other companies of the local battalion of the Essex Volunteer regiments at Hainault. The men were told to parade 'at Highams Park Station at 9.15 a.m. sharp'! Recruits were to report to Mr J. Eagle, The Nook, Clevedon [*sic*] Road, Highams Park or at headquarters. 'Sky Peals any drill night between 8-9 p.m. The rifle range is available for the public at certain times.'

The local newspaper reported that the owners of some of the larger houses in Hale End district did their best to keep up the morale of casualties from the Front:

> Owing to the inclement weather, the arrangements made for entertaining a party of wounded soldiers on Saturday, July 17th by the kind invitation of Mr and Mrs

59 *'Highams', the Manor House, was used as a Red Cross Hospital during the First World War. The first-floor room at the right of the building was the Operating Theatre for wounded soldiers but, when Highams became Woodford County High School for Girls in 1919, it was used as the Staff Room.*

Walter Smee in the grounds of 'St Moritz', Falmouth Avenue had to be cancelled. Mr and Mrs Smee have, however, very kindly offered the use of their grounds to the association for this purpose at a later date.

In August soldiers were entertained at Brookfield by Thomas Armstrong, and a week later it was Mrs Halfhead at Beech Hall who was pleased to open her gardens to wounded soldiers, 'where they made full use of the delightful grounds, with bowls and cricket or in quiet strolls along the grass walks in the garden'.

In December of that year All Saints Church had a service honouring fallen heroes, 'the brave lads of Highams Park who fell in the war'. The organist was George R. Mason and the Hale End Volunteers were there under their Platoon Commanders, G. Atkin and W. Vincent. On Christmas Eve 1915 an appeal for a new Red Cross Hospital to be built on Mr Armstrong's land by Brookfield Path was launched.

Frances Bowler was 10 years old in 1916:

> Mrs Halfhead lived at Beech Hall during the First World War, and her daughters put on an entertainment, which we performed in the Church Hall of All Saints. I was 'Britannia', and we sang patriotic songs – we were *very* patriotic. My father made me a marvellous helmet and a trident, and mother made me a long robe and put gold paint around it, and worked like mad on it!

On Empire Day in 1916 the Headmaster of Selwyn Avenue Boys' School wrote in the Log Book:

> All the departments of the school assembled in the playground, where they saluted the flag and sang patriotic songs. Scouts attended in uniform, the band playing selections, whilst the Juniors marched from their playground between the rows of Scouts holding poles to form an archway. Girls dressed in representative national costumes danced

60   *The First World War took many men away from Highams Park and Hale End. 'My father, Lance Corporal Arthur Edward Marshall of the 8th Battalion, London Foot regiment (the Post Office Rifles), with a wound stripe. He was wounded in France and was due to go back to fight again in about 1916.' (Alan Marshall)*

typical dances. Twenty-two wounded soldiers and three nurses from the local Red Cross Hospital were also present at the celebration.

Edith Upton was a schoolgirl at Selwyn Girls' School:

During the First World War, men came up and down the road, blowing a whistle to sound the alarm for possible air raids, and a trumpet for the 'All Clear'.

There was a fire station in Winchester Road, next door to Gaze, the chemist, which had big red-painted double doors. I went to school with Nellie Clements, who lived above the fire station, where her father was a fireman and her family kept the brasswork clean. Outside the fire station there was a solid round post, about four feet high, with a bell covered by a pane of glass to be broken if there were a fire.

On Empire Day, at Selwyn Avenue School, Nellie Clements was always chosen to be 'Britannia', because she could borrow her father's fireman's helmet, but one day her father rushed to the school railings saying, 'Hi, quick, Nellie! Give me the helmet! There's a fire!'

In March 1917 the teachers' room at Selwyn Avenue Boys' School was reported as being 'unfit for use owing to dense clouds of smoke the greater part of each day' (presumably due to a faulty boiler). On 20 April the Headmaster, Mr Humphries, caught mumps.

The school Log Book records that the school closed early on 14 June because of a 'Fire Station notice that an air raid was pending'. More air-raid warnings were given during October and parents reacted by keeping their children at home. Mr Humphries commented, 'attendance affected by the removal temporarily of several families from the district' – the first evacuation.

Frank Payling was born in 1912 but he remembered incidents in the war quite clearly:

First of all there was the Zeppelin raids. They were quite frequent. We always came downstairs and what was a great delight for me was that the people next door came in as well. They brought the little girl, who lived on her own, and we had the most delightful romps on the sofas!

On Saturday 7 July 1917 I was playing in the hayfield attached to Beech Hall Farm. I looked up, and there was a squadron of planes coming over. There were, if I remember rightly, about 15 of them. They were Gotha planes, based in Ghent in Belgium, and they came over to attack London that morning. As soon as they came over the 'Ack-Ack' guns started shooting and I ran home. Mother was out shopping, and I remember sheltering in my neighbour's passageway. It's very, very strange to relate that the very first bomb that was dropped on London fell in a field in Chingford. It didn't do any harm anyway.

The Zeppelin raids always took place at night. You could look above our front doorway, where there was a clear window, and see the red flashes of the 'Ack-Ack' guns at 'Spion Kop' at Higham Hill. In the Second World War they had a battery of guns on that very same site. I can't recall seeing the shooting down of the Zeppelin at Cuffley, but I must have been there because I remember my mother, in common with a lot of other people, shouting with joy, only to be rebuked by our neighbour, Mrs Haines, who was a rather straight-laced lady, saying, 'They are only some mothers' sons perishing there!'

Mrs Jane F. Matthews lived through both of the world wars. When she was 100 years old, and living in Vincent Road, Highams Park, she talked about the devastating effect of the first war on her family:

61   'Mr Sloss, my grandfather, had served in the Army in China, and my grandmother was a midwife in Highams Park. They lived in Winchester Road.' (Alan Marshall)

All of my brothers were born at home (in the Mile End Road area). There was George, Alf and Ted – one in between died. In the First World War my youngest brother was called up. He had only been in for three months and he was killed, and it caused my mother to have a stroke. After the first stroke she spent nine months getting over that, and then she had another one. Mother was 53 when she died.

I was the eldest, and some months after my mum had the first stroke I wanted to go back to work again, and she said that I could. At that particular time my sister, Edie, was working but she came home that same day and said she'd got the sack, so she was the one who took over. She brought the others up after that.

My work, at that particular time, was stitching uniforms – a machinist really. I made tunics, but it depended on whatever was coming in – sometimes greatcoats. It was all under the Borough of Bethnal Green and we borrowed the machines. Sometimes I was in Shoreditch, and I worked in Bow. It was wherever machinists were needed.

January 1918 brought heavy snow to Highams Park and there were floods in the corridors of Selwyn Avenue School as it melted. The Head Teacher suffered from a very bad cold, and the air raids continued to affect the number of children attending school. The bad weather continued into the spring and on 16 April Mr Humphries wrote: 'School very cold (39 F). Caretaker had not lighted the furnace fire although there had been a fall of snow – reason given that no wood had been supplied by the Architect.' Later that year a circular sent to the school suggested that precautions should be taken against influenza. The virus was extremely dangerous to young and apparently healthy people and caused more deaths worldwide than the First World War!

Frank Payling remembers the end of the First World War:

62 *Mr Armstrong's home, Brookfield House, off Oak Hill. Brookfield School for children with special needs now stands on the site. 'Mr. Armstrong was almost the Squire of Highams Park. He gave money to build All Saints Church Hall – and he lost a son in the First World War. His name is on the War Memorial Board in the church; Captain A. S. Armstrong.' (L. Frances Bowler. Photograph from Mr Ring, a nephew of Thomas Armstrong.)*

63 *Skating on Highams Park Lake, c.1909. Frances Bowler remembered skating there in 1918. 'That was delightful. Oh, I learned to skate on Highams Park Lake! Two winters – it was gorgeous! That's when the medical students were at the* **Eastern Hotel** *(opposite the station in the Avenue). I was a 'Flapper' then. Mr Warboys, who built Warboys Crescent, was a great skater from the fens. He used to dash up and down!' (L. Frances Bowler)*

> I can recall the Sunday before Armistice Day. We were in the Sunday School in what we called the 'Tin Chapel', attached to what was then the Congregational Church in Malvern Avenue. The Superintendent gave thanks and a prayer for the cease-fire, but it would appear that, although the Armistice wasn't signed until the following Thursday, the cease-fire was actually on the Sunday. We were at school on Armistice Day, 11 November, a typical November day – damp, drizzly and miserable. We were let out at lunch time and called at a confectioner's shop in Hale End Road, which was opposite the new Post Office, and bought little paper flags of the Allies. I can remember that as clear as if it was yesterday.

Most of the male members of Selwyn staff came back from their military duties in 1919, and to celebrate the return to civilised life groups of boys were taken to see performances of two Shakespeare plays. The members of staff in April 1919 were A.E. Outridge (Singing), F. Walmsley (Geography), V.G. Davey (Nature Study and Pastel Drawing), E.R. Spragg (Nature Study), S. Adams (Nature Study and History), H.E. Robinson (History), G.C.L. Smith (Geography) and H. Ridgwell. Later in the year Mr Smith went on to Queen's Road School, and Mr J. Walton and Mr J. Gibb were appointed.

Ted Jones lived in Marion Grove, Woodford Green for 37 years until 1997. He said that the wartime experiences of his schoolmasters had benefited their pupils:

> I was born in 1918 and I left school in 1932. I went to school in the City of London, and the name of my school was Bath Street. (It would be between two roads, The City Road and Old Street.) It was a big new school and it had a part for the girls and a part for the boys, on the lower level that is. We were all in one big building – very like Chapel End.
>
> I went to school in Bath Street and left at fourteen but I feel, when I look back now, I had a wonderful education because most of the teachers there had come out of the First World War and they had been on active service. Some were very, very nice, and I got on well.

7

Schools and Scholars

Edith Upton remembered the Attendance Officer (or 'Superintendent of the Attendance Department' – as the Selwyn School Log Book described him in 1921). 'Mr Longman was the "School Board man", and it is said that when it was raining he used to ride his bicycle around Highams Park with his umbrella up!' Samuel John Longman (known as John) was born in Canada in 1874 and lived there until he was three years old, when his parents returned to England and settled in Walthamstow. Later he came to live in Hale End Road. Miss Sylvia Bird is John Longman's granddaughter and she has written a full account of his life in a book, 'Family Chronicles'. She has kindly allowed some of her grandfather's story to be told:

> As the eldest of a family of five children, with a father who only worked spasmodically, my grandfather had to leave school at the age of 12 and went to work at Sainsbury's in High Street, Walthamstow, working very long hours (until midnight on Saturdays). But he found another job at a workshop in London where braids were woven for trimming the furniture that was used on luxury Atlantic liners. He had been brought up to value education, and he spent his lunch hours sitting on the steps outside the workshop, teaching himself Arithmetic.
>
> In 1901 he took the job as a Schools Attendance Officer, working for Walthamstow Urban District Council. He married Clara Hastings but, unfortunately, in the winter of 1904 their children, Alfred and Katie, contracted diphtheria and became dangerously ill and were sent to Chingford Isolation Hospital. Alfred caught measles as well and became so weak that when his father took him, on his first outing, to see the trains at Hoe Street Station, he caught a chill which turned to a fever from which he never recovered. My grandfather blamed himself for the death of his child and suffered a breakdown brought about by the tragedy.

After the birth of another son in 1905 Mr Longman was transferred to Chapel End and Selwyn Avenue Schools and the family moved from Warner Road to the old part of Hale End Road, renting a house from Hitchman, the local dairyman.

Mr Longman was a kind-hearted man who was distressed by the poverty he found in the homes of some of the schoolchildren he was asked to visit, and his daughter Katie recalled that her father often came home asking for spare food and blankets for the families who were suffering hard times. He and his wife, Clara, raised money for charity, particularly for the Invalid Children's Aid Society. He rose to become Superintendent of Attendance Officers, working from an office in the Water House, Lloyd Park (now The William Morris Gallery), and one of his last responsibilities before he retired in 1939 was to make arrangements for the wartime evacuation of Walthamstow children.

Selwyn Avenue Schools after the war

Frank Payling started school in the last year of the war:

> I went to school when I was five, in January 1918, at Selwyn Avenue Infants', and I was absolutely, firmly convinced that it would be like going to prison, and it would

be some considerable time before I saw my brothers and sisters again. I went into Miss Andrews' class – a very forbidding lady, she was – and about half-past ten in the morning my elder sister, Kath, came into the classroom with a message from her teacher. It so amazed me to see her again that I stood up and exclaimed to the class, 'That's my sister!' and Miss Andrews temporarily lost control of her class.

What I do remember about going to school was that we had slate boards and slate pencils. I learned my letters on a slate, and I was so enthusiastic that, instead of putting two loops on the letter 'M', I managed three. Our school-days were quite happy and, of course, unlike today we walked home at midday and walked back, and to do so we had to walk underneath the railway bridge, by the Ching, on a footpath owned by the Great Eastern Railway. To demonstrate proof that they owned it, this footpath was closed once or twice a year. It was closed, not on a weekend, when we didn't need it, but always on a Friday. There was a policeman posted at either end, one in Beech Hall Road and one in Winchester Road. The net result was that was we had to walk an extra half a mile to school, right up to the level crossing at Highams Park and back down Selwyn Avenue. If I remember rightly, it was always a cold, wet day when it happened! You can imagine how popular the G.E.R. was with us!

64 *Mr S. John Longman, who lived in Hale End Road, was a Walthamstow Schools' Attendance Officer for many years. Just as he was due to retire, he was asked to organise the evacuation of Walthamstow schoolchildren in the Second World War.*

65 *'The Keeper's Lodge was a detached two-storey brick-built cottage near the lake by the Ching on the carriageway that became The Charter Road. Later, this was demolished and a bungalow, which was set back from the road farther up the hill, was built for the Forest Keeper. That did not survive for long and there is now very little sign that there were ever any buildings.' (F. Revell)*

66 *Selwyn Avenue Boys' School class of 1927 with their teacher, Mr Geoffrey Grantham.*

Sid Marchant remembered Selwyn for the football teams, singing practices and Mr Walmsley, who retired in 1928 after an illness.

Tubby Walmsley was the Deputy Head, and other staff at Selwyn Senior Boys' School in about 1925 were Messrs Humphries (Headmaster), Ridgewell, Walton, Davey, Shackleton, Fisher, Spragg, Outridge and 'Wally' Green, who lived in Church Avenue, Highams Park until he died in 1998 aged 95 years.

I went to Selwyn Avenue School for three years, and during that time I played for Selwyn Avenue Football Team. Mr Fisher used to take us for football, and at the end of the season he was so proud of us because we were 'runners-up' in the Cup. Then we all left the school – and he gave up! In the team were Les Prime, Ali Oakley, Day, Jarvis, Reg Pattison (the goalkeeper), Doug Coliver, and a chap called Took, who was a back. I always remember Stan Took because of Mr Walmsley, who came from the north of England, saying, 'Took, look at your book, boy!' (to rhyme with 'spook'!)

My last game for Selwyn Avenue was against South Chingford, an evening match and if you played for the school in an evening match, you were allowed to leave the class a quarter of an hour earlier. Of course, we used to go to school dressed in our football gear – boots as well. It was all sheer swank! At 4 o'clock our teacher, Mr Walmsley, would say that the boys from the football team could go and we used to strut out. We walked down Highams Station Avenue and caught the tram to Chingford Mount (there were only a few shops then), and we played on Cherrydown Farm, where the football pitch was just at the foot of the hill. I always remember looking up the fields to the church in ruins. It was really a lovely sight.

67 *The Staff of Selwyn Avenue Boys' School, 1933-38. Top left: Mr Stemp, Mr Davey, Mr Ernest Spragg, Mr Geoffrey Grantham, ?, ?, seated left; Mr Fisher, Mr William (Bill) Dunseath, ?, Mr Humphries, Mr Walton, ?, and Mr Greaves. (The other members of staff at this time were Mr Outridge, Mr Woolf and Mr Sopwith.)*

After the match (we beat South Chingford quite comfortably) I sat on the crossbar of my friend's bike and we cycled up Chingford New Road. It was then just a lane, and when we got to the top we turned right into Hale End Road [now Larkshall Road]. There were no houses and the trees used to meet overhead like an archway, and we cycled down to Ropers Farm, which had wooden Essex-boarding. It was a lovely ride to Highams Park Station.

The log entry for March 1921 records, 'Mr F. Walmsley, whilst playing Cricket in the playground before afternoon session, fell on his shoulder and severely sprained the muscles of arm and shoulder. He will be unable to resume duties for a few weeks as he has to attend Barts for special treatment.' In 1922 circulars stated that cricket could be played on Chestnuts Farm, School Camps were being organised in Walthamstow, and special lessons taken with reference to the meaning and importance of the census on 19 June 1921.

In the autumn term of 1922 Selwyn Boys' School held mock Elections and three pupils, Stanley Milbourn, William Beckling and Norman Wilkinson, tested their powers of rhetoric (with varying degrees of success). Afterwards the school had an opportunity to listen to a real politician, the Rev. R.W. Sorensen, who gave an address on 'The League of Nations'. Sorensen was the Deputy Chairman of Walthamstow Education Committee at that time, but he became the MP for Leyton and later, when Harold Wilson was Prime Minister, was elevated to the Peerage.

In November 1928 the pupils and teachers of the school had a 'near-miss'. Mr Humphries wrote, 'Owing to the fall of chimney stacks across the front entrance during the gale, this entrance and the cloakroom could not be used, nor the stores in the teachers' room.' Four months later, another hazard for teachers was demonstrated when Mr Grantham caught measles.

One member of the Selwyn staff, Mr V.G. Davey, was extraordinarily unlucky. In September 1929 he had an accident on his way to school, breaking a collar bone and suffering a bent rib and bruising. Five months later he sent a letter to the Headmaster to say that he had met with yet another serious accident and had broken the other collar bone, his shoulder and his wrist, and his leg was badly cut. He was away for three months.

The Charter of Incorporation of the Borough of Walthamstow on 10 October 1929 was celebrated by pupils of Selwyn Avenue, who joined other Walthamstow schoolchildren at 10.15 a.m. at Blackhorse Road School, where they were all given apples, bananas, buns and sweets. Charter Day Commemoration beakers were distributed to schools at the end of November. The next year, the senior Selwyn boys, with their Headmaster and Messrs Fisher, Grantham and Stemp, attended the Historical Pageant at Walthamstow Palace. (A great deal of effort went into this production: a series of episodes related the history of Walthamstow, including the visit of the diarist, Samuel Pepys, to the old Rectory Manor House, and a Handbook was published with photographs.)

In October 1931 Mr Humphries recorded that a measure to help the National Economy by reducing the salaries of all teachers by 10 per cent from 1 October 1931 was announced in a School Circular news sheet by the Government. Frank Payling remembered that the cut in salaries was not confined to the teaching profession:

> In 1931 there were 3,000,000 unemployed and there was no Unemployment Pay. The government decided it was only right that those who were in settled jobs should accept a 10 per cent cut in their salaries and wages. I started work in April 1932. My salary was £70 – a year! They didn't take the full 10 per cent off, but they reduced it to £65.

A Successful School

Douglas Insole, OBE played Cricket and Football (as an amateur) for England:

> I went to Selwyn Avenue Junior School in 1931 and remained there until I moved to the Sir George Monoux Grammar School in 1937.

68 *Selwyn Avenue's McEntee Cup Winners, 1936. (A great success.) Mr Ryder, who became the Headmaster (c.1937) is holding Mr Davey's dog, which used to come to school and sit in the classroom all day. Mr W.T. Dunseath is on the right. Top left: Maxted, David Norfolk (who became Headmaster of Kent College, Canterbury – Tony Blair's Headmaster!), Ken Linford, Cyril Kay, Ron Keeble and Charlie Stringer (who became Manager of Granada Leisure). Doug Insole is seated, holding the cup.*

Selwyn Avenue was an outstanding nursery in both the academic and sporting spheres. The 'scholarship' master was a man named Walton, whose class was located in a chapel in Cavendish Road – opposite the school playground. He was a disciplinarian, but his record of success in 'scholarship' (11-plus) exams was remarkable. In my year, 30 boys went on to the Monoux School, out of a total first-year intake of 90. The staff, and notably Geoffrey Grantham and Bill Dunseath, were very keen to develop the sporting side of the school's activity, and in my time I played twice, aged 9 and 10, in Selwyn football teams that won the McEntee Cup for Under Elevens. The support was terrific and the supporters song, 'Selwyn on the Ball', is fresh in my mind 60 years on. The cricket was less competitive in the borough, but at Selwyn it was taught with skill and enthusiasm.

I am still in touch with several of my class-mates who were at Selwyn Avenue in 1937. There are two headmasters, an Admiral, a managing director of Granada – all retired now, of course – among them, and to my knowledge at least ten of us went on to universities – Oxford, Cambridge, London and Edinburgh.

The examination successes of Selwyn were exceptionally good. In 1933, 21 out of 77 were able to go on to the Monoux School and Frank Bishop was No.1 boy on the pass list. Later that year 'Cllr Mrs Bailley visited in the afternoon and presented medals to the boys who played in the final match and won the Walthamstow Schools' Football Challenge Trophy' ('A very happy day for the sports-mad boys of Selwyn,' said Doug Insole).

An entry in the Selwyn Log Book in 1933 showed that 51 children were absent – 'the attendance greatly affected by Influenza'.

Cliff Payling recalls:

I started at Selwyn Avenue School as an infant in 1933. When they built Thorpe Hall Infants' School, I was one of the original intake. We moved because Selwyn Infants' was very crowded. Then I went to back to Selwyn Boys' School for three years, right up to the war.

When Mr Humphries retired in 1937, Mr Ryder came. Afterwards he became the first Head of Sidney Burnell Senior School, now The Highams Park School. When I first started teaching, Mr Glasgow was the Head Teacher of Selwyn, but soon after Alan Child became the Head, and he organised the move when the Boys' and Girls' Schools of Selwyn became one Junior School.

Jim Davis remembers:

I went to St Saviour's Church School, over in Markhouse Road, but in my young life, before World War Two, I used to come to Highams Park and I was very friendly with Alan Spong. He was exactly my age. Of course, he had a lot of friends at school, and I knew a lot of the Selwyn boys (not the girls) and we all used to meet up.

Before the war Stan Hatton lived in Church Avenue, and he was quite well-known in the Walthamstow Swimming Club because he was a very, very good swimmer. He went to Selwyn, and Selwyn has always been a 'swimming school'. They always won everything that was going! When Mr Childs was the Head Teacher there (which is not so many years ago) they used to go swimming before school in the morning, at about 7 o'clock. He kept up a very high standard of swimming there at Selwyn. Even before the war, they always won the team race. We could never beat Selwyn Avenue School.

The activities of Selwyn Avenue School in the following years included taking part in the Town Music Festival, which also made use of the Public Baths. When the swimming pool was covered by flooring the acoustics were very good. The children were kept up to date with current affairs by various outside lecturers who came to the school to talk, including Mr C. Barn of the Columbia Gramophone Co. Ltd, who gave a lecture on Music Appreciation.

The Honours Board of Selwyn Avenue School gives the names of some of the boys in Highams Park who went on to lead exceptionally successful lives. Two of these former pupils had a profound influence on aviation history. Lt Col V.C. Richmond, OBE was the designer of the R101 Airship, and Sir George (Robert) Edwards, OM, CBE, FRS, F.Eng, DL, designed the 'Viscount' and 'Concorde' aircraft.

Lt Col Vincent C. Richmond, OBE and the R101 Airship

Before 1930 airships were considered to have a great commercial future. An air disaster brought government investment in airships to an abrupt end and resulted in the development of the alternative option – aeroplanes. The story which led to the air crash and the resulting change of direction in the history of aviation began in Highams Park.

A very large wooden propeller from an airship was on display on the wall of one of the school halls at Selwyn Avenue School for over 60 years. It is explained by the school Log Book entry of 10 October 1930, when the Headmaster wrote, 'Brief Service in memory of Lieutenant Colonel V.C. Richmond, OBE', and, in the February of the following year, 'Many dignitaries came to see the unveiling of a memorial to Lt. Col. Vincent C. Richmond at the School.'

Vincent Richmond (born in 1893) was registered as a pupil at Selwyn Avenue School by his mother, Florence, who gave their address as 24 Silverdale Road in Highams Park, and later he served as a church warden at All Saints Church. But he became known to the British nation as Assistant Director/Technical (AD/T) Lieut Col Vincent Richmond, the designer of the R34 and R101 airships at Cardington, Bedfordshire. He was described as a very able engineer and a good administrator who had served with airships during the First World War, working on the development of fabrics. He joined the Cardington team and the R101 was made to his design, assisted by Sq. Ldr Michael Rope, 'widely considered to be a designer of genius'.

The airship was huge, three and a half times longer than a Boeing 747 and twice its height, and when it was stretched the outer cover measured more than five acres! It was the latest in a long series of highly successful experimental airships, including the

R34 which had completed the first double crossing of the Atlantic Ocean piloted by Major G.H. Scott in 1919. But in October 1930 Lieut Col Richmond and nearly all the crew and passengers aboard the R101 were killed when the great airship crashed at Beauvais, France, at the beginning of a journey to India which should never have been attempted. It was recorded in the Selwyn School Log Book that both airships had passed over the school the year before, on Remembrance Day, so what went wrong? The causes of the disaster have fascinated historians and engineers ever since, and books and articles are still being written on the subject. Most agree on what happened.

After several test flights in 1929, large sections of the R101 had to be modified – in fact, more or less redesigned – and the team of engineer-designers stated that many more test flights were necessary before the airship was put into service. Unfortunately, what have been described as 'political shackles' bound the Cardington team, and they were forced to use heavy oil diesel engines, which resulted in the R101 being grossly overweight. It was

69 *Lt Col Vincent C. Richmond, OBE, the designer of the world's biggest Airship, R101, who lived in Highams Park. As a boy, he lived in Silverdale Road and attended Selwyn Avenue School. Later, he was Church Warden and Reader at All Saints church, Highams Park.*

thought production was lagging behind German airships and it was important to hasten the development of large commercial ships to link distant parts of the British Empire. Although Richmond and the rest of the team were constantly modifying and testing the R101 from the time of its first flight in 1929, Lord Thompson, under pressure from the government, insisted that it should embark on a flight to India before Christmas 1930. The Imperial Conference was to be held in the autumn, when commercial prospects were to be discussed, so, in spite of protests from the engineers, many delays, much official interference and overcast, windy weather, the ill-fated journey of the R101 began. It ended a few hours later at Beauvais, France, when the airship crashed into a low hillside, causing an explosion which ignited the millions of cubic feet of hydrogen gas, and the whole 'ship' immediately burst into flames. Of the 54 crew and passengers on board only six survived.

Mrs Letitia Morris's father, Joseph Luttrell, was one of the R101 office staff:

> In 1930 we lived at Cardington, at No.1 in The Crescent, where most of the R101 officers lived. The officers' houses in The Crescent all belonged to 'The Royal Airship Works', and the offices, where Dad worked, were right on the main road and so, of course, anything to do with the 'ship' Dad knew all about.
>
> They said that the R101 airship had *got* to go that night. It wasn't ready to go, but it left – and it left in a hurry. My father worried about it, and used to say that it was not ready. He reckoned that they put barrels of beer on board that weren't accounted for, and he said that *everything* should be weighed!

It is recorded that Lord Thompson took 254 lb. of luggage, including two cases of champagne at 52 lb, and a Persian carpet weighing 129 lb.

> I was quite friendly with the wireless operator, G.H. Atkins, and he would take me to the pictures in Bedford. He was 26 and I was about 18 years old. He was killed when the R101 crashed. One of the others was Mr Leech. We had a little Morris Minor in those days and he would service our car for us. He was our neighbour and he didn't charge us anything.

H.J. Leech was one of only six people who survived the disaster, and his last tranquil moments aboard the airship before it crashed are described in Stanley Stewart's book, *Air Disasters*. 'In the smoking room aboard R101, the Cardington Foreman Engineer, Harry Leech, was finishing a final cigarette before bed, when the airship went down.'

Mrs Morris saw the R101 begin its last flight on 4 October 1930:

> I was in Boots the Chemist in Bedford at the time and I saw the R101 come flying over the town. I'd seen it dozens of times before because we lived right by the mast and we used to walk underneath the airship at night-time, but that day it looked very big because it was so low as it came over the town – it didn't lift.
>
> The day after the R101 came down was a Sunday, and we read the notice which was put up on the gate with the names of all the people from the Airship Works who had been killed. It was dreadful – because we knew them all! Of course, I went to the funeral at St Mary's Church in Cardington. It was a *very* big funeral.

The notice on the gate included the names of Sq. Lr Michael Rope, Major G.H. Scott and Lieut Col V.C. Richmond from Highams Park. All who had perished in the disaster were laid in state in Westminster Hall for a night and gun carriages awaited them at Bedford Station for the funeral on 10 October 1930.

At All Saints Church in Highams Park a commemorative inscription can still be seen for Vincent C. Richmond carved into the choir screen of the parish church in Selwyn Avenue and transferred later to the church on the hill, Castle Avenue. It reads: 'Greatly adventurous for peace, he found a pioneer's death and immortality. (Laus Deo in Christian Faith) Lieut. Colonel Vincent C. Richmond, OBE, sometime officer in this church, Designer of HM airship R101, is remembered in this gate of prayer – when his ship was wrecked 5th October 1930. "Stand by."'

Sir George Edwards, OM, CBE, FRS, F.Eng., DL

Concorde has earned itself a place in aviation history, not only as one of the most successful and graceful aeroplanes ever built, which gave nearly 21 years of safe flying, but also as the amazing product of 15 years of continuous British-French co-operation. People in Highams Park are proud of the fact that Sir George Edwards, the designer of Concorde and the Viscount aircraft, was born in Hale End Road and then lived in one of the 'Coronation Villas' in Handsworth Avenue and went to Selwyn Avenue School when he was a boy.

Sir George joined the design staff of Vickers Aviation Ltd in 1935 and became the Experimental Manager of Vickers-Armstrong Ltd at the Weybridge Works in 1940 and its Chief Designer in 1945. He was the Director of Vickers Ltd from 1955-67. In 1957 he was knighted, and in the following years he was showered with honours by many universities and awarded Gold Medals by various internationally renowned institutions for his outstanding contributions to aircraft design. He had been married to Lady Edwards (née Marjorie Annie Thurgood) for nearly 60 years when she died in 1994.

Doug Insole had a great respect for Sir George:

> An earlier pupil at Selwyn was a scientist of world renown, Sir George Edwards, whose family had a toy shop at the corner of Beech Hall Road and Hale End Road. He was chief designer of Vickers Aviation Ltd., and then became Chairman of the British Aircraft Corporation Ltd. (until 1979). His influence on civil aviation was enormous. Sir George was a sporting fanatic, and among his sporting appointments was the Presidency of Surrey County Cricket Club.

70 *Sir George Edwards (right) with the test pilot, Andre Turcat, and Brian Trubshaw after a flight in 'Concorde'. Sir George said that this was his favourite picture because he had enjoyed being allowed to fly the aircraft that he had designed.*

Frank Payling remembered his early days in Highams Park:

> There were two brothers in the Edwards family. One kept a small paper shop in Hale End Road (between The Avenue and Handsworth Avenue), and then there was the toy shop, which had three storeys. And the building is still there. Sir George Edwards' mother died about nine days after he was born in 1908 (mother said she had dropsy), so he was brought up by his uncle and aunt.

Dennis Webb remembered Sir George Edwards' aunt:

> The dear old lady who owned the shop used to say when he was knighted, 'Award of Merit too – my nephew!'

In fact, Edwin Edwards owned both the newsagent's and the Toy and Fancy Goods shops in Highams Park. Sir George Edwards said, 'My father was a strong disciplinarian and he was an intelligent man who chose his stock carefully, filling his shop only with high quality goods.

Frank Payling remembered Mr Edwards' son well:

> Prior to every Christmas time they opened up the second floor of the shop – a 'Toy Bazaar' they called it. They had a lovely display of stations and steam engines, marvellous it was, and I can remember George Edwards serving. He'd be about 12 or 13 then and he let some of the things go cheaper than his father would have done! I have a picture of him with my brother, John. He was in his class at Selwyn Avenue School.

Sir George enjoyed thinking about his early years in Highams Park:

> I lived in Handsworth Avenue. My mother died when I was born, and I think my father was very bruised by that – they were very young. There was an old aunt and uncle: they said to my father, 'Look, Ted, we'd better take the boy in!'
>
> I first went to school in The Avenue, and I remember the notice outside – 'Warner College for Girls (Little Boys Taken)'. I was one of the little boys. Ada Davis was a '5 star' teacher who, in addition to Maths, taught English and French. Rhoda Parsons taught Singing and Elocution – a magnificent female, with a voice rather like Dame Clara Butt's!

From Warner College he transferred to Selwyn Avenue School, where the Headmaster was Mr Humphries, who he remembered as 'a severe disciplinarian at times'. Mr Walmsley was one of his teachers, and also Mr Spragg, who took Nature Study.

Young George made it clear that he was not interested in becoming involved in the running of a shop, and his father knew that his son was a bright boy and was likely to succeed in whatever he chose to do in his adult life. He was expected to do well at Selwyn, but when the time came to make out the application forms for the Sir George Monoux Grammar School it was discovered, to the consternation of his teachers, his father and George, that he was four days too old to apply. 'They said, "There's nothing else for it – you will have to go to Walthamstow Engineering and Trade School!"' George Edwards continued his education by gaining a London University Degree in General Engineering, becoming Pro-Chancellor, University of Surrey in 1964-79 and, later, Pro-Chancellor Emeritus.

Douglas J. Insole, CBE

This well-known sportsman graduated from Cambridge University, where he played soccer for the university and was the Captain of Cambridge University Cricket team, and afterwards played for Essex County Cricket Club being Captain from 1950-60. Doug Insole and his great friend Trevor Bailey have been described as 'the backbone of Essex County Cricket' during their years of playing for the club.

David Lemmon and Mike Marshall in *Essex County Cricket Club – The Official History* wrote:

> Doug Insole, besides being a prolific run scorer, was a fine fielder. He considered this aspect of the game to be of paramount importance, and in his ten years of captaincy, raised Essex fielding standards to a new peak. One of Doug Insole's fiercest contentions, and he himself is a soccer man, is that the excesses of professional football have robbed first-class cricket of some fine players, for it is no longer possible, as it was with Compton, Watson and Hilton, to follow both professions.

Doug Insole played Cricket for England on many occasions, then was chosen as a Test Selector and was appointed Chairman of the Test and County Cricket Board in 1975. As the Manager of various MCC touring teams, he travelled to South Africa, Australia and New Zealand and, not surprisingly, he is mentioned in many books which have been written about Cricket, including those by Brian Johnston and John Arlott.

Teddy Sheringham

A present-day sporting hero, who is another ex-pupil of Selwyn Avenue School, is Teddy Sheringham. For five years before his transfer to Manchester United in June 1997 he was a striker for Tottenham Hotspur and a first-choice player for England. In a recent TV programme he showed that he had always had a competitive attitude to life when he said, 'As a young lad growing up – you want to win things', and he did, superbly, in 1999, when Manchester United won the 'Treble'.

Darren Hall

Darren Hall's name has been in the news ever since his name appeared on the Honours Board of Selwyn School in 1977. He carried on the school's great sporting tradition by achieving All England Champion and World No. 2 status in Badminton, and he is still winning. He reached the final of the Liverpool Victoria English Championships for 14 years and won it ten times.

John P.W. Dankworth, CBE, FRAM, ARCM

John Dankworth (b.1927) and Cleo Laine, who he married in 1958, are known internationally as fine musicians, particularly in the world of jazz. His schooldays were spent at Selwyn Avenue and at the Sir George Monoux School and his childhood in Hollywood Way, Woodford Green, where his parents continued to live for many years after he moved to Wavendon in Buckinghamshire. His sister, Avril Dankworth, a very accomplished pianist, continued to live in the district and became well-known for her work with music and drama for children and adults.

8

More Schools and Scholars – and Mr Chips

Jeanne May was a pupil at the Selwyn Avenue Girls' School:

> I was born in 1914, and I was almost five when I started school. The classes were always very, very big. We all went to Selwyn, which had three head teachers. Miss Kindell was the Infants' Head Teacher for all of us in our family, and was still there when I was a student teacher, and Mr Humphries, who lived in a house in Handsworth Avenue, was the Boys' School Headmaster. Miss Elliott was our Headmistress and there were three separate buildings. The Infants' School entrance was in Cavendish Road, and both the Senior Boys' and Senior Girls' entrances were in Selwyn Avenue. The Infants' School was the larger building, and when I was a student teacher there they had thirteen classes: there were three classes in the hall, two on one side of the partition. But then Thorpe Hall School was built, which relieved the pressure. My brother had to leave Selwyn to go to Thorpe Hall School for his final stage. Can you imagine the parents of today putting up with their child having to change school in the middle of his last year, especially as he was the youngest of the family?

The last house in the Bridle Path (before you got to the lodge of the White House) was called 'Matson'. One of the three teachers from Selwyn Avenue sent to Thorpe Hall School was called Miss Trott, and her aunt owned 'Matson' so there was quite a bit of money in her family.

When Cliff Payling was at Selwyn Avenue School, his elder sister returned to the school as a student teacher, and he amused the older teachers by calling at the staff room to ask if 'Miss Payling' was coming home.

> Jeanne [May] mentioned Miss Trott. She was my teacher in the first class in the spring of 1933. Between then and December 1934 I moved class twice and always had Miss Trott as my teacher. (Perhaps I was her favourite pupil.) On one occasion she brought her young nephew to school and he sat next to me in class. We thought him a very strange boy as he wore long woollen stockings – and his strangeness was confirmed when he suddenly grabbed my arm and bit me! I was also invited to his birthday party at a house in Leyton. This was an experience I did not enjoy very much as I was a shy little boy who was not very keen on parties. When I was transferred to the brand new school (Thorpe Hall) in January 1935 Miss Trott was one of the teachers who came with me. Luckily, I was never in her class again.

Jeanne May recalls:

> I remember all the teachers at Selwyn Avenue. Miss Andrews took all the 'babies', as we called them in those days, and she was quite a tartar! There was Mrs Bolton, the only married one, and Miss Rawlings was in the Girls' School. Miss Garrard-Cole (and I'm not sure how you spell that) became a head teacher, and eventually she came back as the Head of Selwyn, but there were three teachers who always took the oldest children: Miss Sizer, Miss Baines, who lived at the top of Preston Avenue, and Miss Martin.

71   *An early photograph of the Lodge in the forest, Hale End.*

72   *The plan was to build all over the forest land from Woodford High Road down to Hale End Road but, eventually, only five large houses were built in Cottingham Road, off Oak Hill. The houses have gone, St Patrick's Court was built on the site, and the road is now known as The Bridle Path.*

73 *The May Queen and her attendants celebrating May Day at Selwyn Avenue Girls' School in 1925.*

Miss Hilda Oliver remembers:

> When I started at Selwyn Avenue Infants' School in 1917, during the war, Miss Ridgeway took all the English. The classrooms had no chairs but wooden desks, two at a desk, and ink monitors had to clean up the ink from the old inkwells. Of course, there weren't any dinners at school in those days and we came home to lunch through the Ching Path. I think we used to have about an hour for lunch.

Miss Renee Weller found the same desks and inkwells twenty years later, and they were still there in 1947.

> From 1934-7 some of the teachers at Selwyn Girls' School were Miss K. Fuller, Miss Elliott, Miss Chaplin, Miss Branch and Miss Curtis. In about 1934 we used to have a needlework class with Miss Chaplin, and while we were working one of us had to read from *Anne of Green Gables*. I am a devotee of the 'Anne' books, and I still go back to them and read them.
>
> Not many homes had a telephone in those days, and men from the GPO came to the school and showed us how to dial and how to answer the telephone, and when I went to work I had no trouble in picking up a phone and answering it.

(Telephone numbers for Highams Park and Hale End began LAR, for Larkswood; Chingford was SIL for Silverthorne.)

Miss Jennifer Bocking was at Selwyn Junior Girls' School until 1948, when she 'passed the Scholarship' to the Woodford County High School for Girls:

> At Selwyn, I remember Miss Pine, the Headmistress, Miss Brooker and Miss Buttle, who had a glass eye. She was really over the retiring age but she came back because they needed teachers. I was quite frightened of that glass eye, because you tended to think she was watching you, but in fact it didn't move. It was her other eye you should have been watching all the time. There was Miss Owen, a plump lady, very nice but rather well-built, Miss Parrott, who used to take us for swimming, and Miss Ridgeway, a friend of Miss Curtis, who was interested in drama. After the war my dad and I went up to one of the theatres in London to see a play called *The Judgement at Chelmsford*, and who should be in it but Miss Curtis!

Mrs Olive Fewell was a later pupil at Selwyn:

> When I went to Selwyn Miss Brooker was the Headmistress and Miss Owen and Miss Parrott were still there. Some years later, when we were first married, we lived in

74 *Selwyn Avenue Girls' School class of 1946-7. (Several of the Old Girls tried to recall the names of their classmates. They offer their apologies for any mistaken identities or omissions. It's a long time ago!) Top left: Valerie Wood, Anne Crawley?, Yvonne Goldsworthy, Sylvia Smith or Ann Wrigley?, Sylvia Outen, Jean Sears, Hazel, Jennifer Bocking. Second row: Patricia Fabb, Mary Grantham, Stella Ellison, Rita?, Christine?, Jill? Barbara Bright, Angela (Hancock or Woodcock), Maureen (Shuard?) Seated: Valerie Coppard, Jean Beard, Lesley Townsend, Kathleen Wade, Wendy (Faulkner?), Shirley Clapham, (?), Denise Marlborough, Barbara?, Brenda Byford. Cross-legged: Molly Day, Janice Rushbrook, Valerie Tinsley, Maureen Lusher, Petrona (Degutis? or Clark?), Thelma Clark(e), Beryl Hancock.*

Walthamstow. Miss Parrott's brother sang in the choir of St Mary's parish church, and I met her again. I liked her because I enjoyed PE.

Jeanne May remembers:

In the late 1920s we could sit 'the Scholarship' at 10 and there was a 'second go' at 11 years old. I got through at 10, and that meant that I was 'earlier' all the way through secondary school. After Selwyn I went to Walthamstow High School. (Most of the girls from round here went to Walthamstow.) We walked to Highams Park Station and went by train to Wood Street, then we walked up Valentin Road and through the churchyard to the school.

By the station were Warrens, the coal men, and there were sidings at Highams Park and Wood Street stations. Some of the trains stopped at Wood Street and there was an engine-shed there for the steam trains.

The third-class carriages had wooden seats and luggage racks. There was a gap at the top between the compartments, and our favourite thing to do when we were naughty little girls was to climb over from one carriage to the next, and see how many you could do between Highams Park and Wood Street! It was only one stop, of course. Wood Street Station had a 'mile' of steps you had to go down, and if you were coming home and you could see the train coming as you came down Valentin Road you all ran, but you knew you had this terrible flight of stairs to get up!

In 1920 the Chingford to Liverpool Street line was known as the 'Jazz Line', because of its regular and reliable service, with a ten-minute interval between trains. Later the service was reduced to 20-minute intervals. Until 1965 goods trains with trucks full of coal diverted to the sidings by Highams Park Station where, with much clashing and clattering, they were shunted by the steam engines. The line began to be prepared for electrification in 1960.

Hilda Oliver recalls:

> When I went to the Walthamstow High School in the late 1920s we came home for lunch from Walthamstow by train. Mother had the lunch ready (and off we went again). I remember Miss Rawling and Miss Norris, the Head Teacher of the High School. Miss Cunningham was the History teacher, Miss Dennithorn was the Science mistress, Miss Squire was PT, and Miss Jacobs. They've added a lot to Walthamstow High School, but they've taken the playing fields away. We had quite a lot of ground and tennis courts at the back, and later on the Greek Theatre was built.

Win Marchant remembered Hale End Road before the First World War:

> There were some big houses in Hale End Road nearer to Hagger Lane (Forest Road). Mr McCartney, who was a master at the Technical College, lived in half of 'Fyfield House', a big, tall grey building which had been a school run by two ladies, and a school friend of mine lived in the other half.

Sid Marchant knew John McCartney after he had taken Holy Orders:

> When I was 13, in about 1925, I passed a scholarship and went to the Walthamstow Technical College in Hoe Street. (This Leyton college shut down, and then everyone went to the new college in Forest Road.) I took English, Chemistry, Mechanics, Woodwork, Metalwork, and I left when I was 16. The English teacher was the Rev. John McCartney.
>
> To get there I had to walk down to the Billet and across the old level crossing where Wadham Bridge is now. By Mrs Foster's house, just before the level crossing, was a little cottage where you could put your hand on the roof it was so low! Over the crossing on the right was a farm with a holly hedge (Wadham Lodge), and on the left at the bottom of Wadham Road was Mr Eastwell, the wheelwright, at King's Farm. I caught a tram from the Billet and the fare was ½d. to the Bakers Arms, and that's where our school was. I went home to lunch at five to 12 (all the way to the Billet and up Wadham Lane again), then after my lunch I rushed back to school by half past one.

Sir George Monoux School

Frank Payling recalls:

> When I was eleven I sat for the scholarship exam for the Monoux School and, although I passed the first part, I failed the second. In those days the second part consisted of an interview with the Headmaster or School Governors in Selbourne Road. Essex County Council had a house there. Reading wasn't my strength, unlike my elder brother, John, who was a reader; I was more practical. Anyway, I didn't pass the interview but my father paid for me to go (it was three guineas a term in those days), and that's how I came to go to the Monoux School.
>
> I had been there just one year and I was in the scholarship class, and I became one of the nine top boys! Mr Midgely was the new Headmaster, and I don't know quite why they did it – whether it was to boost the numbers of the fourth form – but we were put up, not one but two years! The result of that was I started to learn Latin a year after the other boys. I had the misfortune to develop a stammer before I went to the school, and it became very much worse when I was at the Monoux School.
>
> You may perhaps remember that James Hilton, the man who wrote *Lost Horizon* and *Goodbye, Mr Chips*, went to the Monoux School in High Street, Walthamstow, and where he describes the scene of his own old school he is so accurate that I can actually *see* what he wrote: 'We were next to the Slipper Baths, the Public Baths: there were the stalls, there was the Pickle Factory – Gillards' Pickle Factory.'

75 *Children at the renamed Handsworth Avenue Primary School, c.1970. This school and the adjoining Highams Park (Senior) School were built on one of the two larger fields behind 'The Manor House', which stood on the site of the block of flats in the middle of this picture. St Patrick's Court tower block can be seen, rearing its head above the forest.*

James Hilton was born in Lancashire and died in California, but he came to London when he was two years old. The Hilton family lived at 42 Oakhill Gardens, Woodford Green, where an English Heritage blue plaque was unveiled in 1997 to commemorate the writer of such memorable stories. His father was John Hilton, who taught in Walthamstow, and his mother also trained as a teacher.

Other Schools Attended by Highams Park People

Mrs Jane Florence Matthews (1894-1997) spent her childhood in Mile End Road, Bethnal Green but moved with her family to the Waltham Forest area during the Blitz. When she was 100 years old she had been living for 50 years in Vincent Road, Highams Park. Her daughter, Irene Owen, went to the same school as Mrs Matthews, before coming to Highams Park, and the classrooms had not altered. This was a typical Board School and very similar in design to many Walthamstow schools:

> Everybody went to that school. Mum remembers children running around with no socks and shoes on. They were so poor, a lot of the families. Can you imagine cold weather, and no socks and shoes on, running around the streets?
>
> I went there when I was five years old, and that was my school until we were bombed in 1940. The classrooms were all the same: we had chains on the gas lights, and they used to have a pole with a hook that we used to hook the little ring. You pulled the hook down then you could light the gas with a taper. In a corner in each classroom were the boilers, where the caretakers or teachers would put coal on. If you were a chilly person, at the beginning of the term you'd nip in the class and get a seat near the boiler! There were big radiators all along the side by the window, and they used to bring the little bottles of milk and stand them near the radiators or the boiler to warm it up a bit – warm, tepid milk – horrible!

76 *View from the back of Hollywood Way overlooking the roofs of 'The Manor House' and its farm buildings that could be seen just above the trees along the Ching Brook. In 1939, building began on Sidney Burnell School in the farm's fields, which went uphill to Handsworth Avenue.*

You went up four or five steps to the back of the class and we had two to a desk (Mum said they had single desks) and there were gangways between each line of desks. There was a big wooden blackboard and easel, not flat on the wall, like you get it now. We used to think wouldn't it be lovely if we had one of those sponges to wipe off the blackboard – like the teacher had. We had ink and pens with nibs (no Biros) and I was an ink monitor. That was an honour! We had a big bottle of ink with a spout on it, and we used to go round filling all the inkwells.

The School in Handsworth Avenue

In March 1933 many of the schools in Walthamstow were re-named after councillors and other names from the history of the area. Sidney Burnell was the first Director of Education for Walthamstow, and in 1940 his name was given to the newly built school in Handsworth Avenue. Irene Owen survived the blitz but lost her home, and when she came to live in Highams Park she went to the new Sidney Burnell School in Handsworth Avenue:

I went in 1941 and, of course, we all left at fourteen in those days. The Headmaster was Mr Ryder, and Mr (Bert) Selwood was a teacher there. He was such a nice chap. His wife lived a long time after him, and she survived tetanus, which she caught through working in her garden along Hale End Road! Miss Martin was another teacher, who did amateur dramatics with Mr Eric Newton, a very tall slim fellow, and Avril Dankworth. We used to go to the Youth Club. Eric Newton was the Headteacher of Selwyn School for a short time.

Alan Marshall recalled:

The Sidney Burnell School, Handsworth Avenue was built half way down a field that belonged to the 'Manor House'. The farm is non-existent now, of course. When the proposed school was put up, I remember the people who lived on one side of Handsworth Avenue had no real objections to the school but did object to having

77 *'At Highams Park Station they used to win prizes for the Best-kept Garden every year! They had certificates hanging up there for the garden. I don't know how much competition they had but it was a well-kept station – nice toilets, nice waiting room with a great big roaring fire in it – no problems there!' (Stan Batson)*

railings facing them on the other side, and so the school was built and there used to be a Youth Club. I went along and enjoyed many happy hours in their gymnasium.

Some day a history of the senior school in Handsworth Avenue may be written, beginning with the ancient fields of Stretmans Farm where medieval pottery was found. The first school building for the children of Highams Park and Woodford Green was planned just before war broke out in 1939. Later, pupils also came from Chingford. Lawyers, clerics, academics, artists, businessmen and women, at least one woman pilot and environmentalists (to mention just a few professions) are among the ex-pupils. The buildings have known Second World War bomb damage, lightning strikes on the gym, the destruction caused by the Hurricane, and a serious fire in the school which was very distressing to the staff and pupils. Additional classrooms built, and recent alterations made to the playing field, thanks to the financial backing of a notable football club. What began as Sidney Burnell Senior School has often changed its name and status: it became a secondary modern then a Senior High School, linked with Heathcote Junior High School in Chingford, then a comprehensive school, and is now described as The Highams Park School, a Voluntary Aided Technology College.

Oak Hill Primary School

Maggie Moncrieff's children attended the newer local primary schools:

My daughter, Joanna, went to Selwyn; the others started off at Handsworth Primary School, but there were too many children in the 1970s so they all trooped down [Brookfield Path] to Oak Hill Primary School, Woodford Green, which was lovely for us because it was just over the road. We were founder-members in 1972.

The Headmaster was John Thorne. He was very theatrical and the school did *Joseph and his Technicolor Dreamcoat*, and Angus, my son, and his two mates, William and Anthony Buckner, were three super little trumpet players and they had to play a fanfare. Anthony now works for the BBC.

9

Dangerous Times

In 1939 Britain was at war with Germany again. This time Highams Park and Woodford Green were in the firing line – *en route* to London – and because of the LNER line and the local factories the area was very badly bombed. The raids began in August 1940, when eight high explosive bombs fell on the Forest and in the grounds of the White House, Woodford Green, the first of many bombs on that target.

'H' District Civil Defence Centre was set up at Selwyn Avenue School, and the first Warden to be appointed was teacher Ernest R. Spragg. In 1941 a cluster of incendiary bombs fell on Highams Park, damaging many houses and the 'H' District Centre itself. A month later Mr Spragg was appointed Officer in Charge of the Supervision of the Use of Shelters.

Renee Weller has studied the bombing statistics for Highams Park and Woodford Green from the lists of incidents for the whole borough given in Ross Wyld's wonderfully detailed and readable book, *The War Over Walthamstow*. She found that the area was a dangerous place to live. In the residential area there were 82 high explosive bombs (which were responsible for demolishing and damaging many properties at a time), 159 incendiary bombs, seven oil bombs and two flying bombs, known as 'Doodle Bugs', which had the capability of damaging 1,200-1,400 houses with each explosion, and there were three of the even more devastating long range V2 Rockets in the area. (Little information was available about the latter, though, because the extensive damage they caused was classified information. In addition, 37 unexploded bombs had to be disarmed.

On the Forest and other open spaces of the area, and in the lake, there were a further 60 high explosive bombs, 31 incendiary bombs, two mines and one oil bomb. Ack-Ack shells, shrapnel and 'Yellow bombs' also rained down on the Highams Park area because it was in range of the defence guns. Unfortunately these missiles were responsible for a lot of damage to property. Because of the terrible devastation inflicted on London by the flying bombs and rockets, misleading information transmitted by double agents to the enemy, suggesting that missiles, which had actually been direct hits on City targets had overshot London. This encouraged the enemy to shorten their range and could be one of the reasons why, in the latter part of the war, Woodford, Highams Park and Walthamstow received so many of these bombs.

Lord Bottomley was the Chairman of Walthamstow Council from 1940-1 but received a government appointment to become Defence Organiser for the whole of south-east England. As Alderman Arthur G. Bottomley, he had been in charge of organising the Civil Defence services for Walthamstow so Alderman Ross Wyld JP took over from him and was the Controller of Civil Defence in Walthamstow from 1941 until the end of the war. Lord Bottomley had a great respect for his colleague:

> Ross Wyld, of course, was outstanding, one of the most able men I have ever known. He was president of the Civil Service Association, and W.J. Brown was the secretary. Then Ross took up politics in a bigger way and became the Leader of the Council.

78 *Highams Park Congregational Church in Malvern Avenue after the Second World War. The picture shows that the bomb-damaged roof had been repaired.*

Jane Matthews' family life was very badly affected by war:

We didn't have any bombs in the first year of the war, but then there were air raids nearly every night – a lot of air raids! When we were bombed out in Leatherdale Street (that's in Mile End) on 21 October 1940 – I always remember that – we went to Whipps Cross, on the borders of Walthamstow and Leytonstone, for a short time. We rented a house – well, really the Council found it for us – and we didn't like it at Whipps Cross. We were on a funny corner there, just by the Drill Hall. I was told that I shouldn't go to Whipps Cross – they were bombing the corner because of the big military place there!

We came to Highams Park in 1940. The bombing was so bad at Whipps Cross and we shared a house with my sister and children – and my husband was a policeman. He couldn't get any rest, couldn't keep the children quiet during the day when he was on night-duty, and he said that he couldn't stand it. He had to get away from there. On his first day's leave we came over to Highams Park and were wandering around Richmond Crescent way when we saw this house vacant, and a person saw us looking at it and asked if we were interested. We'd found what we were looking for, so she said that she had the key if we would like to look at it. There was one room occupied: it had got furniture in it because they were evacuated and just wanted to let the other part while the war was on.

My husband was a policeman for the Port of London Authority, down East India Dock, West India Dock and Tilbury Dock. The station was the East India Dock Road, but they were the three docks that he covered. He had to live within three miles of his job: it was only the war which allowed him to move away. He had a little push-bike, but towards the end he had a little auto-bike. He worked shift hours – 2 'till 10, 6 to 2, 10 'till 6 – all hours of the day and night. I always used to be afraid on a foggy night – for him walking around the docks, you see. On a foggy night he could easily slip into the 'pond'. He had to make reports every night on everything, and they met a detective at certain points and had to report things. No walkie-talkies in those days.

> We'd been in Richmond Crescent for about four years, when the people wanted to
> come back. This house [in Vincent Road, where she was living], which belonged to my
> brother, George, and had been bombed in 1940, had been repaired – all the back, a
> complete new kitchenette and bathroom – all that side and the wall, all the bathroom
> went, all the ceilings down, windows – all out. They put that all back again, so they
> were able to come back again if they wanted to, but my brother didn't want to come
> back here – well, *she* didn't [his wife], so we took over. We paid rent for several years
> and then we decided to buy it. I took over and I've been here ever since.

Irene Owen continued the story:

> We had a shelter in the garden in Richmond Avenue but we slept in the front room in
> Vincent Road in the Morrison shelter. The shelters filled with water in Vincent Road
> because the Ching is here: you dug down four feet and the shelter filled with water!

Mrs Webb, who lived in The Avenue near the Jubilee Sports Ground from 1937, also had
trouble with flooding, and she commented that during the war their Anderson shelter
soon became full of water and her family had to resort to sheltering in the garage.

Some of those who Served

Irene Owen told how the Second World War brought tragedy to her family:

> My brother was Flight Sergeant William Matthews, who was a flight engineer based at
> Mildenhall. He went out in Lancaster Bombers which were bombing the Fly-bomb sites
> in northern France. They used to try to shoot down the bombers as they went out over
> the Channel. William had done his 'tour of duty' and was due for leave, when he was
> killed on the night of 5 July 1944 aged 22.

(Later Irene's mother, Mrs Jane Matthews, received a photograph of William with his
squadron taken on the day before her only son died.)

Flight Sergeant Douglas Presland, who lived in Oak Hill, Woodford Green, also
flew Lancaster Bombers, but in November 1944 his aircraft crashed soon after take-off
from Fulbeck, Lancashire, and four members of his crew were killed. He was lucky to
survive, but he lost a leg as the plane crashed and then burst into flames. The story of
Doug Presland's rescue from certain death by another heroic crew member (and Doug's
courage and good humour in the ambulance, when he claimed to be more concerned
about damage to his moustache from the burning aircraft than the loss of his leg) is
in the book *Looking into Hell*, by Mel Rolfe, an ex-reporter from *The Guardian* newspaper.

The Presland family lived for some time in Gordon Avenue, Highams Park. His
parents, who married in 1915, were both film actors at the Walthamstow Film Studios
in Wood Street; Douglas and his brothers, Roland and Gerald, were all pupils at Selwyn
Avenue Boys' School. When the Second World War broke out all three brothers joined
the RAF. Wing Commander Roland Presland was awarded the DSC quite early in the
war; Gerald and Doug Presland got their wings and went to Canada, but then Gerald
went out to the Middle East, where he flew Wellingtons on coastal patrols but, sadly,
did not return from one mission.

After the war, Doug Presland was a teacher at Coppermill Lane School (later renamed
Beaconsfield School) in Walthamstow, where he showed the schoolchildren how to build
a 'Cadet' yacht, which was proudly displayed on the pond outside Walthamstow Town
Hall. When his own boat sank at sea on 19 September 1954 he showed tremendous
courage and presence of mind, and the story was reported in the *Daily Express* newspaper:

> When well out to sea, the yacht capsized and eventually lay on her side before sinking.
> By that time, I had prepared myself for such an eventuality by swimming down to the
> fore locker and retrieving my artificial leg and an air bed, which I blew up by mouth
> and lashed my leg on to.

Mr Presland swam about a mile and a half to the shore, where he had to crawl across deserted mud-flats:

> The trouble was that I put on the suction pad for my leg but the mud sucked off the leg when I tried to walk. I waited until the water came into a channel and then pushed the lilo and my leg in front of me until, at about 10 p.m., I found a longshore man, who said, 'Wait there!' – and he came back with a glass of water and slice of bread and jam!

Leon Frank managed a tailor's shop in The Avenue, where he worked for about five years with Cliff Amos, but he lived in Highams Park for over 45 years. Before the war he had worked for his father, a Jewish émigré from Russia who had come to England via Vienna before the First World War and started a tailor's business in Grove Road, Leyton. 'My father was a bit of a slave-driver. I used to come home from school and start working. I could do pockets when I was 10 years old!'

Leon served in the 7th Column of the 77 Brigade, known as 'The Chindits' (after Chindi, a Burmese god). Leon considered himself lucky to have survived the jungles of Burma and his imprisonment in a Japanese prisoner-of-war camp in 1943 because very few men of the 7th Column came home:

> My Regiment was 13th Battalion, King's Liverpool Regt. We became part of the 77th Indian Infantry Brigade, which included British, Indian and Gurkha troops, and we were the 1st Expedition in January '43. There were mules, some horses, bullocks and an elephant in No. 3 Column (the Gurkhas), and later we became known as 'Wingate's Circus'! The columns of men used to walk through the heat of the jungle in a long 'snake' and I used to sing as I went along. One day, an officer said to me, 'What makes you do that?'
> I said, 'Well, there isn't anything else to do!'
> 'Well, you are the first person I have known to be inspired by the back view of a mule!'
> We were supposed to go into Burma and cause disruption behind the Japanese and make it easy for the British frontal force, but that was cancelled. We were 300 miles into Burma and were told when we were marching that if anyone dropped out they were to be left behind. So *many* people died of disease.

After the war Leon realised that his eyesight had been permanently damaged by vitamin B deficiency. His war experiences have been recorded by the Imperial War Museum, and a photograph of Leon with comrades and part of his account describing the deprivations, illnesses and conditions in which the British troops found themselves have been included in a recently published book, *March or Die* by P.D. Chinnery.

> My tailoring skill helped me through later life, and I have been fortunate to have so many kind friends. The last eight years of my working life were getting too stressful, so I applied for a job at the British Museum (uniformed staff) and the years working there, until I reached retirement age, were the happiest of my life.

Bombing and Civilians

Irene Owen talked about Civil Defence during the war:

> The ARP hut was at the end of the row of houses in Vincent Road, where there was a fence across the road, so Vincent Road was blocked off. It must have had a gate in it, because that was the ARP Headquarters, 'J' District, and where Joseph Clarke School is now there was a hut and a big underground dug-out.
> Mr Overal, who had taken over Mr Howard's job at Hale End Library, and Eunice Clark's sister, Joyce Clark, were in the ARP, and they used to go on duty there at the hut.

Miss Frances Bowler had a busy time:

I was in Civil Defence – a Walthamstow ambulance driver! We were based in Vincent Road, Highams Park (by the 'Manor House'). They built the air-raid shelter, all under sand-bags, all reinforced, so we lived in that. The vehicles were round about. Sometimes it was the 'sitting-case' car we drove but generally the ambulance. There was that famous time when a false alarm was sent out, so we all trotted into 'J' District down there, and they said, war was declared, and we had got to be there all night. However, it was a hoax so I went home, and that was that! We had periods of duty, 24 hours on, 24 hours off. We went everywhere to incidents but mostly in Walthamstow. By Jove, I learned the roads of Walthamstow! We had to know them by heart. It was pretty hectic, but you did feel you were doing some good.

We lost one of our ambulance attendants. She was on leave, and she was coming up Falmouth Avenue, the side where Captain Hewitt lived (about 35 Falmouth Avenue, a biggish house), when the bomb dropped. She fell down, terribly injured, and she died the next morning. That was pretty awful.

Fred Revell joined the ARP in 1937 and was also an ambulance driver at 'J' Division, Vincent Road, which was a Heavy-rescue, Ambulance and First Aid Station. He said that the victim of the bomb incident in Falmouth Avenue was Jean Old, who lived in Richmond Crescent and was a member of the team at Vincent Road ARP Station. He remembered how she was badly injured by the bomb, which fell on the kerb beside her as she walked back from a quiet stroll by the lake on her day off. Fred was on duty and he took her to the hospital: 'John Harrison, the owner of 'The Garden Shop' in Highams Park, was a stretcher bearer during the war, and we worked on alternate days in the shop and at the ARP station until I joined the RAF in 1942.'

Douglas Woolf's father, Dr A.D. Woolf, and Dr F. Sanders, who both had practices in Highams Park, were appointed to 'J' District First Aid Post. Dr Douglas 'came of age' during the war:

I have a 21st Birthday 'key' that was signed and given to me by members of the ARP, including Snowden, Cline, Frances Bowler and Gladys Sanders (Dr Sanders' wife).
We had a very active ARP in Highams Park, and at the end of Vincent Road was an ARP Shelter, which was run by Mrs G. Kennard (from 1938 to June 1941), who was a State Registered Nurse and had a Nursing Home in Falmouth Avenue, the big double-fronted house on the left just before you get to the park.

Heathland Private Nursing Home at 91 Falmouth Avenue had been run by Miss G. Warland in about 1927.

On 6 September 1940 a high explosive bomb scored a direct hit on our house in Marion Grove, near Highams Park lake. It was the first home to be demolished in the Borough of Walthamstow. The bomb was one of a stick of bombs jettisoned from a German plane being pursued by fighters; another bomb fell nearby on Mason Road and the rest landed on Forest land and by the lake. All that my parents were able to save from the rubble was a carpet, Dad's desk, a green china rabbit and a little ashtray with a picture of HMS *Victory* on it!

We would have been killed if we had been at home but, luckily, a few weeks before the raid my father had taken me and my mother to Blaenavon in South Wales with evacuees from the George Gascoigne Central School in Walthamstow, where he taught. We came back with the schoolchildren in 1943, but we were homeless and my father's parents also needed somewhere to live.

My mother was expecting another baby and so she and I went to live in Hemel Hempstead with her mother for safety, but my father had to remain in Walthamstow to teach and to brave the bombing with his parents until the end of the war.

The Ercolani family

Victor Ercolani of 'Cabinet Industries' in Walthamstow Avenue and 'Ercol' Furniture came to the rescue of our homeless family. He was a life-long friend of my father and grandparents from the days when they had all lived at Higham Hill. Victor was an exceptionally generous man, and he bought a house in Highams Park where he allowed our family to live, rent-free, until our own house was rebuilt.

Douglas Woolf knew the Ercolanis for many years:

> Victor Ercolani lived in Nesta Road, Woodford Green, and then he moved to 'Broad Oaks' in the High Road, Chigwell. He was a devout Salvationist and he was a very good man. He married a doctor, called Margaret Carrick, whose brother was a Brigadier in the Royal Army Medical Corps.
>
> Victor Ercolani *was* 'Cabinet Industries', and he was associated with 'Ercol' Furniture.

Mr Ken Roberts was the nephew of the late Dr Margaret Ercolani:

> Victor was born in England in 1899 (he died in 1987) but at least one of his brothers was not. The family came to England before 1899, and Victor was brought up as a Salvationist. In about 1926 William and Victor started the factory, Cabinet Industries, in Walthamstow Avenue. Victor's father had been a cabinet maker and had made picture frames, but at Cabinet Industries radio and later television cabinets were made. In about 1940 the name of the factory was changed to Cabinet Industries because of its Italian name, Ercolani.

During the war, Cabinet Industries concentrated on war work.

The Oak Hill Crescent Bomb

Jennifer Bocking recalls:

> Not far from where I lived in Oak Hill Crescent was the little group of four houses that was bombed in 1940. That's one of my very early memories. I hadn't long been at Handsworth Avenue Infants' School and my Dad was away in the Royal Air Force. Mum and I were on our own and I can remember I was in bed. The siren must have gone. Mother got out of bed, pulled me from my bed, flung me across her shoulder and got on to the landing. Fortunately all the doors were closed. She'd had the presence of mind to do that.
>
> I can hear the bomb coming down, the whistle that it made, although I was only small, and then of course the big bang, and of course everything *went* in our house – the windows and a lot of the roof – everything, but we were on the landing because we couldn't get down to the shelter in time, so we weren't affected by the flying glass. If we had been going down the stairs, all the glass from the front door would have come up and injured us in some way. So we were in the best place to be at that moment! We were protected by the wooden doors.
>
> Nos 50, 48 and 46 were the three houses which were virtually demolished, and of course the ones either side were very badly damaged as well. One of our neighbours, Mr Gilkes, was killed and his wife's sight was impaired by flying glass: their son was in hospital for a long time.
>
> I had an aunt and uncle living opposite when the bomb fell, and their house at 43 Oak Hill Crescent was virtually demolished. (Uncle wasn't in the war because he was older than my dad.) He and Auntie were shaken but they came across to see that we were all right. In fact, they had to stay with us for a while, though *our* house wasn't all that wonderful! Their house was repaired eventually, and we had to have quite a lot done to our house as well.

Hilda Oliver's life changed during the war:

> I started work in a fashion house when I left school, and then the war broke out and so I had to go and do war work. I worked in the West End until 1942, so we had to go up to London between all the bombs.
>
> My aunt, Mrs Davis, got the one in Oak Hill Crescent. She happened to be here, with us, that evening, and when she got back home – there was no house!
>
> There was another bad incident in Hale End Road – three or four houses were bombed. They have built them up now, and they look the same – you wouldn't know where it was.

In 1942 I was called up. I really would have liked to go on a farm, but mother was a nervous wreck so, as my sister was evacuated, I thought that one of us ought to stay at home. So I went into Munitions, where we made wings for aeroplanes using metal-sheeting and putting in the rivets – very noisy. We were doing a 60-hour week (a fortnight days and a fortnight nights). Mother wasn't very happy about that, but it had to be done! Fortunately it was at the centre in Edmonton, behind the North Middlesex Hospital at Sage's builders, who went over to war work. I walked to Wadham Bridge to catch the 144 bus, which took me straight there so it wasn't far, but it wasn't always easy during the Blackout. It wasn't a bad journey – but it was wondering what you were going to find when you came home, really.

There were about forty of us working there. Of course, we were never short of food. We did night shifts and we sat down to a lovely dinner in the middle of the night, and very often at 1 o'clock in the morning we were walking around the grounds. After a night's work, when you'd get on a bus, instead of your head going forward, it would go back! You couldn't keep awake – it was terrible.

Bombs on Hale End and Highams Park

Jennifer Bocking recalls:

At school there were lots of sandbags everywhere, and I can remember Avril Dankworth taking us into the shelters at Handsworth Infants' and playing musical games with us. She would say, 'Now, I'm going to sing you a song, and when I get to a certain word, all put your heads down and cover your heads with your hands,' and of course, it was really protecting us from the bombs.

I wasn't evacuated with the school, but my dad was in the Air Force for four of the six years of the war and he got very worried when there was a lot of bombing on London, and made Mother and me go to stay with one of her sisters and her husband, who lived at Totteridge, near Barnet and Wexton. That wasn't any safer really, but he just felt happier that we were with somebody, rather than just the two of us on our own. For about a year we used to come back at weekends to see that the house was all right. I went to the Church School, St Andrews, at Totteridge for about a year until Mother said, 'Let's get back home. It's just as bad here as it is at home, so we might as well be back there!' I suppose she was worried about the house. So we came back.

Jeanne May remembered bombs falling near her home in Hale End Road:

Highams Park had a number of incidents, but early in the war what we called 'a stick of bombs' was dropped. The bombers would hop over from one road to the next road: there'd be one bomb in each road. People survived a lot of them if they were in shelters, providing they weren't in a house when it got a direct hit. There was one lady, two houses away, and she wouldn't go into the shelter. She lived with her nieces, but she *would* stay in the house. She was killed, but her nieces were all right in the shelter.

Miss Renee Weller recalled the strange brightness at night, when enemy aircraft dropped flares to light up their targets.

The air-raid siren had gone, and so we had all gone down into the air-raid shelter – Mother, Father, my sister and myself. It was springtime, and the apple blossom was all out. Father poked his head outside the air-raid shelter and said, 'Quick, quick, girls! Look at this!' and the flares had fallen, and the apple blossom was absolutely beautiful. He said, 'Oh – look at that! Have you ever seen anything so beautiful in your life? It's just like a transformation scene in a pantomime!'

And then his instinct was to jump, '*Down girls – quick!*' and he shoved us down, and our next door neighbours came flying up the garden path. She fell into the air-raid shelter, back first, and he came on after her, and of course we were all splitting our sides with laughter, and then – BOOM, BOOM, BOOM – three bombs fell, and the air-raid shelter rocked. That was the night the bombs fell in Malvern Avenue.

There we had been, admiring the beauty of apple blossom (in the middle of a war, mind you), and that's what happened. You see, my father was in the Battle of the

Somme; he never talked about it but I suppose those men had an in-built instinct. He realised something was going to happen, and 'whooshed' us down into the shelter.

Jeanne May recalls:

I bought the house in Malvern Avenue in 1946 with my mother's help, but it had to be repaired because it had been damaged when there were two bad bomb incidents in the road. It was the last bombing raid (although we had Flying Bombs and V2 afterwards). Two high explosive bombs killed 11 people! Some said it was because they had come out to see what was happening – a man and his son across the road – but most people, who were in their shelters, were quite OK.

The bomb that fell in the road in Malvern Avenue ruptured a gas main, and it burned all night. That looked *awful*, you know, this eerie light showing everything around. There were a number of other incidents in the Walthamstow area that night, so the relief people were very much stretched. One family died as a result of not getting the right equipment quickly enough. They were alive some time after the incident, in one of the inside shelters, but they had an 'Ideal Boiler', and apparently the smoke from the boiler burnt through the rubble to them in their shelter before they were got out. The man, his wife and two young children were among the 11 who were killed.

We had raids at any time – during the day-time as well – but this one was in the night, and our house in Hale End Road was damaged at the same time and the windows at the front of the house were blown out. We knew we were very close to it. Eventually the 'All Clear' went. It was getting towards daylight by the time we got outside, and of course there was a terrible mess. Over the top of our front door there had been three numbers, made of a sort of porcelain, fixed on to the glass, and my young brother, Cliff, found them in the rubble. He was dead worried because we hadn't got the number up! Silly things you think of afterwards, you know, but it rather takes off the tension.

At the beginning of the war they had what was called an Anderson shelter. They were outdoor corrugated-iron things, and they were semi-sunk into the ground, and my mother asked about having one. Mother was comfortably off, and she said, 'Oh, I can afford to pay.'

'Oh, well, if you can afford to pay, you can't have one!' So that was it!

Later on in the war they produced what was called a Morrison shelter, and that was a steel construction which you had inside the house, a sort of table shelter, with wires round it: you got under it. Well, when they were coming around, my mother decided she was not going to say she could afford to pay for it; she would just apply for it! We got the Morrison Shelter and, of course, every time there was a raid we all got under it. For the latter part of the war we did sleep upstairs and just got down as soon as the warning went. Cliff was quite young, and Mother used to call him on the way downstairs, and I got Rod, my son, and my younger sister, Joyce, and her child, David. Mother always went down first to put the lights on for us to get down. Of course, we were all blacked out so the lights wouldn't show outside.

Jean McCabe lived near the station and recalled the night when 'Pop' thought his last moment had come:

We have lived here since I was three, and during the war, when I was about ten, I remember Nan and Pop were staying with us. (He was called 'Pop' because he was mum's stepfather.) The air-raid shelter, up here in the garden, was an Anderson shelter, one of those circular, corrugated things, and our pear tree was hanging over it. (It must have been September time, mustn't it, for the pears to be ripe?) It was when London was having its bad blitz. It was dark, and all round us there was sort of flashing going on. We were all rushing up the garden to get into the shelter, and Pop was the last one. (He was only a little man, you know.) A bomb went off, and the next thing we knew, Pop suddenly sort of dived in – he *threw* himself in the Anderson shelter. He said, 'I've been hit! I've been hit!' He was a bit stunned, but we were laughing our heads off! We realised that, with all that squashy stuff on his face, he had been hit by a ripe pear that had dropped on his head from the tree!

79 *Mrs E. Miller, Mayor of Walthamstow, did voluntary work during the Second World War in a mobile canteen, providing tea for rescue services and people who had lost their homes in the bombing. (The Mayoress was her daughter, Mrs E. French.)*

Later on we had a land mine at the back of the house, which did a bit of damage: it broke one of the windows. My sister, Yvonne, says she remembers we didn't spend much time in the shelter after a while, except when it was bad. I always remember we used to sleep in the cupboard under the stairs, or got under the table. Pop and Nan stayed here for a while, and mum's sister, and my Aunt Edna and Uncle Arthur were living here for a while too, when he was in the RAF.

Mum was Mayoress when Nan was the Mayor of Walthamstow, from 1942-3, Alderman E.M. Miller, JP. (Her name was Ellen, and because mum's name was Ellen she was called 'Nellie' as well.) She and Nan did a lot of WVS work in the war, on the bomb sites. She used to go round with a mobile tea canteen. She was a councillor for a very long time. She was on the Housing Committee and was dedicated to her council work.

We weren't here all the time during the war. For almost a year we were sent down to Winton, Bournemouth. Yvonne and I went to school for about two days, and then a land mine hit the school and we couldn't go any more because they couldn't fit us in anywhere else, and so we used to go into Bournemouth itself. We often used to walk through the gardens down to the beach part and there were big rhododendrons and all sorts of other lovely bushes.

One day, Yvonne and I were going through the gardens, when suddenly an American soldier pushed us into the bushes! There was a lone German plane coming over, machine-gunning where we were, and that soldier may have saved our lives because when we got up and looked out there were bullet holes in the pathway! That frightened the life out of us! Anyway, the American took us down to the beach and left us there. Being young, it frightened us at the time, but we were all right afterwards.

Fire-watching

Frances Bowler had a great interest in Woodford High School. She was an 'Old Girl' of the school from its earliest days and after the war she worked there as a technical assistant in the science laboratories:

> The girls were evacuated from Woodford High School, then a bit of it was opened because the Red Cross were there, and the Queen herself came to see the Red Cross. Then they shared a school with another school, and the girls started to come back. It was the time of the Flying Bombs, and the staff would keep watch on the roof, and when the bombs came over everybody went down to the 'twisty passage' in the basement. (They supervised an exam once down there.) I know that Miss Chapman, the Headmistress, and the sixth-formers used to sit up, night after night, to be fire-watchers over the building. They went through it!

War Work

Ted Jones recalls:

> Soon after I left school I joined an instrument-making firm in Hatton Garden, of the name of H.J. Elliott. I learned the job on the ground floor and the firm made mostly glassware and instruments for the chemical industry. It was quite a job. When I left in 1935 and went to live with my sister in Higham Hill, my sister really wanted me to get work locally, so she had spoken to a few neighbours. One man asked why didn't I go to work at Short and Masons, on the corner of MacDonald Road and Hale End Road, so in 1938 I joined Short and Masons and, once again, I had to start from the ground-level.
>
> Short and Mason was an old-fashioned firm, and some parts of it were much the same as my previous firm, but there was the engineering section which I was interested in. The chemical part of it and glass-blowing were separated, in a different building, but I wasn't interested in that part: I was interested in the engineering side. That's where I started, but after about a year I was one of those blokes due for a term of two years in the Army. I was 21 in 1939 so I went for my medical and was called up.
>
> I didn't want to be in the Territorial Army, but when I got my call-up papers I was down for the Territorial Army, which was the Royal Fusiliers. They were based primarily at the Tower of London, but I joined them at one of the little Territorial centres, and from then on I went for training.
>
> Early in 1940 I was asked to call in to the company office and was spoken to by my company commander, who said that he had a memo to say that the firm I worked for had come under the Air Ministry, so every person who was called up for the Army had to stay and work in their job. As the work I was doing fell into that category, I carried on at Short and Mason.
>
> Before and during the war, Short and Mason remained a very good instrument-making firm. They made some of the instruments, specially the air-speed instruments, that went on the Halifax Bombers, as well as mercurial barographs used on some of our boats in the Navy.

Mrs Doris Jones, Ted's wife, was also involved in war work:

> I used to do welding at Holmes Bros. at the Billet Road, and we were bombed. It happened overnight, and luckily it wasn't dangerous because we weren't there working. (I worked there for about 13 years.)

Ted Jones continues:

> We were trying to keep production going at Short and Mason, carefully watching for Flying Bombs. If any of us spotted one, anybody who was near a glass window had to pull the chains down and close up the shutters, and we had to get to the shelters quickly. We all came out when the 'All-Clear' went. That was one thing, but V2 rockets was another – because, when they went over our 'dug-out', you hardly heard them. You just heard a 'swish' – and they went.

One day a chap came up to me saying that he had heard that a rocket had fallen in the area where I lived. So quickly I was on my bike and when I got home to Carlton Road it was terrible – the devastation. My sister was in a bad way, and the children, and the Higham Hill Road was completely devastated. Some of the families that we knew well were killed, and the road was actually divided in half by the Flying Bomb. Terrible.

I was Platoon Sergeant, and while I was on Guard Duty with about thirty men at 'Sunnyside', which was an old house just off Billet Road, the Officer in Charge, one of the directors of Short and Mason, Mr Paxton, and my officer came in. He said a Flying Bomb had landed at Stoffers in Hoe Street, Walthamstow, and he took over the guard in the evening and said that we had to get the platoon up to Stoffers area. I remember this very clearly.

We marched along to the Granada and I was ordered to mount men around the area, to stop looting, so I mounted men along by Church Hill, and there was an old-fashioned drapers there. All the other shops in Hoe Street were in danger of being looted, so I mounted men armed with rifles, and they took over guarding the area, and we cordoned off Hoe Street from the Granada and we watched the rescue work going on in Stoffers to get the people out because they had literally vanished in the back. I remember the man whose shop was opposite Stoffers. He was an undertaker and he came down to see if his shop was all right – very sad. Another building that was knocked down was Burton's shop, right on the corner of High Street, so I stayed there all night with my platoon. They were very tired and, of course, all of us had to go to work the next day, and we marched back to Sunnyside, where we got on our bikes and went home.

'V1s' and 'V2s' – the Rockets

Cliff Payling was a schoolboy at the Sir George Monoux School:

As I had been evacuated until Easter 1943 I missed most of the conventional air raids, but I can remember some, including the night in April 1944 when Walthamstow took a 'pasting'.

The advent of the V1 flying bombs coincided with the taking of the School Certificate Exams. Two incidents stand out in my memory, the first being as I cycled home from school over Wadham Bridge. To my right I heard, then saw, a 'doodle bug' coming over Hale End Road. Suddenly the engine cut out and the bomb appeared to be heading towards No. 222 (my home)! Luckily for us, but not for some other people, it veered away to the right and came down in Fullers Road near the *Napier Arms*.

The other incident occurred in the summer holidays. August had been a hot sunny month and I had spent some time sitting in the garden reading a collection of mystery and murder stories. When the V1 raids first started, they sounded the siren in the usual way when one was approaching, but by August they had modified this by sounding loud klaxons whenever one was close. When this happened I used to dash inside to tell my mother and we would take refuge under the 'Morrison'. On one occasion, early in the evening, we heard one extremely close, and then the engine cut out. We held our breath, fearing the worst. We actually heard a whistling, whooshing sound as it passed overhead. Again, luckily for us, it travelled on for another mile or so before coming down.

Renee Weller remembered the 'doodle-bug' incident in Oak Hill, which demolished the large house known as Forest Hall:

I was here all the time, and I remember Forest Hall: it was a large house. It wasn't exactly an orphanage, but I have the memory of neatly dressed children, who were being cared for there, walking in a 'crocodile' to Selwyn Avenue School and back. The children weren't there during the war.

The Fly Bomb caught on the trees, you see, and exploded there, which sent the blast over quite a large area and damaged a lot of houses.

Nearly 600 houses, according to Ross Wyld! Cliff Payling continues:

> To me the V2 rockets were more frightening as they came with no warning, the noise of their approach being heard after the explosion. Probably the closest incident to me was when one landed in Sturge Avenue just behind the Monoux School. It was lunch time and I was in the school library, which was situated in the front of the building. I was standing by a cabinet looking for a title in the card index when part of the ceiling came down. There I was with white dust and small pieces of plaster on my head and shoulders. Some other boys took refuge under tables, but I just stood there!

80 *Miss L. Frances Bowler, Ambulance Driver, checking the cars used for 'sitting case' casualties outside the ARP Station in Vincent Road during the Second World War.*

Halex During the War

Irene Knight remembers the Highams Park Halex factory's contribution to the war effort:

> During the war, Halex made silver leaves – little bits of silver – I don't quite know what they were: it was a kind of secret but when they dropped it from the aircraft it upset the radar. They made all sorts of things in the war. One thing that was special was disposable plastic fuel tanks for aircraft.
>
> They dropped two bombs on Halex. One dropped on the main pathway, going up towards the canteen. If they had dropped it at five to one everybody would have been streaming up there, but it came down at about 1 o'clock. I *think* it wrecked the First Aid Post but it didn't do any serious harm. The second one dropped on the hill, between the factories, which was all allotments. It just spoilt somebody's allotment!

Mrs Evelyn Maynard wrote about her war experiences at Halex in a letter to the chairman of the Chingford Airforce Association:

> The work force had, in fact, gone to the main Eyeshield Department in order to receive our weekly wage. The air-raid siren had sounded and we were told to stay put because enemy planes were in the vicinity. Fortunately the mechanism had been operated to shutter the glass roof. When the first bomb fell the lights went out and it seemed as if a ton of earth had fallen on the shutters. Women were screaming and the noise was horrendous. I was dragged under a workbench.
>
> My mother had heard that the factory had been bombed and, because I was late home, feared the worst. Such tears were shed on my arrival. On returning to work we found that our workshop had been hit by another bomb. To our horror, we realised that any other day but a Friday we would have been killed, because the bombs landed where we used to wait to go home at 12.55. We felt that the gods were smiling on we four 17-year-olds on that day. Needless to say, not much work was done that afternoon.

When one of the Morris family of Woodford Green visited a war museum in the Channel Islands he noticed a pilot's neck scarf on display which, to his amazement, was printed with a map of the area around the waterworks in Woodford High Road. John Leatherland comments:

> Actually, the Xylonite Factory was marked on the maps which the German pilots had because, if they could get a hit, there it was – poof! – up in smoke, but much of the

81   *Local Defence in the Second World War. The soldiers are pictured in front of Salisbury Hall Manor House, which by then had fallen into a poor state of repair.*

usual production went on. After all, the Forces had to be supplied with toothbrushes, hairbrushes, combs and whatnot! Additionally, there was more made in way of the industrial production – periscopes, and so on – and they did a lot of gas-mask assembly. They made certain products for sending to prisoners-of-war, which were in fact useful for other purposes, like, for instance, a map concealed in the handle of a toothbrush!

The Halex War Memorial had names on just one side. The big list was the First World War; the small one was the Second World War. As you went in the entrance of Hale End factory, what was known as the Front Office was immediately on your right, and it was past there. It was sent to the Brantham factory but later on the Brantham factory was sold and I don't know whether it still exists. You see, the Brantham factory had a similar memorial, and they were put side-by-side.

There's a rather sad story about the Hale End memorial. There was a blank in the Second World War list – the bottom one. Well, I had the job of having that done and put on the memorial and, according to the company records, there were a certain number of people who didn't come back, and so I had the plate made and it was put up. I had a very indignant letter from a lady who said that her son had *not* been killed in the war. She believed that one day he would come back, which I thought was most pathetic. I couldn't placate her in any way. After she first complained I went to the War Office and got the records 'dug out' and that showed him as 'believed killed'.

The 'V2' on St Leonards Avenue

Frances Bowler remembers:

A rocket fell in St Leonard's Avenue and it did a good deal of damage. It was pretty grim. I was lucky because I was at the back of the house somewhere, and my father was in the bathroom, also at the back of the house. It was Sunday morning, and he'd been working in the garden. Mother thought she would just go downstairs to the kitchen to see about the pudding, when all the glass from the windows of the front room came crashing in.

82 *The Halex War Memorial stood in the grounds of the factory near the entrance in Larkshall Road. Its present location is unknown.*

I remember that at least one man was taken to hospital, and a girl who had come to see her husband, one of the Civil Defence leaders, got glass in her hair and she came in to us for help. I remember her in the kitchen, bending over, and I was picking out bits of glass from her hair. It looked as though I was looking for nits! I said, 'For goodness sake, go down to the First Aid Post and get an anti-tetanus injection!'

Jim Davis remembers how part of Falmouth Avenue and Gordon Avenue used to look before the V2 rocket fell:

All the ground where those flats are built – the council flats – belonged to the Smees. They were big market-business people and they had a garden that came from Falmouth Avenue, and the end of their back garden came right out on to the edge of Gordon Avenue. They had a whole corner, right round! Smee's entrance was in Falmouth. At the back of their house I remember they had a 'patio', as you would call it nowadays, with steps going down, and they had these great big stone lions on the corners of the steps!

As you went down Gordon Avenue from Church Avenue, Mrs Spong's garden ended and there was a gap, then there was a house owned by Mr Clay. It was a big house, and he had all that ground, with big trees, right from the back of these houses in Church Avenue to where there was a ditch and a big hedge and wide unmade road, which was a pathway, that led from Gordon into Handsworth Avenue. (St Leonard's

83   *V.E. Day celebrations outside the old hall of Winchester Road Methodist Church.*

Avenue is there now.) He used to have big garden parties in the back, on the grass, and his garden used to back right on to ours. They were quite 'posh' people.

When the rocket fell it hit Clay's and flattened his house, and it blew our back wall out, right out to the front – and all next door, the back to the front – all the way through. Grandmother and my grandfather were here, and they were blown right through the house. He was in the shed, the old boy, and he was blown down, but they didn't get killed. They were very lucky, but Clay's was finished and so was Smee's house, and somebody was killed.

They cleared all the ground, and that was the end of the unmade road. The Council built flats on the corner.

I never visited my grandmother much during the war because I was away. When I got sorted out after that, I didn't come down here so much. I was enlisted for a while, and then I got invalided out because of my chest. I had pleurisy and pneumonia. I had spots on my lung, and they invalided me out. Then I spent quite a while in hospital, in Chelmsford.

Alan J. Marshall was one of the schoolboy evacuees from Walthamstow who went to Blaenavon in South Wales. He came home before the end of the war, just in time for the 'V2s':

Gordon Avenue was just round the corner. That was one of the first rockets, and it landed there on a Sunday morning. I always remember being at home, where I lived at Alma Avenue. There was no explosion as such, but complete compression of the ears, that was all. That was the rocket exploding.

In 1945 one of the last V2 rockets fell near St Peter's-in-the-Forest, the old parish church of Hale End, and it was very badly damaged, but after the war ended the church was not only repaired but extended.

Many years later, in 1973, two bombs were detonated by the IRA at the waterworks buildings at the junction of Forest Road and Woodford High Road. The blast was heard for several miles, but fortunately little damage was done.

10

Highams Park Shopping Centre

efore the revised Haile Estate Plan was published in 1897, the first shops in Highams Park had been built: two in Hale End Road and a small block of shops up the steps opposite the station in The Avenue. Until then one of the small Oak Hill Cottages in Hale End had served as a little store, selling sweets to the children. In 1906 more shops were built in Hale End Road and Winchester Road. Will Hebbard lived in Highams Park when the shops were newly built:

> The shops were in The Avenue as they are now, except for the Bank Corner, which was then a field, but in Hale End Road, between Handsworth Avenue and Beverley Road, there were only two shops and no *County Arms*. The shops on the opposite side were built about 1909. Gibbons the butcher must be the oldest name in the district as the family came there a year after the shop was built. I recall Clarks the grocers, Thoms' drapers (later to become Brutons' shoe repairs), Exalls' hardware, Salmons' furniture, Butlers' greengrocers, Gibbons and Goodwins the bakers. (I was their first customer and was presented with a tin of biscuits.)
>
> From Beech Hall Road to the railway were shops as now. On the other side of the line, the first shops were, opposite the off licence, from the opticians to Gazes the chemist, and the Victoria Wine side as they are now.

Victoria Wine, on the corner of Selwyn Avenue, closed in the late 1990s.

> The Post Office was originally immediately in front of the station entrance – later removed to 'Wavy Line' shop – and was incorporated with a grocers shop, while the letter box was part of the shop front. From Harris's Post Office to Beverley Road was Rootes drapers and two shops, Lovells and Bennetts, the fishmongers.
>
> The next shop was Swain the music shop, whose owner played the piano for the silent films of those days. He also had four sons who have become well known in the borough since. Gibson and Rumble's dairy completed the block to Beverley Road.

Will Hebbard went on to describe shops in The Avenue, starting with the bakery which many people remember as Chalkleys but then it was owned by Robert Brookes. When the 'Chalkleys' sign over the shop window was taken down the old name of 'Shearings' was revealed.

> It is most interesting to note that milk was purchased (other than from farms) in the bakers, and the big containers marked 'Cream Milk' stood on the counter for many years afterwards. I was always glad when Mother went to Shearings because Mrs Shearing always gave me a bar of chocolate: her husband, Harry, the baker, was very short and was always working in the recognised baker's garb of vest and trousers smothered in flour. They had four children and were fed up with Highams Park snobbishness. Their children could not go to the Misses Hickmans' private school because the parents were tradesmen!
>
> They left before the first war and the eldest son, Eddy, went down on the *Queen Mary* at Jutland, while only 18.

> They sold to Cakebreads. Nat (Nathaniel) was the boss and very fat and jolly. Joe
> did the bakery round and Kate looked after the shop and house. They were there
> for many years until Joe died, and although everyone thought they were all single it
> transpired that Nat was married and had a son of about 10 or 12, which caused quite
> a stir in the village. On one occasion when I was in my teens Nat got me to crawl into
> the oven to do a small repair which only someone small could attempt because of the
> limited space, and although the fire was out for a whole weekend it was still hot in that
> oven.

Hilda Oliver recalls:

> Our bread was delivered from Cakebreads by horse and cart, and milk was delivered
> from Kays Farm (Beech Hall Farm) in tin-cans, with a horse and cart, three times a
> day! Mid-morning was supposed to be for the milk-puddings. Everything was delivered
> in those days! At the top of Beech Hall Road (behind the shop on the corner – if you
> come back a bit there's an opening and it's now a joiners) was Warrens Horse Stables,
> where the coal merchant kept his horses.

Melvin Harrison now has a health food shop in South Chingford:

> Chalkleys, the bakers shop, was bought by Robert Brookes, who originally bought what
> was Hellingman's Bakery, in Hale End Road. He bought Chalkleys as the main bakery,
> and then he bought three other shops in Walthamstow.

Next door to Chalkleys was Harrison's grocer's shop, and many people remembered the
shop's delicious home-cooked ham-on-the-bone, a very welcome luxury after the shortage
of food in the war. Mr Rolph, the manager, left and the grocer's shop continued under
new management until it became a lino and paint shop. Then 'Manhattan Cocktail
Bar' and a series of wine bars followed, including 'The Greenhouse', and in 1997 it
became de Graag's public house and then *Birdie's*.

Will Hebbard remembered the first owners:

> Stephenson, the grocer, had two sons and a sister and was a widower, but Miss
> Stephenson (when in the shop) ran the office, which was overhead to make more
> room in the shop. She looked so funny sitting over the shop window, peering into the
> shop making notes of debt and credit.
>
> They went to Australia in 1922, but not before young Willie had pinched my motor
> bike from our plot of land in The Avenue, dropped the lamp and got two fingers cut
> off by the chain!
>
> After Arnolds, the tailor, came Law, the butcher, who was one of the oldest
> tradesmen in the village. Poor old Frank was badly knocked about in the war, but
> managed to run his father's shop for many years afterwards.
>
> On the other side of The Avenue were Walkers the dairy, and two shops for
> Watlings' [the builder's merchant, later Pamphilons], then Gazes, the chemist, Bon
> Marche, a drapers, the Temperance Hotel (two shops), and an off licence.

There was a space between the off licence and Barclay's Bank. The block of shops was
built much later.

> Then there was Barclays Bank, Kellands Toys, a wool shop, the laundry, a sweet shop
> and a coal order office. I can also remember Duncan's hairdresser and Quelch shoes.

Vera Mason remembered:

> My father-in-law ran a coal business, and his little office was down by the level-crossing
> gates. Everything was done by horse and cart in those days and Nobby, the horse, was
> stabled up in the place they called The Mews, at the back of Beverley Road. Well,
> round about 58 years ago (before the war) on a Saturday morning, Mr Mason – Bert,
> we'll call him – used to do a round with all the 'overs', and he used to use sacks for
> the coal. It was about half a crown a hundredweight, or something silly like that, you
> know. He had a special round: he had customers who took some in every weekend,

84   *Law's butcher's shop was taken over by George French after the Second World War. Until 2005, it was a high class butcher's shop, run by the Gibbons family, who were butchers in Highams Park for three generations since about 1908.*

every Saturday, and Nobby, the horse, knew the round, and they had a little dog, called Jack, and he knew the round! They set out with the horse and cart, and Jack used to travel under the cart. I can see it now. Along Studley Avenue Nobby would come along, and stop at a house, and Jack would stop, and Mr Mason would off-load his half-hundredweight of bits-and-bobs, and then, as he came out from the door, Nobby would start off again, stop at the next house, the next one in line, and Jack would stop and they would do another delivery. They'd come out, and off they'd go again. Those two animals knew that coal round!

The first two houses in Beverley Road, where the Masons lived, have been knocked down and there is a block of flats there now, but at the back, behind the shops in Hale End Road, there were stables at one time. I think Nobby's was the last stable. The others became garages. Gradually the horses went, and the cars came in.

Stan Batson recalls:

My father was a builder and decorator, and around 1929 he rented the shop at 23 Winchester Road and opened it as a paint and wallpaper shop, and carried on with his building and decorating business which he operated still from Fulbourne Road. My brother, who had just got married, lived in the flat over the shop at that time. Gradually the business expanded, but when the shop opened it was just a few tins of paint because 'ready-mix' paint was just coming into its own then.

Of course, there was a limit to the paint colours in those days. You couldn't, for example, use blues for painting outside, because it would very, very quickly turn green with the sun; the whites would turn yellow. At the time when we opened the shop, when I was about nine, the main colours were browns and creams and greens. There was a kind of maroon colour, a reddish-brown, but you couldn't use red, of course – that would go pink.

To whiten the ceiling you'd buy a big ball of whitening – that was about the size of a small football, not round, but an irregular shape, and you'd dissolve the whitening in water and put size in it. Now size, in those days, was jelly-size, and that used to be bought by the stockist in little barrels called firkins: it would be like a barrel of stiff jelly sold by weight and you would grab up a handful – more or less. (Nobody was very particular about weights in those days.) Ceiling distemper was made of balls of whitening, size (which was the adhesive), and I think there was some other ingredient they put in to stop it 'going-off'!

Our shop in Winchester Road and all of the block of shops along there were built to the self-same pattern. In those days most of the people who ran a shop of that nature would live above it. There was the small shop at the front and then there was the 'shop parlour' behind it, just joined by one door, and at the side of the door there was a big window between the shop and the shop parlour, so that the owner would be sitting in his shop parlour until somebody came in, and the little 'dinger' (the clapper bell that was over the door) would go, and then he would be able to look out of the window and see who was coming in the shop.

Just beyond the shop parlour, there were three steps going up to a large kitchen with a big, black 'kitchener' stove in there with a chimney, where all the cooking for the family would be done, and you'd also eat in there. Behind that was another fairly big room, which was the 'sitting' or 'drawing' room. Upstairs you went up to a very, very big front lounge, a bedroom behind that, then another smaller bedroom – what we used to call a box room. Behind that was a bathroom, a toilet, then a bedroom, so the accommodation was quite substantial in those shops.

Business started to pick up because Highams Park was developing in those days. On the corner of Cavendish Road there was old Mrs Spencer, who had the shoe repair shop. That consisted of a little low building with a little shed attached to it, which is still there, and I bought it shortly before she died. Since shops change hands from time to time it's difficult to remember at which point the various shops were trading together, but we'll start from that shop, which was Spencer's, and next door to that there was a lady who lived up in Larkswood Road, who ran that shop as a needlework and wool shop.

Next door to that shop was H.G. Chainey (Jack and Queenie Chainey), a very good friend of mine. He would be 15 or 20 years older than me and he died some time ago. When the shops were built up at the Hatch Lane level crossing, Jack Chainey also had a shop up there – the corner shop in Manor Way. In the very, very early days, when people used to come to Highams Park from the East End – coming out to the country, to the lake and beyond – they'd buy picture postcards the same as we do when we go to the seaside! Jack Chainey had a whole series of postcards commissioned, and when he packed up his shop I went over there once and he was clearing out a load of stuff and he had literally thousands of pictures of Highams Park!

Edith Upton remembered him as a very lively member of the Walthamstow Antiquarian Society. In 1926 Fred Chainey and 'Hy. Gordon Chainey' were at No. 14 Winchester Road.

Stan Batson continued:

Next door to Chainey's was a gent's outfitters run by Mr Deacon. Now Mr Deacon had lost a leg during the First World War, as I understand. He was a very quiet, gentlemanly man.

When we came to Highams Park in 1929 the Co-op was there, and then I think that Pearks Stores was next door to that. Pearks must have come after Iverson, the greengrocer in 1922. Then there was Mrs Westley, fishmonger.

Going back to the shops on the other side of Winchester Road, and starting from the Walthamstow end again, I recollect there was always a garage there (about number 39). That was Harwoods. They seemed to have quite a lot of cycle and garage businesses around here. As I came, they were going. Harwood was a motor mechanic, you see, and Harwood's also had a garage opposite. They used to have big petrol pumps outside – the old-fashioned ones with a big round glass dome on the top.

At the back (of what is now the car salesroom) is a building that opens up into Selwyn Avenue (which I now own). We ran that for a time in 1950-60 as a timberyard, and for heavy stuff like sand and cement. It's just under a thousand square feet, and it's very, very high.

On the corner, where Victoria Wine used to be, was an off licence, called The King Edward VII, and Bob and Win Ketteridge used to run that. Win, in her very young days, had been a stage dancer and Bob had been a theatrical electrician. They must have met backstage and married, and they ran the off licence for many, many years. Bob and Win Ketteridge were great.

The first shop after the garage (which is now a pet shop) was a 'Tuppenny Library'. In those days, before television, I think there was a lot more reading done and there was no Public Library in Highams Park. There were a lot of these lending libraries around. In the City there was a whole chain of shops, where you went in and paid two pence and got a book out for a week, and I remember when I was working in Moorgate as Audit Clerk for a firm of chartered accountants I used to go into a Tuppenny Library, quite a well-known chain, but there were quite a lot of these little lending libraries locally. There was also one fellow who used to come round on a tricycle with books on it. He used to have a regular round and knock at the door in the evening and people would have a book for a week or two for about 'tuppence' a week.

Up to about 15 years ago the A-Z maps showed the Fire Station in Winchester Road, outside Penny's Stores, where there was a Fire Alarm Post, a metal post about 4ft. 6in. in height, with a roundel on the top.

Along from Penny's Stores there was Gazes, the chemist shop, and then Westcotts, the laundry people who had shops all over Walthamstow and the surrounding districts, and then next door to Westcotts was our own shop, Batsons Ltd. That was our first shop in Highams Park, though at one time we had three outlets.

When we first went there in 1929, next to us was Billingtons, a hairdressing shop. Old Mr Billington was a rather tall, thin, gaunt figure, a bit 'gingery' as I remember him, and he had two daughters. He used to do the gents' haircutting in the front, and Miss Billington had a little hairdressing salon at the back of the shop. There was another daughter as well who was married (Mrs Twitchett). Next door to that was a jewellers shop, although later, when Mr Billington packed up, his shop was taken over by Mr Walker, who was also a jeweller, but in 1929-30 there was a jewellers shop at number 19 Winchester Road.

Just along the road there was an oil shop called Murrays. Mr Murray was a very old gentleman, as I remember him, with a beard. A couple of sons worked with him, and it was a real old-fashioned shop, which sold all kinds of oils, firewood, various bits of chandlery and ironmongery. In later years, after Murray had gone and we were selling paraffin in our shop, we had two 600-gallon tanks in the backyard. It used to be delivered to us from a tanker, 500 gallons at a time and we used to wait until one 600 gallon tank was nearly empty and then get it topped up, but that was in the days after the war when a lot of people were using paraffin oil for heating purposes.

After Worths, the corn chandler, closed, Hunts (another corn chandler) opened next door. Dear old Kathy Evans worked in the sweet shop along there for a long time, and when that changed hands and Kathy lost her job she came and worked for me, part-time, for countless years. She was always known as the 'little Welsh lady with the pink hair', because she used to have her hair dyed pink. She was a very popular person.

Anyway, there was Greenleas, a shoe shop, along there, and right at the very end was Daflons, the butcher, a family business that had been there for many years. After that was the Broadway Parade, with a couple of little shops tucked back. One was (until 1999) a home-brew shop and the other one is the barbers that was originally Fred Allen's little chemists shop; the other little shop was Henry Morgan, the optician. Well, of course, Morgans the Opticians is still trading in Highams Park.

James Hawes, the Funeral Directors, started out somewhere towards the East End of London, and then in the Broadway Parade, Highams Park. I knew the sons and Dick Willey, who was their main man. He lived over the top of the undertakers shop, and he was also the Chief Mourner for the funeral processions. He was a very tall, distinguished-looking man, dear old Dick Willey, and rather had the appearance of Alastair Sim. As he led the solemn procession down Winchester Road, all the shop-keepers would stand outside their shops with their heads bowed.

There is still a branch of James Hawes, Funeral Directors in The Broadway, Highams Park. The present chairman and owner of the family business, Mr Keith Goodchild, is a direct descendant on his mother's side of the original family which started the business well over a century ago. There are now four other branches of the firm, covering East London, Herts and Essex.

Stan Batson recalled:

> On the other side of the Broadway Parade, of course, there was a newer block of shops and flats above. The one that I remember, just after all that had been built, was the Coronation Florists on the corner. Next to that, coming back from the level-crossing area, there was J&J Libraries, and that was run by an old friend of mine, old Reg Jermy, who has long since passed away, and that was another of the old tuppenny lending libraries.
>
> The shops over in that part of the Parade used to change hands quite a lot, and as Coronation Florists vacated their shop on the corner Reg Jermy took over and it became a toy shop, which young Ron ran for many years after the war.

One of the casualties of Dutch Elm Disease was the very tall elm tree on the corner of Larkshall Road and the Broadway, by the Jermys' shop. A wooden seat was built around the trunk, making it a pleasant place to sit and wait for a bus.

Stan Batson continued:

> Another shop in the Parade was Stitchers. They had one or two shops in the East End of London. Stitchers, the Grocers, a Jewish family, were running Stitchers Stores from way before the war until way after. Opposite the first fish shop in Broadway Parade was the Macfisheries, part of a big chain of stores, next to the little corner shop. After the war Alf Bush ran the fish shop, and that was one of the shops that went on for a long time in The Parade, and then Alf's son, Ray, ran his fish shop, across the road. His wife, Pat Bush, who did a bit of modelling and appeared on TV, became a florist. They had another shop in South Chingford, and eventually shut the one in Highams Park.
>
> The 35 bus used to run along Fulbourne Road from Clapham Common, in south London, and it finished up at Highams Park Broadway, because a lot of people were working at the British Xylonite factory, later known as BX and Halex. The buses were run by the London General Omnibus Company before London Transport came along.

Hilda Oliver recalled shops near the station:

> In The Avenue, more or less where the wine shop was (Threshers), there was a Gas Showroom and an Electricity Showroom, and there were two wool shops. Before the war one of them was kept by Evelyn and Mabel (who were related): this was the same shop which was used by the Walthamstow Building Society. Just to the right of the steps, there was a hotel (where Meade's, then Kennedy's Estate Agents were). When Meade left they found a nameplate, and it showed the name, the *Great Eastern Hotel*.

A branch of the Walthamstow Building Society, founded in 1877, was in one of the original shops up the steps opposite to the railway station, and for many years its manager was Mr James Pringle, an ex-Mayor of Walthamstow. He was a cheerful, sociable man who enjoyed meeting customers, and he made his office seem more like a club than a building society. His desk was in a room up some steps at the back of the shop, and new customers were in for a shock. One of the office walls had been built with glass bricks but the others were covered by Pringle Tartan wallpaper. The other surprise was 'Pringle-the-Bard', and Mr Pringle's poems were sometimes known as 'Pringle's Jingles'.

Fred Revell remembered that a 'Tardis' style police box stood at the junction of The Avenue and Station Approach.

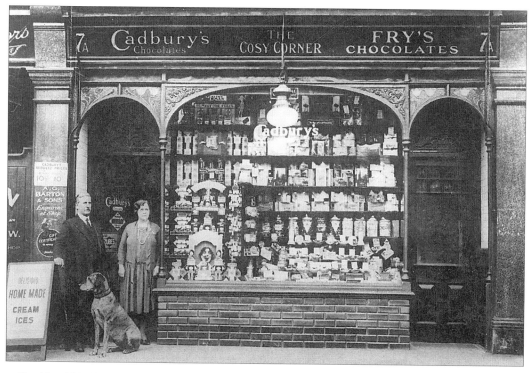

85 *Mr and Mrs Howchin and their dog, Peggy, outside their sweet shop, the 'Cosy Corner' in the Avenue. The shop premises were taken over by a business distributing balloons, then by Coldham, Shield and Mace, solicitors, and are now used by an accountant.*

Dr Douglas Woolf's father, Dr A.D. Woolf, was one of the first GPs in the new urban village and Douglas knew of all the doctors who had practised in Highams Park from 1918:

> Dr Roberts resided in The Avenue and had a small practice there, but his main practice was in Wood Street. Some of the doctors in Highams Park I remember were Dr Rogers, who was in Castle Avenue and Cavendish Road and was succeeded by Dr Cuddon-Large, then my father, who came to Highams Park in 1910, and Dr F. Sanders, MC, who took over the practice of a Dr Brown. Dr Sanders retired in about 1955, and Dr Rogers would have died at about that time. Dr Marien and Dr Sanders became partners.
>
> In The Avenue, Highams Park, is 'Marien Court', called after Dr Marien, who died tragically at the age of 39 in 1962. He was a very good friend of mine. He went into the practice with Dr Sanders in 1950, and he was there for 11 years – a very clever doctor. We worked together at Willesden Hospital so I knew him well. He was married to Joan, and they had a son, called Brian Marien, who qualified as a doctor and practised in Midhurst, and they had a daughter, called Angela.

A window to the memory of Dr Marien can be seen in All Saints Church, Highams Park. Dr Elizabeth Chester worked for a while at his surgery at 27 The Avenue, until she married Leonard Wigzell and left the district. Dr John Raiman had joined Dr Marien in 1961, and Dr Geoffrey Norris, who came to work at the practice in 1962, went into partnership with Dr John Raiman in 1963 and they continued to use the house as their surgery until moving into what was originally known as Highams Park Family Doctor Group, Handsworth Avenue, where Dr W.L. Brace and Dr Robin Winch, who had their own practices, also had surgeries. Dr R.B.J. Cuddon-Large's practice was also associated with

86 *George French was a popular butcher in Highams Park for many years. He is pictured here with his wife, known as Edie, and their children, Jean and Yvonne.*

the health centre, although he continued to have two surgeries, including the one at the top of Cavendish Road, which has now been named The Park Centre. The group practice was renamed The Health Centre and became a fund-holding practice until recently. It is still Highams Park's main medical centre.

Dr Woolf recalled:

Avis, a builder and decorator in Beech Hall Road, Highams Park, was a former employee of A.J. Barton, the well-known builder and decorators. Barton's Builders Yard, at 7A The Avenue, was between the 'Cosy Corner', a tobacconist, and Law's, the butcher. Law sold the shop to Mr French, who was manager of the Co-op.

Mrs Jean McCabe's father was George French, the butcher:

I can't remember what year it was when he moved to The Avenue. I should imagine it must have been after the war. He was at the Co-op at first, across the level crossing, the butcher's shop there, and then quite a few years later he rented the shop in The Avenue.

Usually, Mondays and Thursdays he went up to the market: he'd go and have his beer, about 4 o'clock in the morning! He'd done butchery all his life. When he was younger, when he first started, he was on the boats – on big boats, you know – a butcher on a sea-faring boat. He went to San Francisco quite a lot.

Dr Woolf mentioned two other shops in The Avenue: 'Pamphilon's opened the first big store, and then Harmer and Simmons, the 'Electrical' people, were where the Launderette was in The Avenue, next to Threshers. Irene Knight regretted the closing of several very useful shops, especially Pamphilon's:

Oh, we did miss that shop! The innumerable little things you could pop in there for! I was sorry to see Gill's go, too, but the owner said he was retiring, so I thought, I can't begrudge you your retirement! There used to be a drapers past the *County Arms*, Roots, I think, but the other shop I miss is Batson's.

Edith Upton remembered shops in Winchester Road:

We had a jewellers and a corn chandlers, and there was a very nice drapers where you walked a long way down the shop and there were chairs to sit down on, and then there was a dairy and Daflon, the butchers.

Mr Gaze, the chemist, was there for a long time. He was a stout body. Holly Gaze, his daughter, ran the Winchester Road chemists shop for her father. In The Broadway, before the modern block of shops was built, the ground belonged to Xylonite and was surrounded by an iron fence.

According to Dr Woolf:

> Mr Gaze, the chemist, was always a very respected person. He had the shop in Winchester Road and one in The Avenue as well.
>
> A Temperance Hotel used to be where the dry-cleaners are now [in The Avenue], and it became a cut-price sweet shop owned by Wright, and then it was the Gas Company Showrooms. Upson owned the off licence but it was only one shop in those days. Another person was Astrop, the hairdresser, and where the card shop is now there used to be another hairdresser's, owned by a Mr Watson, who had a manageress called Miss Harris.
>
> Then there was the Digby family, who owned the *County Arms*.

When Arthur Hemmings was asked what the *County Arms* was like in the 1930s, he replied, 'Oh, sawdust on the floor and spittoons!'

> The Masons, who were the coal merchants, lived in Beverley Road, close to the garages behind Beverley Road where there are now little houses. My father used to park his car in one of those garages, which were owned by Mr Bennett, a confectioner in Hale End Road.

87 *The Avenue in the mid-1990s and, below, the same view in about 1909.*

88 *Highams Park Stores, The Avenue, is now a small public house. It was a well-stocked grocer's shop until the latter part of the 20th century. Delicious hams were cooked at the back of the shop.*

Mrs Vera Mason talked about her late father-in-law:

> Mr Mason died in 1940 (he was not very old, about 52) and that was virtually the end of the coal business, because when Bert took it over the war was already on. Bert was exempt because of the coal business, and also he was not a really healthy man.

Dr Woolf remembered that:

> Mr Wren was a local boy who became a dentist and was in practice at 507 Hale End Road (above what used to be Lily Shoes Co., then Wirewell's Radio Shop), and Mr Hunt had his dental practice opposite the station.
>
> Barrett's, the greengrocer, was on the corner of Handsworth Avenue next to Edward's, newsagent and confectioner, and the Home and Colonial was next to Barclays Bank. Further down in Hale End Road was A.C. Gibbons, the butcher, whose grandson now has the shop in The Avenue, and Butler, the greengrocer. There was also Pettit of the Cycle Shop in Hale End Road.
>
> Next door to Bennett's was a fish shop (the owner was Stevens, who was active in the Salvation Army). Later Hellingmans, the baker came, but before that it used to be a Gentleman's Outfitters. Another well-known shop was the 'Ham and Beef' shop, and then there was a corn chandlers, where the racing shop is now, and a dairy on the corner of Beverley Road.

Hilda Oliver recalled:

> We got our butter from Hitchmans Dairies. It had to be made up, by patting it into shape. Gibsons, the corn chandler, was next to Bennetts in Hale End Road and he always had biscuits. You could buy broken biscuits too – they were cheap. You see, nothing came in packets in those days! Next door to him was Rumbles, another dairy.
>
> The drapers looked very different. I'm thinking of Roots, where things were draped around the window: it was absolutely *full* of things. That was a draper's shop for a long time. And then there was Liddells, the grocer, next to them.

Mrs Jenny Miller remembered a shop which, until recently, was 'Christine's' in The Avenue, but it was known as 'Bon Marche' for many years. The owner had retained

89 *When it was built, this section of Winchester Road was well-named as The Market Place because it was a very busy trading centre with many small shops.*

all the original glass counters, wooden drawers and shelves of the old shop, and two bent-wood chairs which the customers loved:

> The tall wooden chairs were the original ones. I don't know who originally owned it, but my aunt, Grace Pickard, bought it about 42 years ago. They bought it as 'Bon Marche' and they kept it as that. Grace never worked there, but Grace's sister, Olive Pickard, did. Then my mother sometimes worked there. She was Elsie Cooke, and another sister, Vi Gwilliams, also worked there, and Florrie Sinfield worked there part-time.

Arthur Hemmings lived in Leytonstone before coming to Highams Park after the war:

> I remember one or two shops in The Avenue: Mrs Farraway in the sweet shop, next to the greengrocers, then there was Harrison's grocers shop which used to sell cooked ham.

90 *'My father, Dr A.D. Woolf, started his Practice in Hale End Road and Winchester Road. He finally settled at 13, The Avenue. The No.13 was over the Surgery but the adjoining house was called 'Amhurst', and that's because my mother was superstitious (and she had lived in Amhurst Park). Then Dr Cuddon-Large succeeded to the Practice and lived there, and now it's a Play School [Nursery].'* (Dr Douglas Woolf)

91 *Haymaking in Hooper's Field with some of the Mason family, who were coal merchants for many years in Highams Park. The field was behind 'Montserrat', a semi-detached house in Hale End Road, where Mr Hooper, an umbrella manufacturer, lived in 1886. By 1891, Mrs Blatherwick was living next door in 'Fernlea' but in about 1908, Mr Hooper moved into 'Fernlea', where he stayed (at least) until 1922. 'Fernlea' was demolished after the Second World War.*

Mrs Matthews described her mother's small Grocery and General Store:

> I lived in Mile End, in Bancroft Road, and I was two years old in 1896 when we went to the shop – a little business Mum had.
> It was a general shop that I called her 'Woolworths'. It sold everything in a small way, one counter for cheese, ham and sausage, and another part for bread and flour – that sort of thing. Another counter was for sweets – jelly babies and mixtures, you know. The children used to come in and say, 'Please can I have a hap'orth of sweets in two papers, one for my sister and one for me?' We would weigh them up separate so they could have one each in little cones twisted round. We would put little bits of food in paper.

Irene Owen, her daughter, recalled wartime rationing in Highams Park:

> We used to go to Beeston's for sweets, next door to the old Post Office – 2oz. a week, that's all! There was another sweet shop in The Avenue (which is now an Indian Restaurant), next to the greengrocers, and Margaret Scott's sister, Eileen Scott, worked there.

Mrs Matthews recalled names of other shops at that time:

> Millers was on the corner of Beverley Road, and Gibson was next door. Weatheralls was next door to the café on the corner of Handsworth Avenue, then the Home & Colonial and Barclays Bank and Pruim's, the shoe shop, and Knight's were along The Avenue.

It is said that the Home & Colonial was demolished with the intention of building a bigger store, but this did not happen after the first supermarket, Kingsway – later Budgen – was built at the other side of the railway line:

> When you went down to the station there was the little kiosk, then there was Harrisons, the florist, and, just behind it, The Garden Shop.

92 *Shops in Cavendish Road. Meophams store, on the left, traded for many years.*

The Garden Shop and Nurseries

Melvin Harrison recalls:

I was four years old in 1948 when the family moved into 36 Castle Avenue. When we left we sold to my brother-in-law, Robert Brookes, the baker near Highams Park Station. [The Village Bakery was next door to the Harrisons' business.] The Garden Shop was there for nearly 50 years and it closed in 1984.

The connection between my family and Highams Park goes back to 1935, when my father, William Harrison, and his brother, John Harrison, started a business, in the Station Approach. It was a new lease from British Rail in 1935, and a building was put on the site then. Originally it was Builders' Equipment and Paints Shop, but during the course of the war things changed, and they decided one day that they would start selling plants, and they turned it into a Gardening Centre. Fred Revell came to work there as a young lad, and that gave an opportunity for the two partners in the business to be away during the war.

A small building next door to the Garden Shop sold dairy products and was owned by a Mr and Mrs White. As the years went by they closed down, and the Harrison family took that over, to use as a florist. That was the corner shop, but the other premises were owned by British Rail. There was the gardening shop, and the little nursery bit next to it, down to the station. In addition to that, a nursery was bought in Brookfield Path, Woodford Green, and that was a series of greenhouses and a shed which was kept in the family for quite a few years, and then it was sold to Mr Stevens.

The produce was actually grown at the nursery – bedding plants, perennial plants and shrubs and there was also storage for bulk items, like peat and potting compost – things like that. The goods were actually brought down to the shop to sell.

John Harrison, lived in Gordon Avenue, Highams Park, then he and his wife, Rose, moved to Wadebridge, in Cornwall, and he started a nursery there. He died a few years later, at the age of 48.

By the time the nursery in Brookfield Path was sold we had bought the house in Castle Avenue, and the garden was a quarter of an acre. It went right through to Handsworth Avenue, with just a fence across the back. There were no buildings between the houses and, therefore, in the bottom half of the garden there was a

93 *This row of shops and the Post Office in Oak Hill provided for the everyday needs of people living in Hale End (now part of Woodford Green). The roof of Forest Hall can be seen beyond the houses.*

storage area, and five greenhouses were built. They were big greenhouses, about 30 feet by 10 feet. As time went on we bought more from other nurseries, so that the bottom half of our garden was sold for building, and we didn't actually own any greenhouses then. Everything was bought in from local nurseries – Sewardstone and Nazeing – round there.

My mother trained as a florist, and with two other ladies, Doris Cokeham and Joyce Wood, ran the florists' shop. A chap called Lew Chapman was there for many, many years. I joined the business in about 1960-3.

Fred Revell, a chap who was here during the war, joined us again for the last few years of the shop. He did a few years during the war, then he went away and worked at Fuller's Electrical. He came back and he worked for us for about five years up to his retirement, so that was his first job and his last job.

The kiosk by The Garden Shop was Apex Travel, owned by Mr Walden. Before that it was Pettingal's Estate Agency. The kiosk was empty for a long while and we had to 'push' the Railways to knock it down so everybody would get a better view of our shop! We were very pleased when they did.

There were the other shops, like Pamphilon's, Batson's, Eve's Stores and Gill Brothers, that started up at about the same time, and they were the hub of the community. Other shops came and went.

Mrs Heales and her cycle shop, at 477 Hale End Road, seemed to have been there for ever. It was started by Mr and Mrs Lionel Heales in about 1938, and at that time some of the family lived in the house next door to the second very small shop (also owned by the family), which was divided by a partition from the cycle shop but had no facilities of its own. It was used for storage by Mrs Wyn Heales, who filled the main shop with bicycles, lights, tyres and so much other cycling paraphernalia that customers had to pick their way with caution through the chaos, but she always knew exactly where to find just what was needed, and was a great help to all local cyclists by supplying spare parts and repairing their bikes. She lived in the flat over the shop, and by working for only a few hours each day, even when she was very elderly, Mrs

Heales kept the shop and repair business going until the end of her life in July 1991. Colin Geyman made a successful career change in mid-life and, until recently, owned Heales' Cycle Shop.

In the early years there was a plan to build some shops in The Avenue near the old stables at the junction with Falmouth Avenue. This did not happen, but shops were included in the Cavendish Road development. According to Renee Weller:

> Trant and Grundy had a shop on the corner of Selwyn Avenue and Cavendish Road. It was a grocers shop, and in the '30s, you see, people didn't necessarily *go* shopping. Once a week the tradesmen would call at the house, and enquire what groceries one wanted, and then you gave them the list and they delivered the groceries to you, so you didn't have to carry large baskets of groceries. The greengrocer's and the baker's carts used to come round so you could get vegetables and fruit, and the cats' meat man used to come round with a barrow.

In the late 1920s a few shops appeared on both sides of the railway at Wadham Bridge. Mr Few, a visiting builder from Wanstead, mentioned that his uncle, Mr Gawn, was the butcher in one of the shops at the end of Winchester Road for five or six years, and like many other butchers of the time he made the sausages which were sold in his shop. Two doors away, De Rosa's fish and chip shop had been in business for about 20 years.

When the new estate around Oak Hill Crescent was built in the 1930s a row of little provision shops was erected opposite the *Royal Oak*. These were so useful that a newcomer to Hollywood Way, Woodford Green in the 1960s recalled that for the first two years she did not realise there were more shops in Highams Park!

Competition from large supermarkets, loss of trade from factory workers and high rents after leases expire have all led to the closure of many shops. Restaurants and 'take-aways' have sprung up and cash points now replace two banks. However, an interesting addition to the area has been *The Guardian*, the local newspaper, which moved from Fulbourne Road into new premises in Larkshall Road.

Since 1981, Cyril J. Moody has made a weekly visit to Highams Park with his van-load of fresh fish for 20 years.

> I was made redundant and so I fitted out my van properly and thought Chingford looked a nice place to try so I bought £50 worth of fish from Grimsby and I went home with £70. I tried bringing more fish and sold that! Highams Park is a lovely little place with nice people but I notice that a lot of the shops have gone.

Mrs Maria Salamonowicz remembered a time when there were four butchers' shops.

> All the shops were doing well and Highams Park was really alive. It was lovely. There was Mr Pruim's shoe shop, a lovely Delicatessen shop in Hale End Road, a big Cafeteria and a Jeweller. Which shops do I miss? That's a good question. Every one!

11

Pleasures and Pastimes

Until the 1960s there were several cinemas and swimming pools in the area. Church halls are still used for playgroups and various societies, but churches and the Halex factory used to run sports and social clubs which provided people with many ways of enjoying their spare time.

Jeanne May (who lived in Hale End Road) remembered a carefree childhood before and during the First World War:

> We had a big garden, but behind us there were allotments and then easy access to the Forest and we had absolutely no fear of wandering around in the Forest and we spent a lot of time there. It was absolute, complete freedom and we had no fear of being attacked or anything like that, and our mother had no fear for us. We might quarrel a bit with one or two children who came from some distance but we had all sorts of families who lived round us as we grew up, and they stayed until the children married.

Cliff Payling said that Jeanne's brother, Ian, was able to defend himself.

> Although he was small, Ian was a lively, boisterous boy, who was not frightened to use his fists on occasions. He was very much an open-air boy who loved to be in the garden, the street or the Forest. After his first day at Selwyn Infants' School he announced that he was not going any more as there were no trees to climb in the playground!
>
> During this period houses in Frinton Drive and part of Hale End Road were built and I can recall joining Ian and his friends in exploring the site and climbing in and out of the partly built buildings. On one occasion we were spotted by the night watchman. I was trapped in a spot from which I found it difficult to escape and I was the last to flee from the irate, red-faced old man.

Jeanne May recalled:

> We children knew a man, who lived in a holly bush, as 'Peggy Wooden Leg'. He had a wooden stump for a leg and we were a bit scared of him when we were young, but there was nothing *wrong* with him: he wouldn't harm us.

Frank Payling also remembered 'Peggy'.

> He was about when we were children up to about 1930. He was a bit of an outcast, you see – we weren't encouraged to talk to him. He had a beard but he was quite an upright figure – he certainly didn't look like a tramp but he lived rough. His leg looked as if it had been sawn off a table!

A few years ago *Essex Countryside* featured two pages of readers' letters about Peggy Wooden Leg, with a photograph of this lonely but well-known man. He was named as either Reynolds or William Reeves, and only became abusive if children taunted him with his nickname. Most people described him as well-spoken, with a soldierly bearing, and two possible reasons for the loss of his leg were the Boer War or blood poisoning after a rusty nail spiked his leg as he broke a piece of wood over his knee.

Hilda Oliver explained how early 'settlers' in Highams Park amused themselves:

> My brother was already born when my parents came here from Clapton in 1905, but my sister, Maude, and I were born in Highams Park. It was a new sort of village and when they came our house was the last but one house in the road.
>
> We had a billiard table in the front room at home, but it was a bit of a nuisance because there was furniture around it and a tall piano, so you couldn't really sit in the room or you would get a cue in your eye! My father always played billiards, my brother played when he was home, my sister and I played, and we had friends in, who played: we spent hours there! Maude played the piano. She was good – she played at the school as well, because she was a teacher.

The Ruda Family of 'Sky Peals'

In 1903 the local *Guardian* newspaper printed an enthusiastic report of a typical concert of the time, given by amateur musicians at All Saints' Institute at Hale End (the Tin Hall). Maurice Ruda, of Sky Peals House, was a very popular performer.

94 *Walter Horace Oliver in the early 1900s. (Little boys wore frocks and long hair until they were about five years old.) This house in Beech Hall Road was built in 1906. There was a piano and a full-sized billiards table in the front room!*

> The Institute gave the first concert of their season, on Monday evening, and in spite of the awful weather it proved a decided success, there being a record audience. The rain came down in such torrents that it almost drowned the third item, a recitation by Miss Colson Phillips.

(The Institute was built of corrugated iron!) The programme continued with pianoforte duets played by Mrs Haw and Miss Agnes Jackson, ARCM, and songs and recitations from Miss Maude Gadsdon, Mr Edwards Davies and Miss Lottie Le Pla.

Unfortunately, Miss Lottie Le Pla and Mr Edwards Davies were suffering from colds, but their songs were, nevertheless, highly appreciated. Mr Fred Heath was in fine form; his humorous songs were full of go, and provided hearty laughter. Mons. Maurice Ruda performed (and encored) twice and seems to have excited the audience so much that when he performed for the third time, the reporter wrote, 'Mons. Maurice Ruda was undoubtedly at his best: the audience fairly rose at him, and each time he played, he met with deafening applause.' In the interval the Rev. Theodore J. Parkes, vicar of St Peter's, who was in the chair, thanked the artistes for their very kind assistance and, in giving the items for the forthcoming fortnightly lectures arranged by the Institute Committee, advised the audience to forthwith become members and so swell its numbers from 80 to 150 or so.

95 *In 1911, Oscar Watling built the 'Electric Theatre' in Hale End Road. It was designed by W.A. Lewis, A.R.I.B.A. In 1928, it was sold to 'Regal Cinema', Highams Park, Ltd (licensed to J. Davis), and it was renamed 'The Regal'. In 1935, structural alterations were made to the front entrance and inside the building, and it was used as a cinema until 8 September 1963, opening as a Bingo Club a few days later. But to meet popular demand, films were shown again – with Bingo on Fridays only. Then films were shown seven days a week but by 1970 they were reduced to matinees and Sunday films. The cinema closed in 1971 and the building is now divided into a Snooker Hall and a Social Club.*

Frank Payling remembered the house where Mr Ruda lived:

Sky Peals stood practically in the Forest and we could see the house from our garden in Hale End Road. (There was just a field behind us.) When the Ruda family were there it became a 'Retreat', and Jewish people would come at weekends: they came up what used to be known as Jews Alley in carriages. That's called Forest Mount Road now.

At the top of the garden we had a plum tree, and below the tree we had a shed. Well, some young Jewish men were admiring these plums, and my brother John (being very generous) decided that it was only right that they should have some. He got up on the shed, and he was picking them up and *showering* them with plums, until my mother discovered what he was doing and stopped him – otherwise he would have stripped the tree completely!

Will Hebbard knew the Ruda family well:

There were ten sons and two daughters there and at one period quite a number were married and living in Highams Park. The large house was used every weekend for Jews to come down from Wentworth Street and Brick Lane. Mr Ruda (who was, I believe, a Russian Jew) fetched them from the station in a wagon, driven by Nattie, about 12 at a time, to have a day out.

My mother sold some art needlework to Eva, and in 1913, when she was married at Sky Peals, we were invited. The bride reclined in all her glory on a chaise longue and received everyone on arrival, and there was loads of food at all times. The ceremony was under a canopy in the grounds with all male heads covered and the groom broke a glass underfoot during the ceremony.

We were also invited to see the baby immediately after circumcision, when literally everyone came to congratulate the parents. Eva's new surname was Schtitzer [or Stitzer] but as no one could get their tongue round it this became Stitcher, which became well-known as the name of one of the first self-service grocers.

Douglas Woolf also remembered Sky Peals:

It was a nice house, built of brick with large rooms and a big conservatory, and there was a large orchard. One daughter married David Stitcher, who was a very prominent member of St John Ambulance, Number 30 Division. They were in the Leather business, and lived at 49 The Avenue, Highams Park.

His brother, Barney Stitcher, was Stitcher's Stores provision shops, which started at *Bakers Arms*, and there was a Stitcher's cut-price grocer on the other side of the line in Winchester Road in Highams Park.

Sid Marchant went to Selwyn Avenue School with Len and Mickey Ruda. (Abraham, Miriam, Higham, Golda and Nathaniel's names are also on the school registers.) Sid was a very good athlete and played tennis regularly until 1997, when he was well into his eighties. He remembered how his sporting career began on a special day at Sky Peals house:

> Opposite Highams Park Congregational Church (Malvern Avenue) were two tennis courts and I used to go and climb the elm trees there and look down and watch them play tennis. My friend and I were not allowed on the courts, so we marked a court out in the road and tied a piece of string across – and that's where we used to try to play tennis!
>
> Well, one day during our holidays we were on the tennis courts, and along came Miss Muddiman who told us to 'Get off!', so we did. We walked up the alley (which is now Forest Mount Road) and standing at the gates of Sky Peals House was Mr Stitcher, and he asked if we boys played tennis?

'Oh, yes, sir!'

'Well', he said, 'I have a court in my garden, which I have just cut and marked out, and my friend was supposed to come and give me a game, and he hasn't turned up. Could you come in, and play me a game?' Oh yes! so in we went, and I played him. And I beat him, and he wanted to know where I played, and I told him that we played on the road. He said that if we would like to come up there during our holidays and cut the grass and mark the court, we could play whenever we liked, but with one condition – we must *not* touch the fruit on the trees! We could pick up the windfalls, but we mustn't pick the fruit! So, every day during the holidays, we were up there playing tennis – and enjoying the fruit!

I enjoyed playing tennis and just after the war, about 1947, I played at Aldersbrook, and won the singles there for three years. Later I was asked to play doubles at Wimbledon, as a veteran. We had a letter, asking if we'd compete, but when we got there it had been raining and was so wet that we couldn't play on the ground! They took us in a car to 'Queens', beautiful dressing rooms, and we played a doubles match at Queens and won the match, so in the afternoon it was back to Wimbledon, and we played on the lovely grass, but unfortunately the other side were the winners, so we went out.

Mrs Edith Upton remembered the sad end of Sky Peals House, 'The Rudas' house had a bad fire one year in the summertime; it was before I was married in 1932'.

The Cinema

Will Hebbard recalls, 'When the Highams Park Electric Theatre was opened in 1911, with celebrations laid on by "Wee Georgie Wood", I was there!' The opening night was on April Fools' Day in 1911, and an account in the *Walthamstow Guardian* gave a full description of the building, promising that future programmes would provide 'a most refined form of entertainment, both interesting and instructive' for audiences of up to 550 people. Edith Upton remembered:

> The Electric Theatre in Highams Park had a very nice entrance, and in the foyer there were pictures of the old Film Stars all the way round, and the ticket office was at the back wall. On either side were curtains, and when you went through them you were actually in the cinema (but we didn't queue in those days, we just pushed and shoved!). Somebody played the piano for the silent films. (My cousin, Doris Lane, played the piano in a cinema called the Carlton, in the High Street, Walthamstow. Her father was Arthur Lane.)

Frank Payling also enjoyed what used to be known as 'the pictures':

> The Regal was always known as the 'Electric Cinema'. I went there to the 'Tuppenny Rush', and we used to get half a pound of locust beans and chew them in the cinema. (It's the bean from the carob tree, and they feed it to cattle! It's got almost a liquorice taste and must be quite nutritious to eat.) Occasionally we would get half a pomegranate for a ha'penny.

Stan Batson moved to Highams Park a year after the name of the 'Electric Theatre' changed to the 'Regal'.

> The cinema was built on the corner of Beech Hall Road and Hale End Road, with some very fine columns going up in front of it, something like the cinema on the junction of Forest Road and Hoe Street, which had very similar semi-circular colonnades on the front, and at one time I remember there was a commissionaire, who used to stand out in his blue uniform with gold braid on the front, controlling the kids for the 'Tuppenny Rush'. Inside there were big columns holding up the roof and the balcony, and if you went in one of the fivepenny seats, you had to make sure you didn't get a seat behind one of the columns! When we were kids we'd go down to the cinema on a Saturday morning or early afternoon at the 'Tuppenny Rush' and we'd sit on forms at the front and watch the silent film.

Later on, of course, the Regal was taken over by the Brooke-Green family. There were two brothers, and they rebuilt the Regal cinema with its present frontage, got rid of the old columns outside and completely refurbished the interior, and installed an electric organ then proudly announced, 'R. Brooke-Green – on the Mighty Wurlitzer!' Their old mum used to sit in the Pay-Box, and R. Brooke-Green ran that cinema.

96 *Now showing … 1944.*

In fact, 'the Mighty Wurlitzer' was a rare and wonderful 'Rutt Theatre Organ', a three-manual 'Kinema Organ' with ten ranks of pipes plus an extensive percussion section, by K. Spurden Rutt of Leyton, and it can still be heard at the St Alban's Organ Museum, which is administered by the St Albans Musical Museum Society. The BBC has broadcast recordings of performances given by leading organists on the 'Rutt Theatre Organ', and live performances are regular features of the Museum, which houses many mechanical musical instruments and other famous organs (including a 'Mighty Wurlitzer').

Mrs Jan Hawkins wrote in *The Village* in June 1999 that just after the war her grandparents, Charles and Lilian Florence Luya, and her Aunt Jess all came to live in Hale End Road. During the war Charles Luya had been in the ARP, but he worked as a lamp-lighter and even after the change from oil and gas lighting he was still employed to switch on street lights up to 1967.

> My grandmother Lilian, known to most as 'Queenie', was the manageress of the Regal cinema for many years, and her son David was projectionist for some years too. Keeping it in the family, I occasionally 'usheretted' and often cleaned! When the cinema was converted to a Bingo Hall, my grandmother ran the tea bar and called the winners' numbers out. Many a Saturday afternoon found me making cheese and ham rolls for the evening supplies.

Stan Batson remembered:

> In the cinemas they used to have stage shows, and in later years we became very keen on cinemas and we used to go at least once a week – at least! It only cost a few coppers. We went to the Palace in High Street, Walthamstow, and you'd sit on kind of stone steps up in 'the gods'. The other cinema we used to go to was the *Crown* in Wood Street.

The Gym Clubs and other Activities run by Local Churches

Jeanne May was full of praise for the various church activities. Some had tennis courts and ramblers' groups, and gym clubs were very popular before the war.

97   *The Winchester Road Gym Club for Girls (1926) was held at the Methodist Church Hall.*

At the Malvern Avenue Congregational Church we used to call the Gymnastics Club
'Gym', and once a year we had the Displays and they were very good. There was one
at the Methodist Church, Winchester Road as well. (Now, *they* were quite famous.) My
eldest sister, Kath, was very good and stayed in our Gym Club long enough to win all
the senior awards.

We had medals – an 'All-round' medal, and then there would be something for
Drill and Apparatus – and when you had your Display, you pinned them all on!

Nothing was paid for by anybody but ourselves. It was only coppers (pennies and
halfpennies), but of course coppers were worth quite a lot of money to big families.

Edith Upton taught at the Methodist Church Gym Club at Winchester Road in the
1920s, and she had kept photographs of the girls:

You don't get Gym Classes as big as this nowadays, do you? I think there were 120
members in the Gym Club, and at one time I had 80 in my own class. I had 50 juniors,
aged 6, 7 and 8, and I had 30 'Tiny Tots', from 4-5 years old. Some of the girls would
be 25 years old, and some of them stayed until they were 30.

Hilda Hunt took the Intermediates, and she was the daughter of Mr Hunt, the
dentist who had a practice in The Avenue up the steps. Gladys Woolford's sister, Ethel,
was a very good pianist and played the Sunday School hymns for years and years, but
I don't think Ethel liked gymnastics. Other girls were Violet Huskinson of Beech Hall
Road, the Moss sisters, Ivy and Eva, who lived in Haldan Road, and Ivy Cousins, who
lived up the hill in Winchester Road and married one of the Silvester family.

I helped Miss Wilkinson to run the Gym Club classes, but I stopped working for her
when I got married in 1932. Miss Wilkinson was a gymnast long before she started the
Gym Classes in 1915, when I was about eight, but as the war was drawing to a close she
got really enthusiastic. Highams Park was developing so rapidly, and all these girls were
most anxious to join.

Miss Wilkinson lived in Winchester Road and ran the classes until war broke out
again in 1939. In those days she was a great worker in Highams Park. I know she was
employed at the Halex factory but wanted to take up nursing, so she became their first
aid lady and was in charge of the First Aid Department. She had to give up because
of her heart in later years and, unhappily, she did die quite young from heart trouble.

The lady who took over from her was Edith Moss.

We all wore a little silver badge engraved with 'WGC' and we had very nice plain uniforms – a tunic with three pleats, back and front, and a white blouse, and if you had long hair a black bow. We wore plimsolls – white ones and white socks for the 'Tiny Tots', and the rest of us had black plimsolls and black stockings. But for the dancing parts we would dress up as Japanese girls, or fairies, or farmers.

Once a year there was a big Display, and there were three days for that Display and I can assure you every day was always sold out, and we used to have people standing to see! The mothers were very enthusiastic and they used to love to dress their children up. First of all it was held in a tiny hall at the back of the church, but then we got the new Memorial Hall. The Church Sunday School was so good and so big that we all had a separate classroom, but it was all partitions and that had to be taken down – quite hard work, but the men helped as well, and the people sat around leaving us a very good hall (and of course it still is a very good hall).

We had competitions and medals and we had a large collection of cups, and there was a board in the Winchester Road Memorial Hall with all our names engraved on it, and it was there for years. I think when they started the Brownies, and that sort of thing, the Gymnastic Club started thinning out, and only a few years ago a lady who was running the Brownies said to me that she wondered what had happened to that lovely board that used to hang in the Memorial Hall. Nobody knows.

Mrs Peacock used to come along and play the piano sometimes. Her husband was a printer in Highams Park. We had the Band of Hope up at this same church, every Monday evening, and Mrs Tracey, Grace's mother, was a wonderful lady who was splendid at getting up concerts. She was such a good actress herself, and, of course, I was always in her concerts and her plays.

Mrs Evelyn Stevens lived in Coolgardie Avenue in the 1940s.

I was never allowed to play in the street, and my friend Barbara Jeffries thought that I was an absolute snob – because *she* used to play hopscotch! Then we went to the same school, William Morris, and we got friendly and that led to me joining the Girls' Life Brigade. Her mother was the captain of the GLB at the Baptist Church at Cavendish Road, and we had the most wonderful young life down there. That church was so thriving, you wouldn't believe it! It was absolutely full up every Sunday night because you were expected to go to church, but we went because we enjoyed it.

The best thing about that church was the 'squash' every Sunday night, when all the young people under the age of 18 used to go to various people's houses. One of the best 'squashes' was at the Harrisons. John Harrison, 'The Garden Shop' man, and his wife were very nice and they lived in Gordon Avenue. He was a very, very big man and used to run 'Christian Endeavour' for the young people. This was during the war, when there was nothing going on for youngsters at all, so these 'squashes' were fantastic, and on a Saturday morning about twenty of us from the church would go rambling in the Forest.

Jane F. Matthews was a young girl in the East End of London before the First World War:

The 'Monkey Parade', we used to call it – along the Mile End Road to Bow Bridge. We used to walk up and down there, the boys and the girls, and then you used to go up the side-turnings and do your courting! We used to go on the horse-buses on outings from St Benet's Church.

Dad used to send us to church, and I didn't like church and I used to ask if we could go to the Assembly Hall, but he said we had to go to church because we were Church of England! The Assembly Hall was towards Whitechapel more and they used to hold big meetings there. We liked it better, because we could sing hymns there – nice hymns. In church it was all so solemn. You know, I used to stand and shiver in church!

12

A Growing Community

Until about 25 years ago a flock of green ring-necked parakeets lived for several years in the Highams Park, near the lake. No-one knew where they had come from but they were an exotic addition to the wildlife of the Forest and wildfowl on the lake and they visited the well-kept gardens of local people for food. (It may have been coincidental, but when Julia and Herbert Fossey, whose business was in peanuts, moved away, so did the parakeets.)

Irene Owen talked about keeping allotments, which were very popular.

> My two cousins used to play on the field by the Ching at the back of my uncle's house (where mum lived later on), and it wasn't allotments then. That must have been a wartime thing. There were allotments right through [The Slip] at the back of Gordon Avenue, and it used to look really nice. Everybody was very keen, and looked after their allotments – and I used to supply the tea over the wall to Uncle George, Jerry, Conrad and anybody else that was standing around!

Evelyn Stevens remembered the electricity pylons and cables which used to cross over Hale End Road by the Ching, then went above the allotments to her garden in Woodford Green.

> We would never have bought our ground if it hadn't been for the pylon. Nobody wanted to move there, but Eddie had lived by the pylon at the bottom of Beech Hall Crescent. It happened all of a sudden really – the pylons disappeared. Actually, I nearly got decapitated when they took them down, because they forgot to warn anybody, and I actually walked out in the garden as one of the cables fell! It was as thick as my arm, and it was only about six inches from me!

Near the allotments is Hale End Horticultural Society's 'hut', which opens to sell gardening supplies to members. The Society began in 1890 with a meeting at the 'Tin Hall', Malvern Avenue Congregational Church. Win Marchant said that the first shows were held in a marquee in the adjoining field, surrounded by grazing cows. She wrote down some other memories of her Hale End childhood in the booklet, *One Hundred Years of Horticulture*, published in 1990 by the Horticultural Society. Win's father, William Bradley, the glass craftsman, was an inaugural member of the Society, and Win described his gardening clothes:

> He wore cast-off working clothes of braced trousers, baggy at the knees, shirt sleeves rolled up above the elbows, a cloth cap and lace-up boots. Father's buddies early on were Jim Eastwell, the wheelwright of Wadham Road, whose son, George, was also a member of long standing, and George (?) Everitt of Handsworth Avenue.

Frank Payling continued to work in the garden that his father had begun more than a hundred years before:

My father won a medal in 1901 for the Hale End Horticultural Society, and the medal reads: 'Hale End Horticultural Society, First Championship Prize – the top prize of the annual event – won in 1901 by Mr Henry Payling'. He was a very keen gardener of fruit and vegetables and he grew a vine in a very large hot-house in the garden. It required to be heated for three months of the year, and it was my job to keep the fire in the coke boiler in till my father came home in the evening. This vine was a black Hamburg grape, the same grape as the one at Hampton Court, and my father would leave the bunches on until the leaves fell off (and when you taste these grapes you realise what a good flavour they have).

Every year he would lend a marrow to the Harvest Festival at Malvern Avenue Congregational Church, and he would leave one marrow to grow really big – the idea being that it was cut up to make marrow jam. (It is flavoured with ginger, and a friend of mine once described this jam as 'heavenly'). Through him, I became a keen gardener, and carried on in the same garden. I'm a compulsive compost-maker, and this all stems from my first-hand knowledge, because I couldn't have been more than two years old when it was my job to sow my father's peas.

Every September my father would order a cart-load of 'good dung' (horse manure) from what was then Warrens, Highams Park, in the goods yard, the other side of the railway line, and it would arrive on a Saturday morning and they would leave a great big heap in the road outside the house. My brother and I would have to cart it in, take it up to the very top of the garden, then we had to tread it down! You can imagine what it smelled like, but it did have an effect on our vegetables!

After the First World War, in the early twenties, the Sky Peals Estate, which backed on to the top of our garden, was split up for allotments, and my father had one of these – and so did his neighbour. He grew some King Edward potatoes; and he dug a root up and the yield was so great that we got the scales out and it weighed five and a half pounds. His neighbour wouldn't believe it. Father told him to pick whichever root he liked, and we would dig it up and see what it was like. Well, this chap dug one up, got the scales out and it was seven and three quarter pounds! We found out that it had only been bettered once in the whole of Walthamstow – somebody had had eight and a quarter.

Hale End Library

Irene Owen worked at the Hale End Library, which began in 'Holly House' at the bottom of Castle Avenue. It was a double-fronted, two-storeyed house with a big faded-blue door in the porch reached by steps, and it had plastered walls painted in the same pale grey as several of the other large houses in Highams Park.

In 1943 I went to work at Hale End Library, which was then just a house with a big garden at the back. It was nothing like it is now! It had bluey-grey metal shelving, with heating pipes about six inches up, on top of the shelves; there were some at the bottom, but they all seemed to have 'blown', so the heat was on the top of the shelves and we were always cold! We used to go in of a morning in the winter time and the thermometer used to say 44°F, and we were perished!

Walthamstow Council had taken over the house and made it into a library in 1935. Part of the back wall had been removed and the Library had been built out into the garden, but in the year before I left they'd started to extend it sideways – it was still open to the public! I left in 1962 and they'd already been at it for about a year then. I think they finished the new building in 1963.

Drummond Clapp, FRIBA of White and Mileson, was the architect of Hale End Library. He also designed several blocks of flats in Highams Park, the Health Centre in Handsworth Avenue and the Selwyn Room and porch of All Saints Church in Castle Avenue. He described how the new library was built by retaining some of the old house on the left-hand side, and putting in new windows at the front to blend with the modern design of the new extension:

98   *'Denmark House' (11 Forest Rise, Walthamstow) was one of the smaller 'Salter's Buildings'. Sir John Salter, who had been Lord Mayor of London in 1740, was Chairman of the East India Company. 'My family rented Denmark House for a few years up to about 1935. My father and grandfather had a very happy time working together in the large garden and orchard behind the house, and Dad could walk out of the back gate to play cricket on the Walthamstow Cricket Ground.' (M.L. Dunhill)*

It was impressed upon his committee by the Borough Librarian [of Walthamstow] that the library should not be closed for or during the alterations and this governed the planning to the extent that it had to be designed to enable the work to be carried out in two stages … The even, artificial light distribution has been achieved with the use of a transparent suspended ceiling which, while masking the joint between new and old work, also conceals the services.

Mrs Owen described Hale End Library during the Second World War:

When I started work there were Mr Howard, who had come from the Central Library in Walthamstow, Joyce Cornish, Beryl Cowell, Joan Lacey (who lived in The Avenue) and myself. It was wartime, so Joyce went into the Wrens, Beryl went into one of the Ministries and Joan went into the Land Army! We were all taken on then as sort of 'temporary' staff, because the girls were being called up. They were just three years older than Eunice Clark, Marjorie Bacon and myself, the three who came to replace them, but of course at the end of the war they had to take the girls back again: they had promised to give them back their jobs.

After the war, Mr Howard returned to the Central Library and Mr Overal got his job back at Hale End Library and became Chief Librarian. Joyce worked at the library for about 23 years and I was there for 19 years, but Mr Howard stayed until he was about 66 years old.

We used to enjoy working there. I used to know *everybody* because the Library was absolutely *the* central place in Highams Park, where most people went.

The William Morris Hall, Walthamstow

My grandfather, Harry Grantham, enjoyed reading library books but he was also a good gardener and kept an allotments because at Upton-cum-Chalvey in Buckinghamshire, where he was born in 1875, growing your own vegetables and market gardening was the way of life. His father was a farrier who moved from the country to Islington, where he employed half a dozen blacksmiths to look after the wagon and cab horses from Kings Cross Station. Harry decided to work at the main GPO Sorting Office in London, but when he was promoted to Head Postman at Walthamstow Sorting Office in 1904 he and his wife moved into a newly built house at Higham Hill (quite near to where the first manor house of Higham Bensted had been).

Before the First World War Higham Hill was just a little village near Walthamstow, surrounded by cornfields. My grandparents kept goats for milking and grew their own fruit and vegetables, and Harry earned extra money for his family as a wedding photographer. (Some of his other photographs have been used in this book.) He was also a keen cyclist and won many trophies.

They joined the Socialist Democratic Federation Sunday School at the William Morris Hall in Somers Road, Walthamstow. Most of the members could agree about things like 'ridding society of capitalism' and were happy to embrace William Morris's ideal of 'Fellowship is Life', but very heated arguments arose as to how to achieve the ideals. All the arguing in the family put me off politics for life. When I was young I was sent to a conventional Sunday School at the United Reformed Church in Woodford Green, but I was fascinated by stories about the SDF Sunday School meetings for families, which included sports, music, drama, art and picnics at Yardley Hill in Chingford and in the Forest. Lively discussions used to follow lectures given by well-known Socialists such as Frances Evelyn, Lady Warwick, who was the last of the Maynard family, the lords of Toni Manor of Walthamstow. (Lady Warwick was also known to King Edward VII as 'Darling Daisy'.)

(Last year the interior of the William Morris Hall was redesigned and an imaginative Adventure Playground built in the yard behind the old building to be used as The Limes Community and Children's Centre, where families and their children with disabilities can join in various activities together.)

My grandmother ('Gertie') was a non-violent suffragette, and I was told she was one of the first women to stand as a candidate for the Walthamstow Council, albeit unsuccessfully. In the early 1930s the Grantham family moved from Higham Hill and, for a few years, rented 'Denmark House', one of Salter's Buildings in Forest Rise. They all loved that house and its large garden and in 1943 my grandparents came back from retirement in Somerset to live very near Hale End Library. Harry immediately began to 'dig for Victory' on a new allotment by the Ching and 'Gertie' joined extra-mural university classes, where Bessie Bottomley happened to be a lecturer. (Luckily they both loved reading as well as arguing.) Lord Bottomley had also attended the Socialist Sunday School:

> Yes, I used to take part, but in the drama part I was hopeless. They tried to enrol me, and then kicked me out! I wasn't a musician, although my father wanted me to be. The Countess of Warwick took a very great interest, and I met her – and at her house as well. Bess and I went, a group went out from Walthamstow, and George Lansbury was there. All the mothers were bringing their babies to sit on his lap! We used to have a Musical Festival at Lloyd Park and George Lansbury came to Walthamstow to open one of the festivals. He was a great character.

Warwick House at Little Easton near Great Dunmow was the Maynard family's house, and when Lady Warwick was living there many artefacts and documents of historical interest to Walthamstow were lost in a serious fire which destroyed most of the house. (For years the Creasey family worked hard to restore the gardens of Easton Lodge to their former glory and have opened them to the public, but the future of the whole

99 *Another of 'Salter's Buildings' in Forest Rise near St Peter's in-the-forest.*

estate is now threatened by new runways planned for Stansted Airport.) Lord Bottomley talked about some of his wife's work in Walthamstow:

> Bess was in the ILP (Independent Labour Party), which was separate to the Labour Party, and then she joined the Labour Party. She became a Councillor and a County Councillor, and was the Mayoress when I was the Mayor [of Walthamstow] in 1945, after the war. Bess represented Hoe Street Ward.

Highams Park wards divide the community very unsatisfactorily, and parts of the urban village are included in Woodford Green, Walthamstow and Chingford. All these areas are ideal parliamentary constituencies because of their nearness to London, and in the 20th century all of them attracted some real political heavyweights. A large bronze statue of Sir Winston Churchill stands on The Green near Woodford High Road, reminding people of his long association with the area. (The Hall of Woodford County High School was sometimes used for his public meetings.) He was the Conservative MP for Woodford from 1924-64 although when he was first elected, after a brief deviation to the Liberal Party, he was described as a 'Constitutionalist'. Clement Attlee (afterwards Lord Attlee, 1st Earl of Walthamstow), lived in Monkhams Avenue, Woodford before the war. In 1940 'Clem' Attlee was Privy Seal, and from 1942-5 he was Deputy Prime Minister of Churchill's War Cabinet. From 1945-51 he was Prime Minister of the Labour government which created the Welfare State, and from 1950-5 Clement Attlee was Member of Parliament for Walthamstow West.

Since then the well-known Conservatives Norman Tebbitt (now Lord Tebbitt) and Iain Duncan-Smith have both represented Chingford (and part of Highams Park) at Westminster. It has been said that the parents of another well-known politician, Denis Healey (who became Lord Healey), lived in Hollywood Way, Woodford Green, Essex.

Weekend and Sporting Activities

Alan Marshall spent his childhood in Highams Park:

> On a Sunday afternoon my brother and I were in our Sunday Best, and off we'd
> go, side by side in front of Mother and Father, out of Alma Avenue (we had lived
> in Cavendish Road before that) and along the parade of shops, down into Larkshall
> Road. The pavements were not then made up: it was just a single-carriageway. I used to
> balance on the little bit of wood that showed you the difference between the footpath
> and the carriageway.
>
> We'd go down to Ropers Farm, where the boys would be playing cricket, and Mr
> Roper senior would be getting all the cows in; they used to operate an ice-cream place
> there, and they made and sold their own ice-cream. That appealed to me, of course!

Hilda Oliver remembered the sports field and tennis courts at the Essex-boarded
Ropers Farm (Ink's Green Farm):

> Father hired a court and we had family games of tennis there. We used to go every
> weekend and if it was fine we would rush home from work, change, and go. It was
> lovely. We had a court right behind the farm house, and the rest used to be a cricket
> field and my brother played cricket there. The far end of the court was actually Larks
> Wood and you could see people walking through. There were some other tennis courts
> there – grass courts – but all the courts have gone now and Ropers Farm has been
> pulled down. Highams Park Cricket Club was actually on Ropers Farm, and there was
> a pavilion where we used to have our tea. Mrs Roper used to run the tea place.

Doug Insole recalled:

> The Highams Park Cricket Club played until about 1936 on Ropers Farm, or 'Inks
> Green Farm', off Larks Hall Road. 'Pa' Roper kept cattle and provided milk for many
> of those living in the district, delivering daily in a horse-drawn cart. There were four

100 *Highams Park Cricket Club, 1932 – a family affair. Standing from left: Frank Casement, Bernie Roper, (?), 'Pa' Welland, Roy Roper, Dick Wray, Stan Welland, Bill Crossley, Robin Roper. Seated: (?), Percy Roper, Charlie Roper (known as 'Pa', (?). The small boy was Doug Insole (aged six) who was the scorer (and grew up to be Captain of Essex County Cricket and was a high scorer of runs for England in Test matches.)*

Roper sons – Bernie, Percy, Roy and Robin – all of whom played for Highams Park
(Cricket Club), while their father umpired. I began scoring for the club in 1933, when
I was seven years old, and carried on when the club moved to Brookfield, off Oak Hill,
because the Roper land was bought by the LCC for housing development.

My family had moved in 1930 from Clapton to a newly built house on the Warboys
Estate in Coolgardie Avenue. Old man Warboys had made his money in the gold fields
of West Australia, and particularly at Coolgardie and Kalgoorlie. He had two sons, Roy
and Jack. The latter stayed with the construction/ development business and lived
in Warboys Crescent, in a large house built on land 'left over' when the allowable
number of houses had been built in the 1930s, until the 1970s.

Alan Marshall talked about Brookfield, the second ground used by the Highams Park
Cricket Club, which had the reputation of being one of the most attractive cricket
grounds in the country. It was in a woodland setting off Oak Hill and near to the
Ching, but during the war, the turf was dug up for allotments and afterwards, instead
of land being returned for recreation, council houses were built (Armstrong Avenue
and Alders Avenue in Woodford Green).

I remember the old cricket field, near Highams Park lake, when Wally Hammond, the
England player, was knocking about 360 (or one of those records), and although it was
at a cricket match here they were broadcasting it.

There's a small footpath leads off the allotments by that cricket field, and the Forest-
keeper's house used to be there. I remember that because during the war, I was over
there once, helping Father, and we had a daylight raid and he told me to dive for cover
because we could see 'Jerry', and we dived in the ditch and these bombs came down!

Jim Davis was full of praise for the field:

Before the war I used to go regularly to the Highams Park Cricket Club. It was a
delightful ground (where all that council estate has been built) – a *delightful* ground!
We used to be able to look down the lane at the bottom of Church Avenue and see
the cricket ground, and you knew if they were playing because you could look through
to the other side of the Ching, up the hill, where the estate is now. You walked down
there to 'Brookfield', and when you got to the top of Brookfield Path you turned
left. Where Alders Avenue is, it was just a track, and you walked straight down to the
cricket ground – into the forest. There was a small wooden pavilion and they used to
have deck-chairs. I loved cricket, and I used to go down there and sit in the ground. I
was never a member but I never used to get kicked out!

It was a lovely cricket pitch and I used to play about in the 'nets' with Doug Insole
and his brother Geoff Insole, who used to go over there when they were boys. It was a
shame it went. A lot of cricket pitches have gone – not only over there.

By 1930 the farms had been sold, but some fields were preserved as playing fields
and for many years the vigilance of members of the Essex branch of the National Playing
Fields Association ensured that Walthamstow fields were available for sporting activities,
but recently various commercial organisations have proved to be irresistible forces, and
many of the playing fields have been lost to supermarkets. According to Jeanne May:

As you go from Larkshall Road and Ink's Green to Ainslie Wood Road there is
another cricket field: that was the sports ground of the company called Caribonum.
The firm was in Leyton and I think it was something to do with typewriting ribbons.
The Council has it now and schools use it. [Waltham Forest Council has built a new
primary school on part of this playing field.] The name of the family that owned it was
Clarke and they lived in Loughton.

Sid Marchant also played football well:

I am the only founder-member left now of the Hale End Athletic Football Club, which
we formed in 1928, and I was Treasurer until 1939 when I joined the Navy. So many
people wanted to join that by the time the war came there were three teams which

101 *Hale End Athletic Football Club's team of 1936, wearing their claret and blue kit. Back row: Norman Clark, Sid Marchant, Jackie Gaskill, Stovel, Jack Bell, Doug Coliver. Front row: Eddie Chadwick (Trainer), Nat Greenleas(f), Johnny Logan, Les Prime (Captain), Les Marchant, Bill Goldsworthy, Mr Prime.*

played in the Walthamstow District League. Now we have four teams and they play at the Wadham Lodge and Jubilee Grounds.

For our first game of football in 1928 we rented the end field, which ran parallel with Brookfield Path, for £5 a year from Mrs Glanfield's nephew. Of course, the ball often used to go in the pond up there, and we used to fish it out, and on Saturday mornings we had to go round with our buckets and spades to remove the cow pats before we played! Then we played on the field where Handsworth Avenue School is now.

Down there, where the flats are now, was the big old house, the 'Manor House', and on Tuesday evenings (in about 1935), after we had practised, we went into that house, and Mrs Stovil had a flat there, a large room and a kitchen with a black kitchen-range, with kettles all steaming away. We used to have a wash with hot water, and she made tea for us.

Musical Societies

Frank Payling recalled:

When I was about seven or eight, I fell in love with Miss Martin at Selwyn Avenue School, and I can still hear her playing Offenbach's 'Barcarole', from the *Tales of Hoffman*. I remember hearing the man who came round playing his gramophone for

money. I don't know where he came from but he'd come about once a week, and he
had the gramophone in a perambulator!

Gerald Verrier was also interested in music and for many years he helped run a very
popular Waltham Forest Music Society, which still meets in Highams Park. (It has now
been re-named the 'Forest Recorded Music Society'.) Mr Harry Waterman, one of the
founder-members and the Vice-Chairman of the Waltham Forest Gramophone Society
for many years, wrote about the history of the society in 1975. On 30 November 1956
the inaugural meeting was held at the Walthamstow Educational Centre (known as 'The
Settlement'), at the instigation of Mr John Howes of the Walthamstow Public Library.
About thirty people were present, and a subscription was fixed at 10s. per annum:

> In the summer recess of 1964, while The Settlement was closed, fire destroyed part
> of the building and we were informed that we would be out of a home. As I was the
> possessor of a large lounge, some reasonably good equipment and an accommodating
> wife, I suggested that we should continue our fortnightly meetings at my house, *pro tem*.
> This 'temporary arrangement', with an average of ten members, lasted in fact for four
> years until February 1968, when I moved house.
>
> In the meantime, with the amalgamation of the London Boroughs of Walthamstow,
> Chingford and Highams Park, Leyton and Leytonstone under the title of Waltham
> Forest (1965), and the formation of Waltham Forest Libraries Music Club, we were
> approached in the summer of 1968 with the offer of a room at Highams Park Library,
> which is the Hale End Library.

(By the end of June 1969 there were 64 members.)
   Gerald Verrier was chairman from 1971:

> I joined at the time when Harry Waterman opened his house for us to enjoy music
> and a chat there, and we used to have some very pleasurable evenings. When we met
> at the Library in 1968, Philip Folkard, who was the Registrar of the Borough for many
> years, was the Chairman and he used to put on the programme most evenings. He
> had made up an amplifier, from the chassis right the way through to the valves, and
> he and Harry knocked up a pick-up to play the records on a turntable, which they had
> bought, and there was one speaker, which Philip provided.
>
> Then we bought our own 'Quad' equipment, and our membership increased to
> nearly 90 at one time, and we were going 'great guns' with so many people there in
> the Library that Fire Regulations became involved and, reluctantly, we had to move.
> Fortunately we found the hall of the Methodist Church in Handsworth Avenue. Again
> the membership jumped up, because the size of the hall was greater than that of the
> Library, and we didn't have that spiral staircase which our elderly members had found
> very difficult to manage, particularly Miss Macropoulas. If there had been a fire at the
> Library, we would have been roasted before she got down, for sure!

Edith Upton recalls:

> Miss Aglaia Macropoulas, known as 'Mac', was Greek in origin, although I am not sure
> if she was born in Greece, but she came to Highams Park in 1911 and lived in Hale
> End Road, in one of those biggish houses. 'Mac' belonged to the Gramophone Club
> and was interested in the Antiquarian Society. She went into the St Francis Nursing
> Home, in Falmouth Avenue, and she was nearly 91 years old when she died in March
> 1994.

Gerald Verrier talked about various members of the society:

> There are other people, like Les Woodward of Forest Glade, and Frank Payling, who
> was the Secretary of the Club for some 21 years. Arthur Hemmings was a faithful
> supporter of the Club for over 20 years. Ted Wood used to come, although he was very
> deaf. He loved to listen to music on records, and to hear the music in stereo: he had
> bought himself another hearing-aid, so he had two, one in each ear! How about that
> for dedication? Derrick Curl was another founder-member and a real help in every

way. He donated so much to the club, including the speakers and the machine we use for a recording of the evening, so that people who are not well can hear it too.

Alan Everson was another member who dipped into his own huge library of recordings to entertain the society. His knowledge of musical works and musicians was so extensive that he used to write the programme notes for performances at Walthamstow Assembly Hall by the Forest Philharmonic Orchestra.

Mrs Jeanne May remembers:

> I produced for the Highams Park Operatic Society. It had started really with the Bible Class girls, who were taught by Doris Smith at the Methodist Church, and they performed at Winchester Road in the old Memorial Hall. I joined in the first production after the war when the society had been going for 21 years. We used the South West Essex Technical College, and an off-shoot of our society became the 'Forest Operatic Society'. Doris Smith ran the Highams Park Operatic Society. Her husband, George Smith, was the Producer and Musical Director. Kathleen Burke was the leading lady for many years (and her sister, Dora, also performed). Pat Lynch, who lived in Beech Hall Road, was a marvellous bass-baritone.
>
> The Walthamstow Operatic Society gave performances at St Saviour's before the war, and Derrick Curl said he was pretty certain they used to perform at the Walthamstow Baths, but after the war I don't think the Walthamstow Operatic Society came into being again. I remember Lettie Cooke singing the main lead, 'Yum Yum', in a performance of *The Mikado*. She was lovely, and she sang very well. Yes, she was a beautiful soprano.

Lettie Cooke, LRAM, ARCM taught in Leyton from 1925-35 and returned to part-time teaching after the war as Mrs Grantham, first at Mayville School in Leyton and then at Woodford Green Primary School.

Arthur Hemmings and his wife, Grace Hemmings, who taught music in the 1950s to '60s at the Warwick Secondary Modern School for Girls in Brook Road, Walthamstow, lived in Forest Glade, Highams Park:

> Our house was built in 1934 but we did not buy it until 1947. Maud and Fred Elliott lived next door, and they were very good neighbours, very kind. We used to go in there alternate weeks for bridge, you know – at the weekend. Jolly nice they were. We played bridge, and Grace played the piano, and a friend of hers called Eric Kember played duets with her. His wife and I used to sing songs like 'Trees,' and 'Boots, boots, boots', songs like that. We always had plenty to do.
>
> We went to concerts at Lloyd Park, and plays: rep companies used to come down there. Grace belonged to the Westminster Choral Society, and they used to meet every month and had shows there, with different people taking part, and she took part in the 'Choir of 1000' with Sir Henry Wood at Alexandra Palace.
>
> Cycling as well as walking was lovely in those days. There were nice roads, d'you see, and there wasn't the traffic about. And we used to like to swim in those days.

Swimming Pools

Swimming was a very popular pastime in Highams Park. There were so many pools. Walthamstow Baths at the top of High Street and the Leyton Baths at the *Bakers Arms* were open all the year, and there were three open-air pools nearby. Whipps Cross Lido was a short bus ride away and, in its forest setting, was a beautiful place to swim, and the Kingfishers' Pool was delightful, but best of all was Larkswood, originally called 'The Chingford Lido'.

Frances Bowler's favourite pool was the Kingfishers' Pool in Oak Hill, Woodford Green, known locally as 'The Kingfisher'. 'There was a lovely house where the Kingfisher Pool was, a very nice house, then it was pulled down and they built the Pool.' The

102 *This swimming pool was in Oak Hill (picture c.1939). 'The Kingfishers' Pool' building was white and the front part had arches and I think that led into the main Club. You actually went in at the side if you were a swimmer.' (J.A. Bocking)*

house was 'Forest Lodge'. This was opposite 'Forest Cottage', which 'Mrs Ball bought from the pig man and served Teas, overlooking the pond':

> The swimming pool was so near to us, and we had one or two good summers when we almost *lived* there! It was very, very good. I remember swimming there, great fun, and we had dances there! (Then they licensed it and it wasn't so good.)

Jennifer Bocking recalls:

> The Kingfisher was an open-air pool which opened in May and closed in September. I used to get season tickets and I was up there as much as possible in the summer. I didn't belong to the Kingfisher Club. That wasn't actually a swimming club but a social club. I was too young anyway, but when I was at college they started up a swimming club and they used to swim for charity, giving demonstrations of formation swimming. I went up there during the summer vacation and was asked if I would like to join. If I remember correctly, a gentleman called Frank Letchford organised us and ran the team. He wasn't at The Kingfisher all that long, but he was really responsible for us.
>
> We used to give shows and were known as 'The Voyagers'. We travelled to pools where they thought we might be able to raise money for charities and we swam in indoor pools quite a bit too, because we'd give demonstrations at any time of year. One particular routine that I used to love doing was called 'Seahorses', when we wore horses' heads! One day, in about 1956-7, the *Evening News* heard about us and came down and took some photographs of us sitting around the edge of the fountain, all wearing identical costumes so that we looked like a team.
>
> The deep end was nearest the building, and at the other end was a big fountain. The water cascaded on to a little shelf, splashed down to a bigger shelf, and then trickled down steps into the shallow end of the pool. The changing cubicles were upstairs and were fairly open, which could be tricky if the weather turned nasty!
>
> The Kingfisher was within a couple of minutes of home really and it was lovely to have somewhere like that so near that you could go to it on a hot summer's day.

103   *'The pool was quite big and at the shallow end, which was the farthest away from the building, it was beautifully surrounded by the forest trees – you could see them all the way round, which was nice.' (J.A. Bocking)*

There was a ballroom at the side, which the Kingfisher Social Club and local groups (like the Young Conservatives) used for dances. A bomb fell on it during the war. Facing the building from Oak Hill, it would have been on the right-hand side, roughly where the car park of the motel is now. I know the pool was going strong in the '50s and it was there in the '60s, but it deteriorated after that and then they let it go to rack and ruin.

Dances

Jennifer also went to dancing classes when she was a child:

Miss Eileen Storey ran a dancing school and all the local children used to go to it in the Roberts Hall, near Wadham Bridge.

Mrs Matthews remembered what dancing was like before 1914:

At first I wasn't allowed out! I had to be in by 10, then half past 10. I mustn't be a minute later! Then I used to go dancing at Poplar Town Hall. We danced the Lancers and Quadrilles a lot, Set Dancing, and then the 'One-step', as they used to call it in those days.
Later on my husband used to run the Police Dances at the People's Palace.

Irene Owen went to the dances and has enjoyed ballroom dancing ever since:

My father used to MC the dances. I used to go but not every week, just occasionally, and there would be dances in the Police Club Hall at East India Dock. I started dancing at Handsworth School, Friday evenings at Youth Club Dances, and then we graduated to the Tech, and then there was the Assembly Hall and Leyton Baths, the Royal, Tottenham, the Majestic, Woodford, and the Palais, Ilford. You just picked it up, and it's only now, in our 'ripe-old-age', that we're going to Dancing School to learn the steps properly!

The Scouting and Guides Movement

Joy Gailer was the Guide Leader at All Saints Church, Highams Park, until she became Assistant District Commissioner for the Guides. She has also taught drama classes at the Church Hall for a very long time.

Frank Payling remembered his scouting days:

When we were in the Boy Scouts we once camped above Chingford Lido, and you could literally count the number of houses you could see on two fingers! That would be in about 1927. Look at it now! Compared with North Chingford, South Chingford is quite modern. It was developed in the late '20s to early '30s.

I was one of the founder members of the 2nd Highams Park Scout Troop, at the Congregational Church. Mr Skippings was the Scout Master – he was an ex-First World War Army officer – a very nice chap, and he formed the troop, and it had about four patrols, and I was in the Owl Patrol, and we hadn't been formed very long when he decided that we should go away for a summer camp at St Osyth, near Clacton. He hired a professional cook – an ex-Army cook, with no references! We travelled down by train on a Saturday and we met this cook at Liverpool Street Station.

On the Sunday morning we had set up the camp in a field on a big farm, and we were all paraded. The farmer came along, and we were all questioned: a lot of his chickens had been stolen. That night the cook vamoosed – he had obviously killed the chickens, and he stole all our petty cash and all the food – and there we were! We weren't more than about eleven, but we managed – we made 'bully beef' rissoles. When we came home, my mother was shocked because I was as thin as a rake!

We used to go to Gilwell Park, and went to Baden-Powell's Campfire on a Saturday night. He'd be there himself – marvellous chap. We'd sit there, with a blanket all round us, and he would tell us a yarn. They wanted a Guard of Honour of about 150 to be present on the lawn at Gilwell Park when the American Ambassador was going to present the Prince of Wales with a bronze buffalo which commemorated the formation of the Boy Scouts in America. We got there early on a Sunday morning, a June day (about 1926-7, it was). Baden-Powell himself addressed us. 'Now,' he said, 'we've got to get this just right. We have got some very important people coming this afternoon.' (He was as well-known as any of them.) I know that it poured with rain, but we stood in this 'horseshoe', and I could have touched the Prince of Wales, I was so close to him.

The 14th Epping Forest Group scouts met for many years in their hall by the grounds of 'Woodlands', Larkshall Road. It took them five years of hard work to raise money to build it, and all possible building work was done by the Scouts, the Rovers and their parents. On 19 April 1932, 450 people squeezed into the building for its opening by C.F. Merriam, Esq., Chairman of the British Xylonite Co. The scouts' annual sports day was held nearby, at the Caribonum Ground, and their President was Sir C.T. Warner, Bt, CB, of 'Highams'. One of the two Vice-Presidents was Mr T.F. Humphries, Head Teacher of Selwyn Avenue School.

The scout hall used to be next door to Budgen's supermarket. Alan Marshall was one of the 'Cubs'.

We had Sea Scouts, Rovers, the Scout Troop and three Cub Packs. The Scout Troop was a very, very strong group, and the 'leading light' there was Gibson, who used to work for the old LNER. We used to call him 'Major Gibson'. Our scouts were not affiliated to a church: we were completely independent. Apparently, Gibson 'had words' with the local clergy and (I remember this well) we went into the Forest and had open-air services there, just down the road in Larks Wood!

My brother was into scouting and we both went to Camp. We used to assemble at Highams Park Station and we got aboard the train and landed up in the West Country – straight through! It's only afterwards that you appreciate it. We used to be in Scout Headquarters there – wonderful! Well, I thought it was wonderful. It was just a wooden building, and they used to put on the 'Gang Shows' there.

A lot of the lads went to war, and of course the Sea Scouts went for the Navy, and my brother, together with a lot of his contemporaries, went into the Air Force.

104 *'This is the 14th Scouts, Epping Forest. That's Gibson (4th from right). Sid Dykes was there, and I can see my brother, Harold A. Marshall (6th). The Cole Twins were in the Cubs. When the Second World War came, a lot of them joined up and were lost.' (A. Marshall)*

Among their 'good deeds' in the *Scouting Year Book for* 1932-3, the scouts collected money for the Dr Barnardo's Homes, and took some of the boys to a pantomime. But a sad note in the 1938-9 magazine reported:

> Gone Home. Scout B. Moore – of the 'M' troop – 15 older members of the group stood by to give their blood; unfortunately unavailing.

Mrs Irene Knight's brother-in-law, Stan, was a quiet, gentle bachelor, who was christened in 1912 in All Saints Church, on the same day as four of his brothers and sisters:

> Stan Knight worked for a firm of accountants, and he used to go around auditing accounts for people. His Scout Troop was the 14th Epping Forest (1st Highams Park) Troop: Stan was the Assistant Scoutmaster and Gibson, who lived at 46 Abbotts Crescent, was the Scoutmaster. In the war, when Stan wasn't called up and Gibson was, Stan ran the troop, such as it was. James Gibson survived the war and he came back and took over again.
>
> Stan had some 'heart condition', and that's why he was never called up, but he used to go up the hill from his house for a train with his case, and I went to pick it up one day and I could hardly lift it off the ground! Stan lived with his parents, and after they died he moved into Preston Avenue with his sister, Mrs Harrison, for a while. His sister was married to Bill Harrison, who lived in Preston Avenue with two aunts, and they brought him up. Stan was 83 when he died.
>
> I was in the Guides, the 1st Highams Park All Saints' Girl Guides. (Alice King took that. I think she lived in Hale End Road.) We went off to summer camps on the Isle of Wight and down at St Margaret's Bay at Dover.
>
> When I started going to All Saints Church, Selwyn Avenue, the vicar was McKinley. They had everything down there: Men's Social, Mothers' Union, Choral Society – you name it, they had it. There was quite a big Tennis Club there, and we used to sit on our bikes and watch them all playing behind the church at the end of Cavendish Road. There was a building at the side of it, which was eventually a Men's Club.

We always used the hall of All Saints Church-on-the-hill and we held guide and scout dances there when they weren't in the Scout Hall. All the same crowd turned up and one of the scouts ran a scouts' dance band. We had very good times.

Church Activities

Mrs Olive Fewell talked about one of the organists at All Saints.

> It was about the mid-1950s when I met Mr C.E.W. Shrubshall, who had been the organist of All Saints Church, Highams Park for a long while. (I think his name was Charles, but in those days, people were very formal, and I only knew him as Mr Shrubshall.) We were doing a 'Bob-a-Job' with the 1st Highams Park, Winchester Road Guides and Brownies. (Our Brown Owl was Miss Dicks, and we met in the Methodist Church Hall.) When I knocked on the door of 126 The Avenue, a very elderly gentleman, Mr Shrubshall, came to the door. (There was also a lady, who I later learned was Miss Pash, his housekeeper.)
>
> I asked if I could do any jobs for him and he said I could, and would I like to come in? So I went into his house. This meeting developed into a twice-weekly visit, and I did his shopping until I left school, and afterwards I still used to visit him. He had employed a housekeeper when he lost his wife, his 'dear Anna', to whom the organ at All Saints Church, where he was the organist, is dedicated – Anna Shrubshall. He had an organ in one of his rooms at home, and he would play to me, but unfortunately the neighbours would complain about the noise! (It did make quite a noise when he played, but he loved to play the organ.)
>
> It was a strange story really, because the housekeeper, who had been employed to look after him, became an invalid herself, and he was looking after her in the end! He was a lovely gentleman, so kindly and caring.

Miss Hilda Oliver made worship much more comfortable for the congregation of All Saints Church in the 1990s, when she donated tapestry-covered padded cushions for all the hard, wooden pews. Her father, Walter Oliver, also used to take an active part in church life.

> Father was a Sidesman at All Saints-on-the-hill. We didn't go to the parish church in Selwyn Avenue. The earliest vicar was the Reverend Pratt and then it was McKinley. It was a flourishing church in those days and they had social clubs, Badminton Club, Dramatics – all kinds of things. There used to be a marvellous Sunday School at All Saints, which was run by two sisters, the Misses Reed, who used to live in Preston Avenue. We always had stories and then sometimes we did some drawings. The children started at five and went on until their teens.

Brian Rayner-Cooke, the internationally famous singer, was once Choirmaster at All Saints, and other organists have included Mr Clifford Pomfret and Mrs Joyce Ellery. (Joyce's husband, the Rev. Arthur Ellery, was chaplain of Bancrofts School and went on to be vicar of Chipperfield's parish church.)

Choirs and other Societies

Les Felgate was a chorister at All Saints Church and sang with the Forest Choir.

> I sang for the Forest Choir for twenty years-plus as a second bass. Godfrey Bramhall was the conductor and Norman Caplin was the accompanist. Godfrey was the Organist and Choirmaster at St Mary's, Woodford and Norman Caplin was an Assistant Organist at one of the City churches, All Saints, Margaret Street.
>
> We sang at St John's, Smith Square quite a few times, and we used to sing Christmas carols at a service for the Freemasons at Waltham Abbey, but our main venue was the Walthamstow Assembly Hall because we were part of Waltham Forest. (They do all the recordings there: all the big orchestras have recorded in the Assembly Hall.) We sang at the Queen Elizabeth Hall for the first time in April 1980, and we went up to

105 *The Choir of All Saints' parish church (c.1920). Miss Hilda Oliver tried to identify some of them. Top row from left: Passmore?, (?), Russell Watson of Beverley Road, (?), (?), Mr Popkins. Last on right, Walter Horace Oliver. Seated men: Peddar – Choirmaster and Organist, Hughes, Revell, Rev. Pratt, Edward James – Lay Reader, Thornton, Sid Harris – brother to the Postmaster. Boys from left: Popkins, (?), (?). Cross-legged: Jenkins,(?), Exley – son of the schoolmaster, who lived in Falmouth Avenue, (?), Ludlow, Sid Span.*

the Festival complex one happy Saturday and they liked us so much that they gave the Forest Choir two bookings the next year! I've enjoyed every minute of it. We had quite a good following – we could pack the Assembly Hall – and we usually had the Essex Chamber Orchestra, led by Reg Adler.

Godfrey Bramhall commented,

When I first took over the Forest Choir in 1962 we sang at All Saints parish church in Selwyn Avenue. We did Handel's *Messiah*, *St Matthew's Passion*, *St John's Passion*, Mozart's *Requiem* and the *Mass in B minor* by Bach, and a lot of those were the first performances in Waltham Forest.

Frank Payling and his brother organised trips for the theatre-lovers of Highams Park and Woodford Green for many years.

We didn't go to the West End. We went to the Provinces, Northampton, Peterborough, Bromley, Croydon, Farnham, and we went to Colchester (the Mercury), Chelmsford, Ipswich – we took anybody who wanted to go and we advertised it only by word of mouth.

Maria Dvorakova Jones was a teacher who was also a member of the local branch of the English Speaking Union although she spoke English with such a strong Czechoslovakian accent that local schoolchildren must have found it very difficult to follow what she was saying. But she really knew how to get the best out of life. She was a brave but cautious globe-trotter, who travelled alone until she died in 1997, aged 84. (She always flew with British Airways and bought British goods to show loyalty to her adopted country.)

Mrs Jones lived near to Wadham Bridge. She really loved music and, as a member of the London Dvorak Society, did her best to promote performances of Czechoslovakian music, played by famous Czech musicians in the great Concert Halls of London. On one memorable occasion she persuaded dozens of people in Waltham Forest to give food and lodgings to an entire Men's Choir from Czechoslovakia (because she knew they couldn't cover their touring expenses thanks to currency restrictions). She then booked a church hall in Chingford, where the surprised choir members found themselves 'singing for their suppers' in order to repay their equally bemused hosts, but they responded by giving a glorious impromptu performance.

Holiday Camps?

Sir Fred Pontin, the wealthy business tycoon who raised millions of pounds for charity and provided thousands of holiday-makers with reasonably priced holidays in his 24 holiday camps in Britain (and 10 Pontinental holiday villages abroad), once lived in Forest Glade, Highams Park, where he was known to some of his neighbours as 'Pat's father'! A telephone call to the office of 'Holiday Club Pontin's' confirmed that, although Sir Fred no longer ran the business, he *had* lived in Highams Park.

In April 1996, he responded in a very generous way to a letter, by sending his autobiography, *Thumbs Up*, a readable account of the way in which he built up his holiday camp empire. Sir Fred sent a letter with his book, mentioning that he was approaching his 90th birthday. He wrote, 'It may be of interest to you to know that on leaving school I lived at Gloucester Road, Walthamstow. When I married I lived at Forest Glade, Highams Park on an unmade road opposite the forest.

The extraordinarily successful Walthamstow businessman was born in 1906, when the Pontin family moved from Shoreditch to Walthamstow. His father was one of a long line of skilled cabinet makers, so although Fred started school at Blackhorse Road he was able to go on to the Sir George Monoux School as a fee-paying pupil. (The Headmaster at that time was 'Wally' Topliss, who was stone-deaf but an expert at lip-reading.) At the Monoux School Fred won every sporting prize available to him as a junior boy and was awarded what was known as the 'Victor Ludorum Cup'. But he was the eldest of six children and had to earn money for the family, so he left school aged 15 with no formal qualifications.

As a schoolboy he had been interested in studying the Stock Market and his father urged him to get a job at a bank, but Fred told him that he intended to become a millionaire and a bank was not the place to make his money, so he headed for the City. Wearing his grandfather's suit, altered to fit him, Fred set off to work with the other 'City Gents', and his knowledge of the Stock Market and an aptitude for figures soon gained him rapid promotion.

His father and mother were enthusiastic supporters of Walthamstow Avenue Football Club, an amateur club which was very successful in the FA Cup competitions. Soon Fred became the Club's Treasurer, and his match reports were a regular feature in the *Walthamstow Guardian* newspaper. Sid Marchant explained where the club used to be.

> The Walthamstow Avenue Football Club ground was in Higham Hill, in a place called Green Pond, where a lady used to sell milk at the entrance. The owners received an offer they could not refuse and sold the ground off for housing. The club then combined with two other clubs, and their ground is now at Hainault.

In about 1909, before the land was sold to the football club, visits to Green Pond Farm were very popular, according to the records of Walthamstow's Moreia Presbyterian Church of Wales. Mr D. Alban Davies kept the farm of 200 acres, and every Thursday afternoon a number of Welsh people, under the leadership of Dr Stanley Owen, met for clay-pigeon shooting. One of the regular visitors was Mr D.O. Evans, later to be a Member of Parliament. Sunday School outings to Green Pond Farm were made and one of the songs written by Dr Stanley Owen (bardie name Hoffnant) for the Sunday School party was called 'Heol y Gelli' (Grove Road).

At one of the social events at Walthamstow Avenue Football Club Sir Fred Pontin met Dorothy Mortimer, who he married in 1929, and they moved from Walthamstow to live in Forest Glade. Sir Fred's City career prospered and he started a football pools business, then a bookmaking one, and his love of horse racing led to ownership of National Hunt winners.

After the war he searched for a decommissioned site to convert into a holiday camp, but instead he discovered a site of eight acres with about 100 derelict buildings which had been a holiday camp before the war at Brean Sands, near Weston-Super-Mare, which he bought. This was the first of his chain of Pontin Holiday Camps. (Pontin's Holiday Camp at Morecambe was advertised as '60 acres of happiness'.)

In 1957 he was lucky to survive after being seriously injured in a car crash at the Billet Roundabout, Walthamstow, when he fell asleep at the wheel of the car late one night. It took two hours for firemen to free him from the wreckage, before he was taken to Whipps Cross Hospital, then to the London Hospital next day, and it was a long time before he recovered.

It was not long before most members of his family were actively involved in the holiday camp business, and they stayed with the venture until, at the height of its success, Sir Fred decided to sell the business in 1978, although he remained as Chairman of the company until 1980.

During a period of over 30 years running Pontin's Holiday Camps and the Pontinental Holiday Villages, Sir Fred found time to raise huge sums of money for many charities, became Chief Barker of the Variety Club of Great Britain, and was made a Companion Member of the Grand Order of Water Rats. A knighthood was awarded to him in 1976, for charitable services. Sir Fred Pontin died in October 2000. His daughter, Pat, who spent her childhood living close to the Forest and Highams Park lake married her husband following the Pontin family tradition and working for 'Pontinental' for a while. But then the couple decided to take their four children to live in the country and become farmers in Kent.

Highams Park Lake and the Lea Avon Sailing Club

For twenty years Ken Ford, in his spare time and on a purely voluntary basis, taught children how to sail and to make their own dinghies. It all began on the River Lea but, after years of negotiations, in 1967 the Conservators of Epping Forest gave their permission for Ken and the children to use Highams Park lake. Ken remembers the effect this triumph had on him.

> I went down to the lake that night with my wife, and I sat in what was the old rowing boats' shed, and I had a terrible headache – the worst headache I ever had. I had never had migraine before in my life, and I sat in there and it was terrible! I suddenly thought, What have I done? I had been down on the Lea, which didn't belong to me, and now all of a sudden I had got a load of kids, a load of boats, and a lake – and I was responsible for the lot! My head was terrible, but then as it cleared I started to get a grip of things.
>
> First of all, the Conservators of Epping Forest had the idea to get some of their money back – to let the rowing boats out on the water at the same time – but I couldn't imagine doing all that work and standing with a ticket machine as well. I'd have had to be a robot to have done it all!

Children from Highams Park joined the club, which soon needed somewhere to make boats and meet because at one time it had 90 members. Ken searched for sources of cheap building materials and organised fund raising by getting the children to collect tons of newspaper. It took two years to build the club house, using great pieces of wood from the railway sidings at Whitechapel.

> The posts were 12 by 12s, and 30 feet long, you know, so it took 60 of the older children to lift them, but it was no real weight, you see, because if you placed one child in front of another, they were only picking up one cube of wood between them, which was really equal to a plank of wood about 12 foot long. They would carry the timber into place, lay it down and then, with ropes and a bar on the top, they would

106 *A 'Merlin Rocket' sails across Highams Park Lake (c.1980), crewed by one of the children from the Lea Avon Sailing Club, founded by Ken Ford. He showed the children how to build dinghies, a sea-going launch (now moored at Benfleet, Essex) and their own Club House by the Lake.*

pull it up, drop it in the hole, plumb it up, and then concrete it in.

After the Club House was finished the children raced their dinghies and enjoyed the club room above the boat house for several years.

Then Ken started another project:

The idea of building a cruiser was to try and encourage the older ones, which it didn't, in actual fact. I thought of it as the 'Red Witch', because that's the boat I really wanted, but the Chairman was Sam Sheppard and I thought the cruiser should be named after him to show respect.

Sam Sheppard, OBE was the Chairman of the Corporation of London's Epping Forest Open Spaces Committee. His daughter, grandson and great-grandchildren still live in Woodford Green, in the old Hale End area. The 40-foot sea-going cruiser was launched and taken to Brightlingsea, Essex, where it was used by Ken Ford and ex-members of the club.

The Lea Avon Sailing Club closed when the children grew up and began to sail elsewhere. The boat house was taken over by the scouts but, unfortunately, was almost destroyed by a fire. Since then it has been rebuilt and the scouts now use it for canoeing. It reopened in 1992 and is now known as the 'Michael Mallinson Scout Lodge', the name being transferred from the other Scout Lodge, which stands a little way up The Charter Road and is now 'The Lady Mallinson Cabin'. The original Michael Mallinson Scout Lodge was built 30 years ago on land owned by Sir Stuart Mallinson in memory of his and Lady Mallinson's son, Michael, who lost his life in the war. Sir Stuart sold the White House and also the land surrounding it to Walthamstow Council around 1960, but continued to live in the White House until he died.

Most of the changes to the area happened in the last 100 years, when Hale End grew into the urban village of Highams Park, and history continues to be made. Shops close or change hands, many of the very large houses of the Haile Estate have been replaced by flats and none of the tiny cottages of Hale End remains. The signal box by the level crossing is now controlled from Liverpool Street with the aid of CCTV cameras. But the Highams Park and Woodford Green area in Waltham Forest retains the appearance of a pleasant community, still surrounded by the Forest. It is hoped that the people who live here now will ensure that the next generation is also able to enjoy their surroundings and the freedom of the Forest, and finds Highams Park a good place to live.

Bibliography

(CHS) Chingford Historical Society
(VHM) Vestry House Museum, Walthamstow
(WAHS) Waltham Abbey Historical Society
(WAS) Walthamstow Antiquarian Society
(WF) London Borough of Waltham Forest
(WHS) Walthamstow Historical Society

Allen, W.H., *The Houndsditch Murders and the Siege of Sidney Street*
Atkins, Ernest, *One Door Closes Another Opens* (WF, Memories 6), 1994
Barns, Stephen, *Walthamstow Deeds 1595 to 1890* (WAS, No.11), 1923
Barry, Septimus, *Chingford Hall* (CHS)
Batsford, M.E., *Non-conformity in Walthamstow* (WAS, No.22) vol.1, 1977
Beeson, Trevor, *Rebels and Reformers*, SCMP, 1999
Berrett's Directory, 1886-7
Bowler, Hewitt, Howell and Reynold, *Bits and Pieces*
Boyes, John H. (notes by), *Beech Hall - Hale End*
Cassidy, R., *Copped Hall* (WAHS), 1983
Clarke's History of Walthamstow (1861), reprinted in 1980 (WAS 23, new series, VHM)
Connor, J.E., *Liverpool Street to Chingford* (Middleton Press), 2003
Deaton, Guy, *Schola Sylvestris*, 1980
Farmer, Jack, *Woodford as I knew it*
Ford, Ken, 'The Lea Avon Sailing Club Oral History' (unpublished)
Forster, B.M., *Introduction to the Knowledge of Funguses*, Forster Linnean Society, 1820
Galey, R.L., *The History of Woodford Green United Free Church*
Gerald, Lucy, *Essex Rock*, Essex Rock and Mineral Society, 1999
Gervers, M., *The Cartulary of the Knights of St John of Jerusalem in England: Secunda Camera, Essex*, for the British Academy, Oxford University Press, 1982
Grantham, G., Oral History Tape 119, 29.5.1985 (VHM)
Hall, John M., Hall, Ray, *Suburbanisation in Metropolitan Essex: the interrupted development of a Repton Park at Highams*
Hatley, Annie, *Across The Years* (WAS), 1953
Hilton, James, *Catherine Herself*, 1920, 1935
Indenture transferring for the purpose of building a School House, c.1808
The Library Association, Vol.66, No.12, 1964
The Macropoulas Dolls and Photographic Collection (VHM)
Masefield, Sir Peter, *'To Ride the Storm' – the Story of the Airship R101*
Plummer, P.C., Bowyer, W.H., *A Brief History of Courtenay Warner and Warner Estate* (WHS), 2000
Pond, C.C., *The Chingford Line*, WAS, new series no.17, 1975
Pontin, Sir Fred, *Thumbs Up*, Solo Books Ltd, 1991

Reaney, Dr P.H., *Place Names of Essex*

Reynolds, Margaret, and Leighton, Angela, *Victorian Women Poets – an Anthology*, Blackwell, 1995

Roebuck, George Edward, *The Story of Walthamstow*

Shannon, Monsignor D., *Essex Recusants*

Shillinglaw's *Walthamstow Directory*

A Short History of the British Xylonite Co. Ltd. (1877-1927)

Skinner, Mrs Georgina, President, *One Hundred Years of Horticulture*

Smith, M.M., *Highams* WAS, no.8, 1966

Some Walthamstow Houses, Bosworth, Monograph 20 (WAS)

The School on the Green (1820-1980), published by Woodford Green Primary School Parents' Association – Head teacher D.J. Stanley

Tuffs, J. Elsden, *Essex Coaching Days*, Essex Countryside, Letchworth Printers Ltd.

The Victoria County History of Essex, Oxford University Press, 1973 (reprint 1992, WF)

Walthamstow Antiquarian Society; Nos. 6, 7, 22, 28

Walthamstow Corporation Report, Manor House, 1932

Walthamstow Guardian Newspapers

Walthamstow Topics – Occasional Publication No.10, May 1968

White, C.M., *The Gotha Summer*

Wyld, Ross, *The War over Walthamstow*, Walthamstow Borough Council, 1945

Index

References which relate to illustrations only are given in **bold**.
(W) Walthamstow, (WG) Woodford Green, (WD) Woodford, (C) Chingford

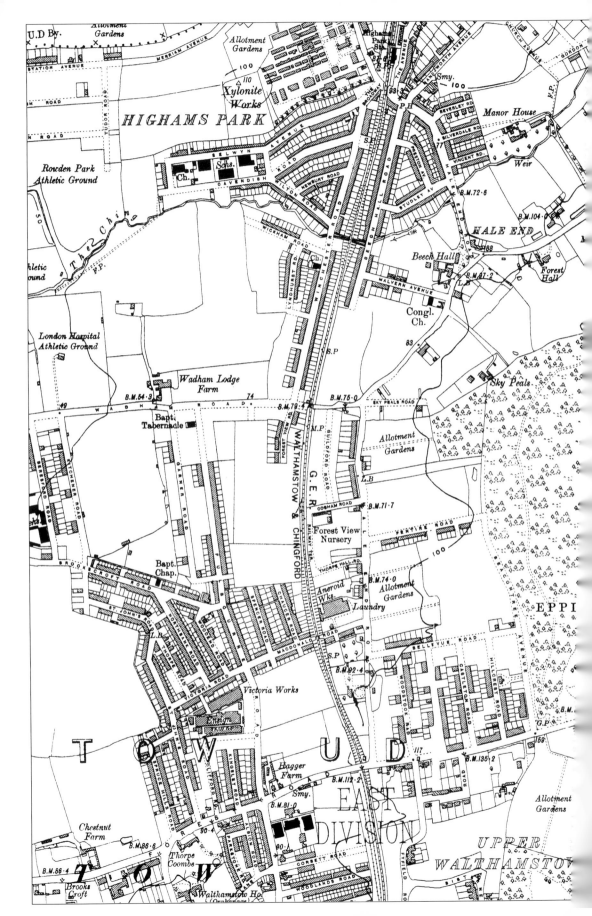

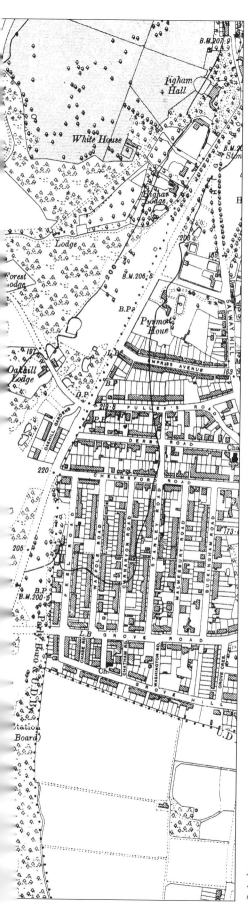

A map of Essex, dated 1921, shows the new urban village of Highams Park and most of the farms, cottages and large houses of the old hamlet of Hale End.